AMERICAN HIS

The Revolutionary Period: 1750–1783

VOLUME 3

Other titles in the
American History by Era series:

AMERICAN HISTORY BY ERA

The Revolutionary Period: 1750–1783

VOLUME 3

Bruce Thompson, *Book Editor*

Daniel Leone, *President*
Bonnie Szumski, *Publisher*
Scott Barbour, *Managing Editor*

**GREENHAVEN
PRESS®**

THOMSON
™
GALE

San Diego • Detroit • New York • San Francisco • Cleveland
New Haven, Conn. • Waterville, Maine • London • Munich

LIBRARY OF CONGRESS CATALOGING-IN-PUBLICATION DATA

The revolutionary period, 1750–1783 / Bruce Thompson, book editor.
   p. cm. — (American history by era; vol. 3)
  Includes bibliographical references (p.) and index.
  ISBN 0-7377-1042-X (lib. bdg. : alk. paper) —
  ISBN 0-7377-1041-1 (pbk. : alk. paper)
   1. United States—History—Revolution, 1775–1783. 2. United States—History—
Colonial period, ca. 1600–1775. I. Thompson, Bruce, 1952– . II. Series.
E208 .R465 2003
973.3—dc21
                                               2002070610

CONTENTS

Chapter 1: Social Change in Colonial America, 1750–1755

1. Benjamin Franklin's Experiments in Electricity

Benjamin Franklin is famous for having flown a kite during a thunderstorm. This dangerous stunt was an important early experiment in the nature of electricity. Franklin was among a group of amateur scientists whose experiments in the practical applications of scientific knowledge marked the beginnings of the Industrial Revolution. Men like Franklin put the American colonies in the forefront of this revolution.

2. Colonial Home Life and the Consumer Revolution

The essential elements of home life—cooking, eating, sleeping, and entertaining guests—underwent a profound change during the eighteenth century. The number of possessions that a family might own increased dramatically. This change is known as the consumer revolution.

3. The Iroquois Confederacy

The dominant group of American Indians at the time of the French and Indian War was the Five Nations, or Iroquois Confederacy. This group had a sophisticated social and political structure that made it an important power in the region.

Chapter 2: The Seven Years' War, 1756–1763

was a common tanner with a love for singing. Both
wrote music expressing the new American spirit.

7. The Boston Tea Party
To protest taxes on goods imported from England,
a group of Boston citizens dressed up as Indians,
boarded a cargo ship, and dumped its cargo of tea
into Boston's harbor.

Chapter 4: Declaring Independence, 1775–1776

1. The First Battle of the American Revolution
The famous "shot heard 'round the world," which
marked the beginning of the Revolutionary War,
was supposedly fired at Lexington/Concord; however, an earlier confrontation occurred at Salem,
which may have been the real beginning.

2. The Battle for Bunker Hill
The first battle fought by the new colonial army
was for a pair of hills outside the city of Boston.
Neither side won a decisive victory, but afterward
the British knew they were fighting a war, not
merely putting down a rebellion.

3. The Declaration of the Causes and Necessity of Taking Up Arms
On June 6, 1775, the Second Continental Congress
passed a declaration authorizing George Washington to begin organized military action against the
British. This declaration was not, however, a declaration of independence.

4. The Loyalist Case
Public opinion was split on the question of independence from England. Only about a third of
Americans actually favored independence. Another third opposed independence, and the final

third was neutral or undecided. The loyalists believed they had a strong case for remaining part of the British Empire.

Chapter 5: Losing Battles and Winning the War, 1776–1781

Fox, hectored the British with a guerrilla-style war
that gave the British no clear target.

Chapter 6: Founding a New Nation, 1781–1783

5. Celebrations at the End of the American Revolution

By Kenneth Silverman

Everybody loves a parade. Most cities sponsored parades and pageants to celebrate the end of the war. The colors and symbolism used in those celebrations differed from the colors and symbolism that we now associate with the quintessentially American parade.

During the sixteenth century, events occurred in North America that would change the course of American history. In 1512, Spanish explorer Juan Ponce de León led the first European expedition to Florida. French navigator Jean Ribault established the first French colony in America at Fort Caroline in 1564. Over a decade later, in 1579, English pirate Francis Drake landed near San Francisco and claimed the country for England.

These three seemingly random events happened in different decades, occurred in various regions of America, and involved three different European nations. However, each discrete occurrence was part of a larger movement for European dominance over the New World. During the sixteenth century, Spain, France, and England vied for control of what was later to become the United States. Each nation was to leave behind a legacy that would shape the political structure, language, culture, and customs of the American people.

Examining such seemingly disparate events in tandem can help to emphasize the connections between them and generate an appreciation for the larger global forces of which they were a part. Greenhaven Press's American History by Era series provides students with a unique tool for examining American history in a way that allows them to see such connections. This series divides American history—from the time that the first people arrived in the New World from Asia to the September 11, 2001, terrorist attacks—into nine discrete periods. Each volume then presents a collection of both primary and secondary documents that describe the major events of the period in chronological order. This structure provides students with a snapshot of events occurring simultaneously in all parts of America. The reader can then gain an appreciation for the political, social, and cultural movements and trends that shaped the nation. Students reading about the adventures of individual European explorers, for instance, are invited to consider how such expeditions compared in purpose and consequence to earlier and later expeditions. Rather than simply learning that Ponce de León was the first Spaniard to try to colonize Florida, for example, students can begin to understand his expedition in a larger context. Indeed, Ponce's voyage was an extension of Spain's desire to conquer the Caribbean and Mexico, and his expedition was to inspire other Spanish explorers to head north from Hispaniola and New Spain in search of rich empires to conquer.

Another benefit of studying eras is that students can view a "snapshot" of America at any given moment of time and see the various social, cultural, and political events that occurred simultaneously. For example, during the period between 1920 and 1945, Charles Lindbergh became the first to make a solo transatlantic flight, Babe Ruth broke the record for the most home runs in one season, and the United States dropped the atomic bomb on Hiroshima. Random events occurring in post–Cold War America included the torching of the Branch Davidian compound in Waco, Texas, the emergence of the World Wide Web, and the 2000 presidential election debacle in which ballot miscounts in Florida held up election results for weeks.

Each volume in this series offers features to enhance students' understanding of the era of American history under discussion. An introductory essay provides an overview of the period, supplying essential context for the readings that follow. An annotated table of contents highlights the main point of each selection. A more in-depth introduction precedes each document, placing it in its particular historical context and offering biographical information about the author. A thorough chronology and index allow students to quickly reference specific events and dates. Finally, a bibliography opens up additional avenues of research. These features help to make the American History by Era series an extremely valuable tool for students researching the political upheavals, wars, cultural movements, scientific and technological advancements, and other events that mark the unfolding of American history.

AMERICAN SOCIETY IN THE REVOLUTIONARY PERIOD

The period of American history from 1750 to 1783 was revolutionary in more than one sense. During this period the American colonies won their independence from Britain; but this political upheaval was reflected in, and to some extent caused by, equally important social and cultural upheavals.

The most prominent feature of American society in 1750 was its remarkable diversity. In fact, no group of people called themselves "Americans." The Quakers of Pennsylvania were very different from the Puritans of Massachusetts. They had come from different regions in England, spoke with different accents, wore different styles of clothing, and practiced different religions. Both groups were even more distinct from the settlers in Virginia, who had come mostly from southern England. A fourth group, from the English-Scottish borderlands, was just beginning to move into the western frontier, bringing yet another mix of styles and customs. There were also German, Dutch, and French settlers. And then there were the Indians. Some eastern tribes had been forced west, and some had been destroyed, but a significant number had been integrated into the society of the invading Europeans, contributing still more variety.

About the only generalization that can be made about Americans in 1750 is that they were practical people. To some extent this practicality was forced upon them by the necessity of carving a living out of the wilderness. But Americans embraced their practicality with a fervor that went far beyond the demands of necessity. Being practical was not, for them, an evil to be endured with reluctance: it was an essential part of their moral character. The Puritans, the Quakers, the Shakers, and others, came to the New World to find a place where they could practice a peculiar brand of Christian austerity, and this "Protestant ethic" of austerity and seriousness was still very much alive in 1750. It might be too much to say that in 1750 Americans actually disapproved of having fun, but it was certainly true that many Americans approved of the "simple life," i.e., a life that found contentment in bare necessities and a refusal to dress up and put on airs. Americans chose to live in small, one-room homes, and own only what was necessary for the functioning of the household. In short, Americans took delight in the simple and practical.

Of course, this meant that Americans had little use for what their European cousins considered the refinements of culture. In 1750 even the larger cities, such as Philadelphia, Charleston, and Boston, lacked concert halls and theaters. No American had established a reputation or made a living in painting, poetry, or drama. Music was confined to churches and used solely for the singing of hymns. The descendants of Europeans had been living in the New World for a century and a half by 1750. This would have been plenty of time to begin making contributions to the fine arts, if Americans had been interested in doing so. In 1750 Americans simply weren't interested in such matters. Culture in this sense was considered frivolous.

By 1783, much in American society had changed. While practicality and a reverence for "the simple life" continued to be typical American characteristics, Americans had also come to appreciate the refinements of culture. Cities now had concert halls and theaters in which people could see performances by professional American musicians and actors. By this time Americans had made memorable and internationally recognized contributions to art and literature. The American style of life had changed as well. Homes were larger, divided into rooms with specialized functions, and they provided a modicum of personal privacy. The number of personal possessions had increased enormously. Perhaps the most significant change was that Americans thought of themselves as "Americans." The re-

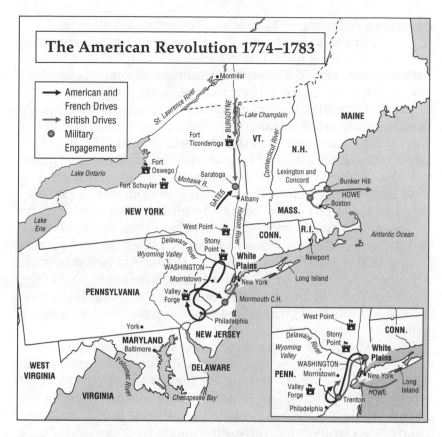

gional and cultural variety had not diminished, but there was now a larger sense of unity and shared history.

Several factors may have contributed to these social changes, including growth of the urban population, increasing wealth, and an influx of new immigrants with less austere tastes. Advances in science and technology also played a role; and, of course, some of the changes were influenced by the upheaval of war.

AMERICAN SCIENCE IN THE REVOLUTIONARY PERIOD

Given the practicality of Americans, it should not be surprising that there were prominent American scientists before there were prominent American artists, poets, and musicians, and that American scientists were typically concerned with practical applications for their discoveries.

Several Americans became prominent in the field of astronomy. John Winthrop of Massachusetts organized an expedition to Newfoundland to observe the passage of Venus across the sun, and he noted the relation between sunspots and the aurora borealis. David Rittenhouse, a Philadelphia clockmaker, also made some contributions to astronomy and to the development of scientific instruments. He is best known for his practical applications of astronomy to the craft of surveying. In the New World astronomy had direct practical applications to surveying since marking out boundaries through a vast wilderness had to be done with reference to the sky. Beginning in 1764 Rittenhouse helped the English astronomers Charles Mason and Jeremiah Dixon settle a boundary dispute between Pennsylvania and Maryland by surveying their mutual border (know as the Mason-Dixon Line, which later figured prominently in the debate over slavery). He then surveyed boundaries between many of the other thirteen colonies, including the New York/Massachusetts boundary. Benjamin Banneker, whose parents had been slaves, also became a prominent astronomer and surveyor.

The best-known American scientist was Benjamin Franklin, who became something of a celebrity in Europe because of his discovery in 1753 that lightning is a form of electricity, and that electricity *flows* from place to place. Franklin's discovery of the nature of electricity has probably produced more profound changes in our lives than any other single discovery, although, except for the invention of the lightning rod, those changes were not felt during the period covered by this book. His invention of the Franklin stove had a more immediate effect. The Franklin stove could heat a room much more cheaply than a fireplace could. It made possible the building of larger homes, and the dividing of homes into separate rooms.

THE SEVEN YEARS' WAR

The most obvious influence on American society during the revolutionary period was the upheaval of war. Between 1750 and 1783 two wars were fought that changed the course of world history. The first big war in that period was known in Europe as the Seven Years' War, but it was known in North America as the French and Indian War. Winston Churchill called the Seven Years' War the first "world" war. It was a war fought on several continents, and it was indeed nothing less than a struggle for world domination.

The Seven Years' War was chiefly a struggle between Britain and France. The war had two distinct phases. During the first phase the French won most of the battles; during the second phase the British won most of the battles. In the attempt to create an empire connecting their northern colonies in Montreal and Quebec with their southern colonies in Mobile and New Orleans, the French began building a chain of forts along the southern Great Lakes and into the Ohio Valley. Some of these forts were built in territory claimed by the British colony of Virginia, which at the time claimed territory as far north and west as Lake Erie.

The first battle of the war was fought by none other than George Washington, who was then a young officer in charge of a Virginia militia. After delivering a warning to the French to withdraw from territory claimed by the British, he was authorized to use force to compel the French to leave. His force ambushed a small detail of French soldiers at Great Meadows near Fort Duquesne. Then, unable to retreat fast enough to avoid retaliation by the main force, he had his soldiers hastily assemble a stockade called (appropriately) Fort Necessity. The flimsy stockade was not adequate to repel the French attack and was easily captured. However, since the French were not prepared to keep prisoners of war, Washington and his troops were permitted to withdraw "with honor" back to Virginia.

The next year, with much fanfare, General Edward Braddock arrived from England in command of two regiments of trained British soldiers. Cutting his way painfully through the forest, his army stretched out in a narrow column four miles long, he managed to come almost within sight of Fort Duquesne before the French and Indians ambushed his flanks and destroyed the entire army, including General Braddock himself. For the next two years the British continued to loose battles, failing to take Ft. Niagara from the French, and losing many of their own forts, including Oswego and Ft. William Henry. At Ft. William Henry the British were also allowed to withdraw "with honor," as Washington had been allowed to do at Ft. Necessity. However, the Indian allies of the French, who did not understand this curious European military custom, fell upon the withdrawing British soldiers and civilians, and massacred them.

Despite these disastrous defeats at the beginning of the war, the British enjoyed some important advantages over the French that eventually turned the war in their favor. The most important of these was simply that the British colonies were larger and better established than the French colonies. The total population of British colonists in the New World was about one and a half million—more than fifteen times the total French population. With more resources to draw upon it is no wonder that the British military finally started to win a few battles.

The first significant British victory was at Louisbourg in Nova Scotia. The battle took the form of a brutal siege. Civilians inside the fort finally convinced the French commander to surrender to prevent the loss of civilian lives. The British then managed to destroy Ft. Frontenac on Lake Ontario including the boats that were kept there. This made it more difficult for the French to supply their troops in the Ohio Valley. Brigadier General John Forbes then led a second assault on Fort Duquesne. This time, after clawing his way inch by inch through the Pennsylvania forests just as General Braddock had done, he arrived at the fort to find the French soldiers nearly dying of starvation. The French destroyed their own fort and withdrew with their guns and supplies before General Forbes could mount an attack.

Next year, 1759, the British captured Ft. Niagara, Ft. Ticonderoga, and Crown Point. Only victories at Quebec and Montreal were needed to finish the war. General James Wolfe was sent up the St. Lawrence River to lay siege to Quebec. For several months the siege was directed at the heavily fortified northern side of the city. Then, under pressure to withdraw for the winter, General Wolfe made a surprise attack, repositioning his army on the Plains of Abraham to the south of the city. Panicked by this maneuver, the French commander sent his army of inexperienced soldiers against a disciplined British infantry line. They were cut down and fled in disarray, leaving Quebec to the British. The following spring, 1760, three British armies converged on Montreal, forcing it to surrender. The war in North America was over. However, the war continued in Europe and other parts of the world for another three years.

PEACE AND PROSPERITY

In North America the period following the Seven Years' War was one of unprecedented peace, security, and prosperity. With their increased wealth Americans improved their standard of living, and took the time to begin enjoying the arts. Ironically it was precisely this security and prosperity that laid the foundations for the next war, the American Revolution.

Prior to 1763 the American colonies received an important benefit from being part of the British Empire, namely, the protection of the British military from France and Spain. But the defeat of France and Spain in the Seven Years' War had been so complete that neither country now posed a threat to the American colonies. Canada to the north and Florida to the South were now firmly under British control, and the American colonists no longer felt they needed to be protected. By winning the war the British had made themselves obsolete.

The British, of course, saw matters differently. They had amassed considerable debt paying for a war the central objective of which was protecting their colonies. They thought it was perfectly reasonable to expect those colonies to shoulder some of the expenses of maintaining an empire. This British perspective seemed particularly reasonable in light of the growing prosperity of the American colonies. American manufacturing and agricultural production had reached such levels that it was providing serious and unwelcome competition with British manufacturing and agriculture. British companies had no trouble convincing the British Parliament to put protectionist laws in place that were widely regarded as unfair and repressive by the American colonists.

The fact that the American colonists felt secure allowed them to feel that the costs of belonging to the British empire were rapidly coming to outweigh the advantages. They began to reevaluate their status within the British empire, and even—encouraged by the philosophers of the Enlightenment—to ask fundamental questions about the relation between citizens and their government. At the same time that peace and security allowed the colonists to begin questioning their place in the empire, it also gave them more time to pursue the arts. The two factors produced a flowering of artistic activity: people began using art, music, and poetry to explore the important social questions they were asking. Previously Americans had been too practical to be interested in the arts; now they realized that important political questions could not be dismissed as frivolous, and that the arts could be used to comment upon and educate people about these questions. Painters Benjamin West and John Singleton Copley became known for paintings depicting subjects from American history. Poems and songs were frequently used to comment on current events. Phillis Wheatley, a young slave girl, became a celebrity in London for her poetry, much of which was concerned with current events.

There were many important events for poets and artists to comment on. In 1764 the British Parliament passed a law prohibiting colonial governments from issuing their own paper money. The colonies had little gold and silver from which to manufacture "hard" currency, so this law had the effect of changing the value of hard currency to favor British importers. They also passed the Sugar Act, which placed a three-penny duty on molasses imported from the West Indies. A more burdensome law, aimed directly at having the colonies shoulder some of the costs of empire, was the Quartering Act of 1765, which required that colonists actually house British soldiers in their homes. These new laws provoked complaints and dissatisfaction from colonists, but no overt resistance.

The law that first provoked direct rebellion was the Stamp Act of 1765. The earlier laws had been tolerated because they were regarded as *external* to the authority of the colonies themselves. The Currency Act affected the value of money in a way that adversely affected the colonies, but no one doubted the right of the British government to regulate legal currency. The Sugar Act imposed taxes on companies shipping products *into* the colonies, which had the effect of raising prices, but it did not impose a tax on the colonists directly. Even the Quartering Act was tolerated since it was acknowledged that the British government had a right to provide for its own soldiers, however much colonists disapproved of the method. But the Stamp Act was different. It was a tax on printed material, including newspapers and legal documents, which were both produced and consumed *within the colonies themselves*. It was an *internal* tax, i.e., a tax placed directly on colonial businesses and citizens. As such the tax preempted the taxing authority of the colonial governments, who felt that only they were entitled to levy internal taxes.

The Stamp Act was generally regarded as illegal. The Virginia House of Burgesses (the colonial government) even passed a resolution, called the Virginia Resolves, stating that they did not recognize the legitimacy of the Stamp Act. This encouraged open rebellion throughout the colonies. Tax agents assigned to distribute the stamps were hung in effigy and threatened with violence. Some resigned, others were run out of town by angry mobs, and some had their homes broken into and their property destroyed. Resistance to the Stamp Act brought trade between Britain and the colonies to a standstill.

In 1766 the Stamp Act was repealed, but at the same time Parliament affirmed that it *did* have the right to impose taxes on colonists without regard to the distinction between internal and external taxes. The British reorganized the administrative structure of the colonies to take more direct control. A number of courts were created that answered directly to the British government in London. More soldiers were moved to the colonies, especially to Boston where some of the worst rioting had occurred. Under the Quartering Act, many of these soldiers were housed in private residences. Naturally this did nothing to ease tensions. The soldiers seemed to be an occupying army, not a force for the protection of citizens, and the requirement to house soldiers, which had previously been a mild annoyance, became a truly objectionable burden.

The British Parliament then passed a new tax bill, the Townshend Revenue Act of 1767 (named after Charles Townshend, who wrote the bill). The Townshend Act was a group of trade duties, i.e., external taxes, but since Parliament had denied the distinction between internal and external taxes, the colonists were now willing to do the same. Again the colonists organized a boycott, which was so effective that the British Parliament was forced to repeal most of the Townshend duties in March of 1770. Only the duty on tea was left in place, as a matter of principle. As a matter of principle, many colonists avoided the duty on tea by buying tea smuggled from Holland instead.

On March 5, 1770, tensions between Boston citizens and British soldiers stationed in the city came to a head. The incident may have begun with a group of children throwing stones at a British sentry stationed outside the customhouse. Perhaps the sentry threatened the children. In any case, a mob of angry citizens soon gathered. British soldiers arrived to protect the lone sentry, and one of them fired into the crowd. Five people were killed, including a free black named Crispus Attucks. He is sometimes considered the first casualty of the American Revolution. The incident came to be known as the Boston Massacre, and it became the subject of many songs and poems. The silversmith Paul Revere created an etching of the incident that sold widely on drinking mugs.

In May of 1773 the British Parliament passed a law known as the Tea Act, which, in their minds, had little to do with the American colonies. The purpose of the Tea Act was to raise money to pay for troops stationed in India and simultaneously to rescue the East India Tea Company from bankruptcy. Taking more or less direct control of the company, the British government lowered the cost of tea even below the cost of smuggled tea hoping to sell large quantities of the commodity in America.

In practice, the Tea Act was like picking at a scab. American merchants feared the artificially low price of tea would create a monopoly. Advocates of liberty feared that it would undermine resistance to import duties. The only solution seemed to be to prevent the tea from even reaching American markets. New York merchants put pressure on ship captains to refuse to carry East India Company tea. Various seaport cities passed resolutions refusing to receive the tea. In fact, when the tea arrived in America, only Charleston, South Carolina, allowed the tea to be unloaded. However, it was promptly consigned to a warehouse, where it sat unused for three years. In Boston, to prevent the tea from being unloaded, a group of citizens dressed as Indians, boarded the ships carrying tea, and dumped the tea into Boston Harbor. This incident came to be known as the Boston Tea Party.

In response to the Boston Tea Party, the British Parliament passed a series of measures known collectively as the Coercive Acts (or Intolerable Acts by the colonists). One of these acts shut down Boston Harbor until restitution was paid for the lost tea. Another made membership in the Massachusetts provincial council an appointive rather than an elective office; that is, members were to be appointed by the governor of the colony, who was in turn appointed by the king, rather than elected by popular ballot. This was, in fact, how the other colonies were already governed, but none of the colonies were happy with the idea that the British government felt it could intervene directly in their governmental structure. The First Continental Congress was convened to coordinate the American response to the new British laws. Members of the liberty movement began actively organizing militias and stockpiling weapons. War now seemed inevitable.

THE REVOLUTION

The Revolutionary War began in Massachusetts, since this is where British troops were stationed to enforce the closure of Boston Harbor. The British troops made forays into the countryside to seize weapons being stockpiled by patriot militias. This led to confrontations. At Salem in February 1774 one such confrontation ended when the British withdrew without firing.

A few months later a regiment of British soldiers tried to march to Concord to seize a stockpile of weapons. Before they could reach Concord they were met by a patriot militia at Lexington Bridge. This time the British fired and the militia returned fire. Aware that they were outnumbered, the British troops then retreated in regular order back down the road while members of the militia shot at them from both sides of the road, hiding behind rocks, fences, and trees. The Americans lost 95 men in the skirmish; the British lost 273.

Following the conflict at Lexington and Concord, the colonies again agreed to convene a Continental Congress to coordinate their response to what was now widely perceived as British aggression. This Second Continental Congress was made up of many of the same delegates who had attended the First Continental Congress a year earlier. All the delegates agreed that American rights were being violated, but most assumed that the British empire could still be held together. Some, such as John Jay of New York and John Dickinson of Pennsylvania, favored reconciliation. Dickinson was eventually persuaded that some armed resistance would be necessary, but hoped it would be limited and not lead to a permanent rift. Radicals, such as Samuel Adams of Massachusetts, favored complete independence. Among those who favored armed resistance, many, encouraged by the success at Lexington-Concord, believed that local militias could do the job. Those more experienced with the British military, particularly George Washington of Virginia, realized that it would be necessary to raise a paid professional army, and ideally a navy as well. Since the Congress had no taxing authority, both would have to be funded through private donations. Once it was decided to assemble a Continental Army, someone had to be designated to command it. For this purpose the delegates chose one of their own members, George Washington of Virginia.

While the Continental Congress debated, militias from around the northern colonies began assembling at Boston and by April of 1775 had laid siege to the city. Although the militias were relatively disorganized and undersupplied, the British commander, General Thomas Gage, was cautious and did not feel he could attack until reinforcements arrived from England. In June the British did finally attack the American positions at Breed's Hill and Bunker Hill. They managed to drive the Americans away, but at the cost of over a thousand British lives, while the Americans lost only four hundred. The American army re-treated more or less intact to Cambridge, where George Washington met them and took command.

That winter, Washington sent a contingent of his new army north to seize Fort Ticonderoga in New York. The regiment re-

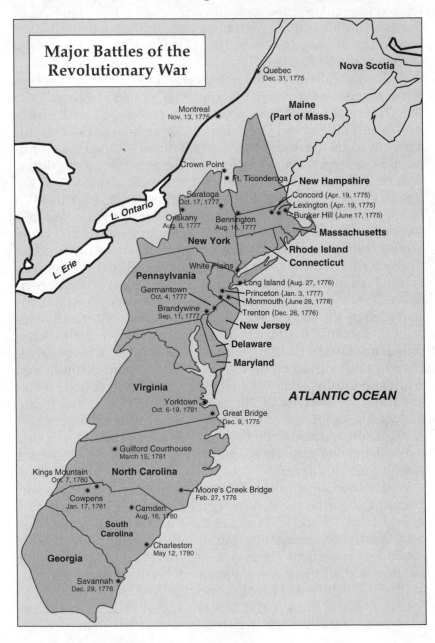

Major Battles of the Revolutionary War

Quebec
Dec. 31, 1775

Nova Scotia

Montreal
Nov. 13, 1775

Maine
(Part of Mass.)

Crown Point

Ft. Ticonderoga

New Hampshire

Saratoga
Oct. 17, 1777

Concord (Apr. 19, 1775)
Lexington (Apr. 19, 1775)
Bunker Hill (June 17, 1775)

Oriskany
Aug. 6, 1777

Bennington
Aug. 16, 1777

L. Ontario

New York

Massachusetts

Rhode Island

L. Erie

White Plains

Connecticut

Pennsylvania

Long Island (Aug. 27, 1776)

Germantown
Oct. 4, 1777

Princeton (Jan. 3, 1777)
Monmouth (June 28, 1778)

Brandywine
Sep. 11, 1777

Trenton (Dec. 26, 1776)

New Jersey

Delaware

Maryland

Virginia

ATLANTIC OCEAN

Yorktown
Oct. 6-19, 1781

Great Bridge
Dec. 9, 1775

Guilford Courthouse
March 15, 1781

Kings Mountain
Oct. 7, 1780

North Carolina

Cowpens
Jan. 17, 1781

Moore's Creek Bridge
Feb. 27, 1776

Camden
Aug. 16, 1780

South
Carolina

Charleston
May 12, 1780

Georgia

Savannah
Dec. 29, 1778

turned with heavy cannons taken from the fort. In March of 1776 Washington's army again laid siege to Boston. This time they were well organized, well supplied, and had heavy artillery. General Gage decided to abandon the city. However, he did so without alerting fellow officers. A regiment of British reinforcements under Lieutenant Colonel Archibald Campbell was captured by the Americans when it sailed into the city a few days later.

During the summer of 1776 American forces were in effective control of the thirteen colonies. Emboldened by this state of affairs, the Continental Congress took the dramatic step of declaring independence from Britain.

THE WAR IN THE NORTH

The sense of American victory did not last long. Even as Congress in Philadelphia debated the question of independence, British ships were sailing for New York from Halifax, Nova Scotia. As the Declaration of Independence was being signed, British troops were landing on Staten Island. Washington moved the Continental Army from Boston to New York, and was ordered by Congress to try to hold the city. However, the British army under General William Howe was overwhelming, and Washington's army was forced out, suffering its first significant defeat. Washington learned from the experience that it was not wise to confront the British directly. The remnants of the American army fled into New Jersey with General Howe's army in hot pursuit. The British chased Washington's army across the Delaware River and then settled down for the winter. Washington, however, made a surprise move back across the Delaware on Christmas of 1776 and won a couple of quick victories at Trenton and Princeton, reminding everyone that the American army was still alive. Then he, too, settled down for the winter.

By the time the war resumed in 1777, the patriot army had had a chance to recover. New recruits had been signed up, trained, and supplied with weapons. Howe spent most of 1777 waiting for more reinforcements. Finally in late August he began pushing toward Philadelphia, the capital of the rebellion. He assumed that taking the city where Congress met would finish the war. Washington tried to slow his advance, making a stand at Brandywine Creek and again briefly outside Philadelphia itself. Both were ineffective and General Howe marched into the city. It was, however, a hollow victory. The American army was still in the field, the people of Pennsylvania did not rally to the British cause as General Howe had expected they would, and Congress merely disbanded and went home.

Meanwhile to the north a second British offensive under General John Burgoyne managed to retake Fort Ticonderoga, and then marched south toward Albany. However, the push south proved to be a mistake. At Saratoga, New York, the British found themselves tired, low on supplies, and outnumbered by two American forces, one under Benedict Arnold and another under William Gates. The British were forced to surrender.

It was clear the British were not going to win an easy victory. The French, who had been secretly supplying the Americans with money and arms, felt it was safe to enter the war openly. They began harassing British possessions in the Caribbean. In order to defend colonies threatened by the French, the British were forced to withdraw from Philadelphia, leaving neither side in complete control of the northern states, and neither side strong enough to mount an effective offensive. By the summer of 1778 the war in the north had reached a stalemate.

THE WAR IN THE SOUTH

Late in 1778 the second phase of the war began with successful British naval attacks on Savannah, Georgia, and Charleston, South Carolina. Within a month Georgia was firmly in British control. The conquest of South Carolina proved to be more elusive. The British were able to defeat the main American army—a severe blow to the patriots—and then defeated a second army sent from the north under William Gates. However, the patriots then reformed into small guerrilla bands that hectored British supply lines and won occasional small victories where opportunity presented. Andrew Pickens, Thomas Sumter and Francis Marion were the chief guerrilla leaders in the Carolinas.

The war in the south was very different from the war in the north. While there were many Americans loyal to Britain in the north, they had done little to directly aid the British. Patriot troops faced soldiers from Great Britain, or in some cases German mercenaries hired by the British, but they rarely had to fight their own neighbors. In the south loyalists turned out in large numbers to support the British. For example, at the Battle of King's Mountain in North Carolina only one person in the battle was actually British, namely, the British commander, Lord Charles Cornwallis. All of the soldiers on both sides were Americans. The battle ended in a massacre of loyalist American soldiers. In other battles loyalists retaliated with atrocities of their own.

In December of 1780 Washington put Nathanael Greene in command of the southern forces. Greene proved to be an effective commander in the south just as Washington had been in the north. Like Washington, he never won a pitched battle against the British, but he managed to move his troops so effectively that each British victory was expensive and accomplished little.

In 1781 General Cornwallis left the situation in the Carolinas unresolved and moved his troops to Yorktown, Virginia, hoping to launch an attack into Virginia. This proved to be a mistake. Yorktown was fairly close to New York, where the Continental Army under General Washington was camped. Washington realized he could move his army quickly south and trap Cornwallis at Yorktown, provided he could prevent the British from escaping by sea. The French provided a fleet of twenty-eight ships from the Caribbean to blockade the Yorktown harbor, and a fleet of British ships from New York was unable to break the blockade. With no escape by sea available, Cornwallis was forced to surrender.

This victory did not bring the war to an end. In the south the British still had possession of Charleston and Savannah, and there were still loyalist troops in the field. The battle of Yorktown merely brought the war in the south to a standstill. Again, neither side had complete control, and neither side could mount an effective offensive.

The standoff continued for another two years.

THE UNITED STATES OF AMERICA

In 1781 the thirteen independent states ratified the Articles of Confederation, which had been written by a committee of the Continental Congress chaired by John Dickinson. The Articles created a weak central government with limited authority over the independent states. At this point each of the former colonies was still used to thinking of itself as a separate country. However, the Articles did create a central government capable of conducting foreign affairs including the negotiating of peace treaties.

The Second Continental Congress disbanded, and most of the same members then reconvened in Philadelphia under the name "The United States, in Congress assembled." The nation known as the United States of America had come into being.

PEACE

The war had been extremely costly for Britain. The British national debt had doubled, and much of what they had gained during the Seven Years' War was now being threatened by France and Spain. For example, in 1780 the Spanish recaptured West Florida, which had been ceded to Britain in 1763. Moreover, it was clear that time was on the side of the patriots. Each winter the Americans were able to recruit and train new soldiers, and each year their armies became more seasoned: their soldiers more disciplined and their leaders more experienced. By 1781 many people in Britain had concluded that there was nothing to gain and much to lose by continued fighting. Due to the unpopularity of the war, Lord Frederick North's Tory party lost their majority in Parliament. The new British government wasted no time offering to negotiate a peaceful withdrawal.

Negotiations to end the war were complicated. Britain wanted to end the hostilities so it could use its military resources protecting its other colonies from France and Spain. Of course, for the same reason France and Spain would have been happy to see the conflict prolonged indefinitely. Moreover, neither France nor Spain was eager to see a strong new nation in North America positioned to expand into territory that they still hoped to make their own. Hence France and Spain wanted to be involved in the peace negotiations, and Congress gave them reassurances that they would be. However, the American negotiators, Benjamin Franklin and John Jay, were shrewd enough to realize that American interests no longer meshed with those of her allies. To prevent the new United States from being hemmed in by concessions to France and Spain, they negotiated a separate peace with Britain without French and Spanish interference or approval. Among the terms of the treaty was a provision that the United States would take possession of British territory between the Appalachian Mountains and the Mississippi River, a provision that France and Spain would certainly have opposed. In order to obtain this concession, the Americans agreed to give up their claim to Canada. The treaty between Britain and the United States was signed in January of 1783. France and Spain had little choice but to come to terms with Britain a few weeks later, bringing the war to an end.

The effect of the war on American society was, of course, profound. The American colonists had been forced to work together to defeat the British, and their eventual victory gave them a shared sense of history. Furthermore, Americans now had something in common that, at the time, they shared with no other civilized people in the world: by their own choice they were not ruled by a king. Instead they had a "republican" form of government. For this reason they expressed their patriotism using symbols borrowed from the ancient Roman republic. The columns of Roman architecture were borrowed by American architects; the eagle, which had been the symbol of Rome, was adopted as a symbol of America (despite Benjamin Franklin's argument that the native turkey was more appropriate). Since a republican form of government had not been tried in hundreds of years, Americans felt they were embarked on a bold adventure. Despite their differences Americans now thought of themselves as one people who were embarked on that adventure together.

Of course, not everything changed as much as might have been hoped. Although the American Revolution was motivated by talk of freedom and equality, this dream was not universally realized. In 1750 slavery had been common in all thirteen colonies. In 1783 slavery was still common and the situation of African Americans had changed little. Women also made no progress during this period. By 1783 families were wealthier, so women enjoyed more free time; but their social status relative to men had actually declined. Women were less involved in public affairs than they had been in 1750. Some people at the time were aware that the Revolution had fallen short of its promise, but so much had been achieved that it was hard not to look to the future with optimism and hope.

Social Change in Colonial America, 1750–1755

CHAPTER 1

BENJAMIN FRANKLIN'S EXPERIMENTS IN ELECTRICITY

DANIEL J. BOORSTIN

In 1752 American printer, author, inventor, and amateur scientist Benjamin Franklin became something of a celebrity in Europe because of an experiment that, as every child knows, involved flying a kite during a thunderstorm. Franklin's experiment proved two things. In a merely practical sense it proved that lightning was a form of static electricity, similar to the sparks that result from petting a cat or rubbing leather shoes on a carpet. Franklin's experiment proved something purely theoretical as well. The idea that lightning would be attracted to a kite was based on an idea that Franklin was the first to propose, namely that electricity was a fluid, meaning that it could flow in certain directions, and that it could be described as positive or negative depending on the direction of its flow. The success of the kite experiment convinced European scientists of the truth of Franklin's theory.

Obviously, understanding that electricity can flow was the first step in learning to exploit electricity in telegraphs, telephones, electric lights, and, eventually, computers. No one at the time, including Franklin himself, appreciated the revolutionary importance of the discovery. The one immediately practical invention to come from the discovery was the lightning rod for protecting houses from damage due to lightning strikes. The metal rod provides a pathway that allowed electricity to flow safely past the house rather than through it. It is the same principle as digging a channel to divert a flood. The lightning rod was the first piece of technology to exploit the fact that electricity flows more easily through metal than through other materials.

Daniel J. Boorstin is a distinguished historian. He has served as director of the Library of Congress from 1975 to 1987, as director of the National Museum of American History, and as senior historian of the Smithsonian Institution of Washington, D.C. His works in history have won numerous awards, including the Pulitzer Prize. In this selection he makes a case that Franklin's great breakthrough in electricity might not have occurred if Franklin had been in closer contact with European "experts" on the subject.

O n a rare occasion, an American could discover something, even in physics, simply because he was less learned than his European colleagues. Ignorance of the respectable paths of scientific thought might leave him freer to wander off wherever facts beckoned. Such was no foundation for a solid tradition of speculative science, but it was not absolutely impossible to advance physics under American conditions. To exploit naïveté in a subject as cumulative as physics required great genius, but at least one colonial American—Benjamin Franklin—was able to do so.

Franklin's concepts did of course grow in the context of Newtonian [based on the theories of Sir Isaac Newton] experimental science, but Franklin was not, and never pretended to be, well read in the Newtonian classics. The evidence even for his reading of Newton's *Optics* is only circumstantial; everything confirms our suspicion that Franklin lacked the mathematical knowledge to understand Newton's *Principia* or other works of similar difficulty. His theoretical equipment for advanced study in any of the physical sciences was meager.

A Triumph of Naïveté

Franklin's actual accomplishment was obscured by extravagant comparison here and abroad to the greatest mathematical and physical theorists. John Adams declared his reputation "more universal than that of [German philosopher Gottfried] Leibnitz or Newton, Frederick [II, King of Prussia, known as Frederick the Great] or [French writer] Voltaire." Lord Chatham [William Pitt] praised him in the House of Lords as "one whom all Europe held in high Estimation for his Knowledge and Wisdom, and rank'd with our Boyles [referring to physicist and chemist Robert Boyle] and Newtons." The great chemist Joseph Priestley declared Franklin's discovery in his kite experiment "the greatest, perhaps since the time of Sir Isaac Newton." Franklin's special genius has been buried under the even less discriminating praise heaped on him since his death.

In fact his achievement illustrated the triumph of naïveté over learning. A clue to Franklin's peculiar success as a "physicist" is found in the explanation for Cadwallader Colden's failure. Colden, [an amateur scientist from New York] . . . aimed at greatness in the European mold. In his *Principles of Action in Matter* (1751), he professed to carry on the work of Newton, even to outdo Newton by providing a general theory of the "cause" of gravitation. Colden did not possess the specialized learning, the architectonic mind, nor the community with other learned physicists without which great works in mathematical physics have seldom been produced. Yet he pretended "to have discovered the true cause of the motion of the planets and comets, and from thence to deduce the reason of all the phaenomena, with that exactness as to agree with the most accurate observations." Happily, he explained, all this would be accomplished, "without any aid of the conic sections, or of any other knowledge, besides the common rules of arithmetic and trigonometry." Franklin, in contrast to Colden, had no illusion that he was at home in Newton's mathematical world; he merely set out to explain certain specific phenomena. Colden's work would probably have been of higher quality had he lived in Europe near the ancient seats of learning, but under such circumstances Franklin's work might not have been done at all.

Electricity was where Franklin earned his reputation as a physicist; only there did he make physical discoveries of lasting significance. Franklin's electrical discoveries were not embodied in treatises nor were they the minor premises of a large theory about the nature, origin, or causes of electricity, much less of all matter. His writings on electricity were diffuse and miscellaneous. His book, which became famous under the title *Experiments and Observations on Electricity, made at Philadelphia in America,* was actually a collection of letters, so loosely organized that some readers have doubted whether the items were intended for publication. They were not published as a book in America until 1941.

"He has endeavoured, said [chemist] Sir Humphry Davy, "to remove all mystery and obscurity from the subject. He has written equally for the uninitiated and for the philosopher; and he has rendered his details amusing as well as perspicuous, elegant as well as simple." Even today the reader is amazed to find that so fundamental a work is so commonplace and non-mathematical in its language. This work, the basis of Franklin's scientific reputation, reads more like a book of kitchen-recipes or instructions for parlor-magic than like a treatise on physics. In explaining "the wonderful effect of pointed bodies, both in drawing off and throwing off the electrical fire," in one of his most important letters, he writes:

> Place an iron shot of three or four inches diameter on the mouth of a clean dry glass bottle. By a fine silken thread from the ceiling, right over the mouth of the bottle, suspend a small cork-ball, about the bigness of a marble; the thread of such a length, as that the cork-ball may rest against the side of the shot. Electrify the shot and the ball will be repelled to the distance of four or five inches, more or less, according to the quantity of Electricity. . . . When in this state, if you present to the shot the point of a long, slender, sharp bodkin, at six or eight inches distance, the repellency is instantly destroyed, and the cork flies to the shot. A blunt body must be brought within an inch, and draw a spark to produce the same effect.

In Franklin's day it was possible to carry on important electrical experiments with kitchen equipment because the subject was still in its infancy, and had not yet begun to become mathematical. Of all the sciences which saw great advances in the 17th and 18th centuries electricity had had the least history. There was a great deal less to know, or to be ignorant of, in electricity than in astronomy or mathematical physics in general. Since it seemed to have no practical application at the time, there was full scope for the play of idle curiosity. Franklin's interest in electricity was, if anything, less "practical" than that of some of his contemporaries, for he doubted that electricity would ever be the medical cure-all that some were then predicting it would be. His amateur and non-academic frame of mind was his greatest advantage; like many another discovering American, he saw more because he knew much less of what he was supposed to see.

When Franklin first became interested in electricity, just after 1746, he knew very little of what had been done in Europe. Returning to Philadelphia after a trip to Boston, where he had happened to witness "electrical entertainments," Franklin was delighted to find that the Library Company had received some glass tubes from [his London correspondent] Peter Collinson. Three fellow-amateurs joined him in repeating the experiments he had seen. Most active was Ebenezer Kinnersley, an ordained Baptist minister who never had a pulpit—"an ingenious neighbor," according to Franklin, "who, being out of business, I encouraged to undertake showing the experiments for money." The other two were Philip Syng (1703–1789), a silversmith by trade, and Thomas Hopkinson (1709–1751), a lawyer and the father of the ingenious [composer] Francis Hopkinson. Both were to be among the founders of the American Philosophical Society. The precise role of each in the important early experiments is not easy to assign, partly because Franklin showed no excessive modesty in his accounts. But no one of the miscellaneous group was primarily a "natural philosopher"; none held a reg-

Benjamin Franklin performing his now-famous electricity experiment.

ular university degree nor could have been called learned by
English standards.

The Philadelphia amateurs were quite out of touch with the
work of European natural philosophers. They thought that
Syng had accomplished something novel and important when
he "invented" a simple electrical machine: a sphere of glass that
turned on an iron axle producing friction which collected the
electricity. This seemed a great improvement over the "fatiguing exercise" of rubbing a glass tube. But machines like Syng's
had long before been used in England and were already popular among electrical experimenters on the continent.

It seems that Franklin's only knowledge of earlier European
work on electricity was what he had gained from . . . Peter
Collinson. That was not a great deal. Franklin reported to
Collinson that he and his three Philadelphia collaborators were
observing "some particular phaenomena, that we look upon to
be new." But he had no way of knowing whether these were
really discoveries or had already been noticed by European scientists. Franklin's later letters to Collinson (which became the
book on electricity) continued to have the tantalizing quality of
a journal by an explorer who does not know whether anyone
has seen his land before.

If Franklin had been better informed of what European scientists had accomplished, he might not have dared to make his
boldly simple suggestion: that electricity was a single fluid, not
varying with the material from which it was produced. This
was Franklin's fundamental electrical discovery. The two forms
of electricity he then described simply as "plus" and "minus,"
depending on what he conceived to be the direction of the flow.

Sophisticated European thinking on the subject had already
"advanced" to [French scientist Charles-François de Cisternay]
Du Fay's more elaborate doctrine:

> There are two distinct Electricities, very different from
> one another; one of which I call vitreous Electricity and
> the other resinous Electricity. The first is that of Glass,
> Rock-Crystal, Precious Stones, Hair of Animals, Wool,
> and many other Bodies. The second is that of Amber,
> Copal, Gum-Lack, Silk, Thread, Paper, and a vast
> Number of other Substances.

Franklin seems to have known nothing of Du Fay's distinction.
He proceeded directly from his own observations to his epochal

assumption that all electricity was a single fluid. Even if Franklin had known the misleading distinction which European scientists had made, he might have offered his own simple explanation. But it would have required boldness of imagination from a man whose forte was not boldness but common sense. It is more likely that he would not have dared even to voice his revolutionary observation.

Fortunately for our understanding of Franklin's work, we know what happened to his thinking after he became better acquainted with the writings of his European contemporaries. From the standard European writings on electricity, many of which Peter Collinson sent to the Library Company of Philadelphia, Franklin learned the respectable ideas and the conventional vocabulary. His own insights lost their freshness. As early as 1748, he showed a tendency to learn from books rather than from observation; he began to see things as his European contemporaries saw them. A pamphlet published in London in 1751 with four of Franklin's letters on electricity offered nearly all his basic contribution to the subject. The more perceptive European scientists themselves feared that if Franklin acquired their learning he would soon see no more than they did. Pieter van Musschenbroek, discoverer of the principle of the condenser and an inventor of the Leyden jar, warned the American scientist. On receiving Franklin's request for books on electricity in 1759, he urged him to "go on making experiments entirely on your own initiative and thereby pursue a path entirely different from that of the Europeans, for then you shall certainly find many other things which have been hidden to natural philosophers throughout the space of centuries." Unfortunately, by this time Franklin had already become "learned" in electricity and the damage was done.

Franklin's writings on electricity, then, were not exceptions to the descriptive, limited character of colonial science. With his usual good luck, Franklin had happened on a subject where his lack of mathematics was no disadvantage, where his lack of learning was in fact an advantage, and where the play of his idle curiosity could bear fruit. Here was hardly enough to justify [Thomas] Jefferson's boast that America was already producing great physicists to vie with those of the Old World. Least of all did it show that America was a fruitful soil for basic scientific discoveries of a theoretical character. If it suggested anything, it was the contrary. American barrenness of other discoveries in

the physical sciences during the colonial period only emphasized the atypical and coincidental character of Franklin's discovery in this field.

LIGHTNING IS ELECTRICITY

The achievement by Franklin which most fired the popular
imagination and which has been hallowed in American folklore, was even further from the rarefied world of Newtonian
physics: his proof of the identity of lightning and electricity,
and his invention of the lightning-rod thus made possible.
Franklin's famous experiment of the electrical kite was not a
basic theoretical discovery. It was a clever way of putting to
practical use the "power of points" and the "single fluid" theory of electricity, both of which had already been developed in
Franklin's letters. It was a combination of applied science and
mechanical ingenuity. The identity of lightning and electricity
had already been suspected by Europeans, but they had found
no way to prove it. Franklin's contribution was a simple de-
vice that, as he said, "might have occurred to any electrician,"
but which somehow had not occurred to European physicists
preoccupied with their "electrical machines," their laboratory
experiments, and their theoretical arguments among themselves.

When Dr. John Lining of Charleston asked Franklin how he
had come to think of the kite experiment to test the identity of
lightning and electricity, Franklin replied by quoting from his
scientific journal:

> Nov. 9, 1749. Electrical fluid agrees with lightning in
> these particulars: 1. Giving light. 2. Colour of the light.
> 3. Crooked direction. 4. Swift motion. 5. Being con-
> ducted by metals. 6. Crack or noise in exploding. 7.
> Subsisting in water or ice. 8. Rending bodies it passes
> through. 9. Destroying animals. 10. Melting metals. 11.
> Firing inflammable substances. 12. Sulphureous
> smell.—The electric fluid is attracted by points.—We
> do not know whether this property is in lightning.—
> But since they agree in all the particulars wherein we
> can already compare them, is it not probable they agree
> likewise in this? Let the experiment be made.

Once Franklin had proposed the obvious and only conclusive
test of the hypothesis, several Europeans made the trial. They

may even have pursued Franklin's suggestion before Franklin himself got around to it.

The Abbé Nollet, one of the most "advanced" and learned of the French physicists and a leading exponent of the two-fluid theory, rejected such a direct appeal to "mere" observation. Franklin recounted in his *Autobiography* that Nollet, already offended by Franklin's omission of his name from the *Experiments and Observations on Electricity*, "could not at first believe that such a work came from America and said it must have been fabricated by his enemies at Paris, to decry his system. Afterwards, having been assur'd that there really existed such a person as Franklin at Philadelphia, which he had doubted, he wrote and published a volume of letters, chiefly address'd to me, defending his theory, and denying the verity of my experiments, and of the positions deduc'd from them." Still Franklin would not be drawn into quibbling over questions that could be settled only by observation. "My writings contain'd a description of experiments which any one might repeat and verify, and if not to be verifi'd, could not be defended. . . . I concluded to let my papers shift for themselves, believing it was better to spend what time I could spare from public business in making new experiments, than in disputing about those already made."

So eager was Franklin for the application of his ideas, that in the very letter in which he proposed his experiment to test the identity of lightning and electricity (and even before the experiment had been made or his hypothesis had been confirmed), Franklin described the lightning-rod. "If these things are so," he wrote from Philadelphia in 1749, "may not the knowledge of this power of points be of use to mankind, in preserving houses, churches, ships, &c. from the stroke of lightning, by directing us to fix on the highest part of those edifices, upright rods of iron made sharp as a needle, and gilt to prevent rusting, and from the foot of those rods a wire down the outside of the building into the ground, or down round one of the shrouds of a ship, and down her side till it reaches the water?" In *Poor Richard's Almanack* for 1753, he published a simple description of a lightning-rod under the heading "How to secure Houses, &c. from Lightning."

The lightning-rod quickly took hold in America. Even though academic learning on electricity was scarce, what men did know about electricity was soon put to more widespread practical use than in the great centers of European learning. We do not have reliable statistics, but observers from both sides of the Atlantic noticed that lightning-rods were more widely used in America than in England. "No country has more certainly proved the efficacy of electrical rods, than this," the Rev. Andrew Burnaby noted as early as 1759 when he traveled through Virginia. Although buildings were sometimes struck by lightning, rods were so generally in use that it had become rare to hear of their being damaged. Burnaby hoped that this American example would inspire others to give up their religious prejudices against using scientific devices for human safety.

Even in America, however, the introduction of the lightning-rod had been delayed by religious prejudice and scientific conservatism. In 1755, soon after rods had first come into use, Boston was shaken by a severe earthquake, which the Rev. Thomas Prince explained in a new appendix to his sermon *Earthquakes, The Works of God and Tokens of His Just Displeasure.* "The more points of Iron are erected around the Earth, to draw the Electrical Substance out of the Air; the more the Earth must needs be charged with it. . . . In Boston are more erected than anywhere else in New England; and Boston seems to be more dreadfully shaken. O! there is no getting out of the mighty Hand of God! If we think to avoid it in the Air, we cannot in the Earth: Yes, it may grow more fatal." But the sensible Professor John Winthrop, who understood Franklin's points, read a lecture in the Harvard College Chapel to refute such wild imaginings; and the cases in which the rods had actually worked seemed in the popular mind to outweigh fancy theoretical objections. In London in 1772, Franklin found it curious that the English were only then beginning to use lightning-rods although in America rods had already been in common use for nearly 20 years and were found not only on public buildings, churches, and country mansions but even on small private houses.

The circumstances of life here had probably prodded the Americans. "Thunder Storms are much more frequent there [in America] than in Europe, . . ." Franklin wrote from London in 1772. "Here in England, the Practice [of using rods] has made a slower Progress, Damage by Lightning being less frequent, & People of course less apprehensive of Danger from it." Meteorologists tell us that, although the frequency of thunderstorms in southern Canada is about the same as in Europe (occurring on the average on about eleven days in the year), the frequency increases as one goes south until thunderstorms are nearly seven times as frequent in states bordering the Gulf of Mexico (occurring on the average on about 72 days in the year). All such figures are crude, and it is possible that the weather was different in the 18th century. But we do have enough information to make us suspect that lightning and thunder were more frequent here than in Europe. At any rate they must have seemed more threatening to colonial Americans dispersed over a half-known continent.

COLONIAL HOME LIFE AND THE CONSUMER REVOLUTION

STEPHANIE GRAUMAN WOLF

Perhaps the most important revolution of the eighteenth century was a revolution in the way people lived. At the beginning of the century it was expected that cooking, eating, sleeping, and visiting with guests were all done together in the same room. This was true even of the very wealthy, for, while the wealthy themselves had separate chambers within their estates, their servants both worked and lived in the rooms where they were employed. While large estates had dining halls and ballrooms for formal occasions, the wealthy normally ate daily meals in their rooms. Rather than sleeping in separate bedrooms, they owned large, enclosed beds located in the same chambers that were used to conduct business and entertain visitors. Even the wealthy had relatively few possessions: Wealth was measured in terms of land, livestock, and servants, not things. If even the wealthy did not distinguish different rooms for different purposes, and owned relatively few possessions, the same was even more true for the lower and middle classes, and for the new, temporary houses of the colonies.

By the end of the revolutionary period American homes had changed dramatically. They were divided into separate rooms, each having a specified function. People, both rich and poor, owned many more private possessions. In America this change might have been explained merely as a change from frontier to urban living. However this alone does not account for the change, which affected rural as well as urban communities and Europe as well as the New World. In fact, the change was a sweeping cultural phenomenon that cultural historians refer to as "the consumer revolution."

Stephanie Grauman Wolf is the author of several books on early American social history, including *Urban Village: Population, Community, and Family Structure in Germantown, PA, 1683–1800s*. She is a senior research fellow at the Philadelphia Center for Early American Studies, University of Pennsylvania. In this selection she traces the effect of the consumer revolution on typical American households.

A house is a physical structure; a home is the vision of life and family that it embodies. During the eighteenth century, Americans molded and shaped their domestic space, within the technological limits of their times, not only to accommodate their daily habits, but also to fit the human values and relationships that were important to them.

These eighteenth-century Americans rarely discussed what they were doing, let alone what it meant. Few people bothered to record where they put the trash, how often and where they bathed, or where and with whom they made love. Nor did they explain even to themselves, perhaps, why it was important to live in a house that was "spacious and well-furnished with linen and silverplate" yet unimportant that three or four persons, including guests, slept in the same room. They assumed that those around them used similar objects, followed similar patterns, and attached the same meanings to them. It was only when travelers from another culture were surprised or confused by everyday habits that differed from their own that the mundane details of American living were recorded at all, and while their descriptions may have been factually correct, their value judgments were based on the traveler's own cultural expectations. A genteel Englishman from London had no way of evaluating the degree of luxury, style, comfort, convenience, or even cleanliness to be found in the rural home of an upstate New York squire. Wealthy Anglo colonists traveling beyond the borders of their own township, region, class, or ethnic group failed to understand how others could tolerate homes so different from their own: Indians were "savage" because they slept on skins and lay their fires directly on the floor; Germans were "boorish" because they expended more effort on their barns than their houses; southerners were "filthy" because they slept together in a single room.

THE CONSUMER REVOLUTION

Most of these derogatory comments came, in fact, from those who were raised in English ways, and middle- or upper-class ways at that. For centuries, decent living as defined by English culture had required that animal and human living spaces be separate, that hearths and chimneys take the place of open fires and roof vents, and that there be some division of the house into rooms that served different purposes. By the beginning of the eighteenth century, respectable English farmers, craftsmen, and tradesmen had long participated in a domestic upheaval so deep and far-reaching that historians refer to it as the "consumer revolution." Even common homes came to be filled with objects of utility and display, in number, kind, and variety previously reserved only for the very rich and powerful. A house became more than a shelter and a workshop: It became a family center where privacy, comfort, and leisure were expected parts of the daily routine.

It also became a measure of its owner's place in society. Before the consumer revolution, chairs, for example, were rare commodities, and only religious or secular rulers were entitled to own or use them. Everyone else sat around on stools or benches, leaned against the walls, or squatted on the floor. The quickening pace of the English economy and the beginning of the Industrial Revolution during the seventeenth century made chairs more affordable and available, and they became less symbolic of power and more indicative of the economic and social position of their owners. As more and more householders filled their homes with chairs, mere possession was no longer sufficient to establish superior status and the owner was judged by the cost of the materials and fancy decoration that went into his seating pieces, as well as by the number of specialized chairs and matched "setts" he could afford. As with chairs, so also with a host of other newly available items, from cooking utensils and tableware to luxury fabrics and looking glasses.

Eighteenth-century settlers from England carried an awareness of the new domestic standards with them to the colonies, and whether or not they had been involved in the consumer revolution at home, they generally hoped to become active participants in their new communities. Other European colonists, Africans, and Native Americans were only introduced to the English ideals of the "proper home" through association with their Anglo neighbors or masters. They often rejected these alien arrangements in favor of their own cultural traditions or were barred from involvement by economic insufficiency. By the end of the eighteenth century, however, the English model of culture had become the dominant pattern of the new nation. A vision of the ideal American home increasingly took a form based on domestic values rooted in the English housing and consumer revolutions of centuries before.

In actuality, of course, there was no typical eighteenth-century American home, just as there was no one kind of eighteenth-century American family. The domestic reality was a combination of physical necessity and cultural choice. First and foremost, the kind of house in which a family lived was dictated by its location in relation to the frontier. We tend to think of colonial frontier life as a seventeenth-century phenomenon, yet there were as many backcountry people at the time of the Revolution as there had been colonists in 1690. The first settlers in newly opened, isolated regions during the eighteenth century replicated the stages of housing typical of the previous century. Their immediate problem was to erect some kind of shelter, however temporary, and begin to clear ground for a first planting.

ENGLISH WIGWAMS

Many of their first houses were called "English wigwams," combining features of the rough, conical dugouts used by itinerant workers like goatherds, shepherds, and farm laborers in the English countryside with those of the mobile shelters erected by Amerindians like the Iroquois, MicMacs, and Delawares during the hunting season. Both had the advantage of quick construction and easily available material: forked poles, branches, bark, turf, or animal skins. The English version also required a handful of nails. Where feasible, eighteenth-century pioneers created a larger, slightly more stable version of the "newcomer's wigwam" by digging into the ground to a depth of about three feet and topping this foundation with the roof structure of a hut. The best-known of these so-called "caves" were built in Philadelphia on the banks of the Delaware River in the early 1680s by William Penn's first settlers. Well into the nineteenth century, the sod houses of pioneers in the Great

Plains reflected a continuing tradition of this sort.

With the exception of these cave huts, the common denominator of most impermanent houses was that they had no foundations; buildings rested directly on the ground, or were attached to posts driven into the ground. Where the crisis of total wilderness was past, or in parts of the backcountry that were somewhat less remote, these temporary homes bore a closer resemblance to permanent structures, with squared walls, roofs, chimneys, and window openings. While they were not sturdy enough to last indefinitely—the wood next to, or directly in, the ground was bound to rot out relatively quickly—these second-stage houses nevertheless were capable of providing settlers with shelter "for some years, till they find leisure and ability to build better.". . .

HOUSING BUILT TO LAST

As eighteenth-century New England farmhouses were enlarged from the single-room dwelling of first settlement, they were built to provide for a household which, though large, contained no real outsiders. While the original "hall," with its great fireplace, remained the general gathering spot for sitting, eating, and, occasionally, sleeping, it shared a central chimney with a "parlor" or "chamber" where the farmer and his wife, and perhaps the newest baby, slept. This new room doubled as more formal space, where outsiders were entertained: If visitors stayed for a meal, it was taken here, in which case mere eating was elevated to the status of dining. A small entryway or lobby provided access to parlor and hall, as well as a staircase to the room or rooms above, where most of the family slept and which served as storage space for household goods and even occasional crops. What was unique about the New England farmhouse was the development of a full-blown "kyttchin" out of traditional, unheated storage space present in English hall/parlor houses. While originally a shed off the back of the hall, by the eighteenth century the "lean-to" extended across the whole back of the house and was actually incorporated into its basic framework. One end was frequently partitioned off for the storage of provisions and utensils, and the other end turned into a small chamber for the ill, the elderly, or women confined to childbed who might require attention. The central portion, however, acquired its own hearth and became the single location for food cooking and processing, moving such activities entirely out of the hall. An underground cellar for cool storage, meat-salting, and dairying completed the innovations to the English model. By the second half of the century, the New England farmhouse had become the northern norm for "decent" country living. Anything less was substandard, as John Adams noted in 1767 when he visited a poor family in Braintree [Massachusetts]. The husband, wife, and five children occupied "one Chamber, which serves them for Kitchen, Cellar, dining Room, Parlour, and Bed Chamber. . . . There are the Conveniences and ornaments of a Life of Poverty. These the Comforts of the Poor. This is Want. This is Poverty." By the 1790s, as New Englanders "hived out" west across the northern territories, they carried their traditional house plans with them, creating a familiar type that has become the modern symbol of nostalgic old-time domesticity.

Southern families and farm life were established on a different basis from the very beginning, and their eighteenth-century houses developed traditional forms that were adapted to these particular patterns. Most southern farmers were a far cry from the great plantation owners and their homes were nothing like our modern national image, based as it is on something like Tara in *Gone With the Wind*. They were described by contemporaries as "meane and Little," referring both to impermanent building techniques and to the fact that perhaps as many as half of all southern whites and nearly all blacks continued to occupy one-room houses right through the 1700s. The little houses of common southern planters were even smaller than those of far poorer New England contemporaries, since they lacked the second story usual in New England "hall" houses. In 1733, [Virginia planter] William Byrd commented on the "rudeness and remoteness" of the immediate backcountry. He felt "quite out of Christendom" and noted that the local farmers admired the house "of a few rooms" that Byrd had had built for the manager of his estates there "as much as if it had been the Grand Visier's tent in the Turkish army." Nor was Byrd, admittedly something of a snob, prepared to accept the hospitality of his neighbors. He preferred sleeping out of doors to sharing a room where the family "all pigged loveyngly together."

Since southern servants were not part of this "loving" domestic scene, the final form of the multiroom southern farm was a physical manifestation of this cultural reality. Some houses retained a cross passage common to one type of older English plan, where the hall lay on one side and a room for storage and farm processing, known as a "downside" kitchen, lay on the other. More and more, however, the passage in the southern house served to separate the family who used the hall for a sitting room from the servants who worked in the processing room and slept above it in a separate loft. Eventually the segregation was quite complete. The Chesapeake farmer eliminated the passage entirely, and provided detached buildings for the "drudgeries" of cooking, washing, smoking, dairying, soap boiling, and all the other heavy domestic chores of preindustrial farm life. He also provided separate "quarters" for the laborers who, under the supervision of his wife, performed these tasks. As newly settled southern, backcountry regions adopted the economic patterns of the Chesapeake, they accepted its domestic arrangements as well.

In the Middle Colonies—New York, New Jersey, and Pennsylvania—the diversity of population, family structure, and farming practice prevented the development of any single, clearly defined "machine" for daily living. Even where immigrants retained something of their Old World common culture, such as the very small number of the thousands of German immigrants to Pennsylvania who consciously chose to isolate themselves, they did not re-create the *hofs* (barn/house complexes built around a courtyard) typical of their places of origin. The true distinctiveness of their homes was often a matter of decoration and style, rather than a radically different organization of space.

THE GEORGIAN-STYLE HOME

It was in the many small towns of eastern Pennsylvania, as well as among middle- and upper-class families of more urban areas and rural gentry throughout the colonies, that the Georgian home came to be the standard by the 1760s. This European import was more than the ideal of exterior balance and classical decoration we have already described; it embodied an organization of interior space as well. A broad hall ran all the way through the center of the house with two rooms opening out on each side. A staircase led directly to an upstairs hall, also flanked by four rooms. Work spaces and servants' quarters could be attached to the back in urban areas, or located in separate dependencies on country estates. They could even be stuffed into the main body of the house—kitchen in the cellar, servants in the third-floor garrets, for example—without disturbing the basic symmetry of the arrangement. So perfectly was the Georgian plan adapted to the middle-class families who formed the fastest-growing segment of the American population by the end of the eighteenth century that, in one form or another, it has continued to symbolize the American home right through the twentieth century.

Initially, of course, it was the Georgian's new and fashionable "look" that attracted the rich, the near rich, and the merely aspiring. For country dwellers wealthy and sophisticated enough to have transcended the status of farmer and entered the colonial equivalent of English gentry, a new, stylish Georgian house carefully set on a rise or by a river where it could be seen and admired by neighbors and passersby made a powerful statement of the owner's "arrival." It was no accident that led Robert Carter of Virginia to locate his huge mansion on a "high spot of Ground" where its forty-foot facade could be seen "at the Distance of six Miles," as his admiring new employee, Philip Fithian, recorded in 1773. Earlier Georgian houses, like James Logan's mansion, Stenton, built near Philadelphia in 1724, betrayed the status-seeking nature of their style by keeping the balanced look only on the front, while punctuating the back of the house with windows and doors wherever they were useful, regardless of symmetry. Mansion houses like Carter's, built beside rivers where both front and back were visible to the public, were Georgian in design on both sides. For town and city residents, use of the new style communicated a similar message to an even larger audience.

The quick and long-lasting popularity of the interior Georgian house plan was due to the way that it fitted in with developing notions of specialization of the tasks and people within households. As we have seen, even ordinary rural houses were being modified to these ends. Although many farm families still cooked in the dining area, slept in the parlor or cooking area, and stored farm implements and surplus crops almost anywhere, the trend was clearly in the direction of separating spaces for special tasks and daily routines. Georgian houses, with their formal arrangement of front rooms around a central hall and back spaces appended or detached that were, in a sense, not part of the plan at all, clearly separated "working" from "living," and "living" into neat compartments. As the century wore on, plans began to specify a function for each of these spaces: parlor or sitting room, dining room, office or study, bed-chamber or back parlor. The priorities involved in determining which household activities required segregation differed radically from our own. There is little question that if we could have only one private room in our houses, it would be a bathroom or, at least, a water closet. Yet, while many colonial Americans used indoor facilities rather than resorting to the outdoor necessary—as indicated by the increasing frequency of "wash basins, pitchers, chamber pots and close stools" on lists of household furnishings—they were content to locate these intimate conveniences in bedchambers which they frequently shared with others.

THE DESIRE FOR PRIVACY

The most important room in the Georgian house, in terms of reflecting the changing concepts of everyday life among middle- and upper-class Americans of the eighteenth century, was the central hall. It not only maintained the segregation of function within the household by allowing access to each room without having to go through another, it performed the increasingly important task of preserving family privacy from the outside world. Privacy itself was not a concept that had had much currency in the seventeenth-century world of communal living, nor was it a luxury afforded to the majority in the eighteenth. It was, however, implicit in the growing separation of household members as we have discussed it. The desire for solitary space is perhaps best expressed by Abigail Adams in a letter she wrote to [her husband] John, in 1776, while staying at her aunt's house:

> I have possession of my Aunts chamber in which there is a very convenient pretty closet with a window . . . a number of Book Shelves [and] pretty little desk or cabinet . . . where I write all my Letters and keep my papers unmollested by anyone. I do not covet my Neighbours Goods, but . . . I always had a fancy for a closet with a window which I could more peculiarly call my own.

Just as important as personal solitude, however, was a growing emphasis throughout the century on the withdrawal of the family as a whole from the rest of the world. The old one-room house allowed outsiders access to every activity of the household. Ordinary houses set off work space from living space but allowed for few subtle distinctions among visitors. The Georgian hall, however, separated callers from all household activities until they could be directed to the appropriate room, depending on the nature of their business and their degree of relationship to the family. Female intimates might be allowed upstairs to the wife's chamber, social inferiors who had business affairs to settle with the master might be taken to the office, servants or menials could be directed around to the back, and those of equal social standing who were privy to household entertainments might attain the parlor or the dining room (or be politely turned away, when the family did not care to receive them). While few reacted as strongly as Mrs. Benjamin Harrison, who fainted when a local farmer appeared unannounced in her parlor, the hall helped to prevent this kind of unexpected confrontation.

Since the hall was the place where the family met the public, its size, grandeur, and furnishings all bespoke the social position of those who lived within. High ceilings, elaborately carved doorways to the inner rooms, and stairways to the upper regions where none might penetrate except by invitation—all at once informed the visitor of the status of the family and fixed his or her own position in the social hierarchy. The slow but steady increase in the use of Georgian house plans meant that by the 1790s even those of modest means and few pretensions had adopted the ideals of household organization and family privacy that were formerly the standard only among the elite.

THE IROQUOIS CONFEDERACY

PAUL A.W. WALLACE

Europeans in the New World represented a wide variety of cultures with different religions, customs, and even languages. Yet Europeans understood the need for high-level political structures so that small communities could act together. By contrast, the Native Americans who confronted the European invasion generally did not recognize any form of central authority. The Delaware tribe, for example, was a widespread and important group, but each local community was completely independent and subject only to its own laws. This, of course, made it difficult for the tribe to enter into treaties or coordinate war efforts.

However, one group of Native Americans did understand the concept of a larger political structure. The Iroquois Confederacy was originally made up of five tribes: the Mohawk, Cayuga, Oneida, Seneca, and Onondaga. In 1722 a sixth tribe, the Tuscarora, was added. Hence, the confederacy is sometimes called the Five Nations and sometimes the Six Nations. Through warfare the Delaware came to be dominated by the Iroquois, but the Delaware tribe was not considered to be a member of the confederacy. Because of its sophisticated political structure, the Iroquois Confederacy was a powerful force on the American frontier. European nations, especially the French and the English, were inclined to treat it as a nation in its own right.

Paul A.W. Wallace (1891–1967) was editor of *Pennsylvania History*, the journal of the Pennsylvania Historical Society, and the author of numerous books on the history of Pennsylvania. His work on the Indians of Pennsylvania was considered a classic and has been reprinted frequently. This selection, taken from a

Paul A.W. Wallace, *Indians in Pennsylvania*, revised by William A. Hunter, Harrisburg: The Pennsylvania Historical and Museum Commission, 1993. Copyright © 1993 by The Pennsylvania Historical and Museum Commission. Reproduced by permission.

1993 reissue of Wallace's classic work and revised by William A. Hunter to incorporate recent scholarship, describes the way of life as well as the political organization of the tribes that made up the Iroquois Confederacy.

T he Iroquois called themselves *Kanonsionni*, "People of the Longhouse," using a familiar figure taken from their housekeeping. They, like the Susquehannocks, lived in long, rectangular, bark-covered houses, each with its central corridor, its hearths, and its several families under the general superintendence of an elder matron of the lineage.

The longhouse was a good symbol, calling to mind as it did both the geography and the government of the Confederacy. The five independent peoples of which it was composed, each speaking a dialect of a common Iroquoian tongue, were seated in a string of villages along a trail—at one time a warpath but after confederation known as the Ambassadors' Road—which crossed northern New York from near Schenectady to the Genesee River. From east to west—as the names of rivers and lakes in that region remind us—they were the Mohawk, Oneida, Onondaga, Cayuga, and Seneca nations.

THE DEMOCRATIC STRUCTURE OF THE IROQUOIS CONFEDERACY

Each nation was virtually independent, having its own council, just as each family in the longhouse had its separate fire. The homely image of the longhouse brought to mind also their highly advanced, (and to us surprisingly modern) concept of democratic rule. The authority of the Great Council (the central government) came from the homes of the people. On the death of a chief, the head matron of his lineage consulted the matrons of other longhouses before appointing his successor to the clan council. The chiefs of the several clans made up each nation's council, and these same chiefs represented their nation on the Great Council of the Confederacy.

The federal congress or Great Council was often known as the Onondaga Council because it met at Onondaga (Syracuse, New York), the principal seat of the Onondaga nation whose territory lay in the geographical center of the League. Meetings were held at least once a year, and oftener if pressing business (matters of peace and war) arose. When Conrad Weiser, Pennsylvania's representative, carried peace messages to the Iroquois, he sent advance notice to Onondaga; and from that place runners were dispatched to both ends of the Longhouse to summon the council chiefs to meet him when he arrived.

In the Onondaga Council, each member nation had certain privileges and responsibilities. The Mohawks, for instance, had a council veto. The Onondagas provided the presiding officer, Atotarho (Wathatotarho, Thadodaho), who was also the Head Chief of the Confederacy; and their chiefs as a body were the steering committee, "tending the fire," which meant preparing the agenda and, in the absence of the Council, attending to necessary business. The Senecas appointed the two war chiefs of the Confederacy.

The role of the federal council was to harmonize, if that were possible, the often conflicting interests of the different nations in the Confederacy. Each nation had its own customs, language (a dialect of the common tongue), and international problems. The Mohawks faced east, the Senecas west, and their friends as well as their enemies were not always the same. In time of great crisis, if feelings ran high and unanimity in the council was impossible (as happened during the American Revolution, when both the Americans and the British solicited Iroquois aid), each member nation was permitted to go its own way, even though it meant that different parts of the Confederacy for a time might be indirectly at war with one another.

In the Great Council, each national delegation voted as a unit. It was a council rule that no important matter should be debated on the day it was first brought up. This was intended not only to prevent snap judgments, but also to give the chiefs in each delegation time to come to agreement among themselves and appoint a speaker to present their united views before the assembly.

The government, though democratic in spirit, was not a pure democracy in form. The chiefs held office by hereditary right. On the death of a chief, the matrons of his line selected his successor from the same lineage, usually a brother or nephew (a sister's son) of the deceased but not his own son. Certain lineages (and they alone) had title to chiefships; others were without direct representation on the council. But, the population being small and the sense of social responsibility high, the selection of a chief was thoroughly talked over before any appointment was made, and it usually represented the general will.

The chiefs' council (whether on the national or confederate level) was much like a modern cabinet. It had responsibility for co-ordinating the affairs of the nation or the League and for making recommendations, but it had no authority beyond what came by concurrence with the council of warriors and women, in other words, with the general public.

THE POLITICAL POWER OF WOMEN

The political position of women among the Iroquois has always astonished white men. The matrons did not, after appointing the chiefs, retire modestly into the political shadows. Scaroyady, the Half King, in 1756 asserted that "women have a great influence on our young Warriors. . . . It is no new thing to take women into our councils particularly amongst the Senecas." Cornplanter in 1790 said that "in the Seneca nation the women have as much to say in council as the men have, and in all important business have equal authority."

Iroquois women did not occupy titled positions on the League Council, but their political influence was profound. For one thing, they had their own councils, choosing representatives and spokesmen as circumstances required. For another, important women—"the Ladies of the Council," as the French called them—sat with the chiefs in council. They listened to the discussions and sometimes took part in them. Often their wishes prevailed, as when the Seneca women, during the crisis of 1794, pressed for peace with the United States and constrained Cornplanter to speak their will. From the chiefs' councils they carried discussion to women's councils or the council of warriors and women. Finally they went into action, exerting their immense prestige among their kin to see that the national will was carried out.

These civil chiefs (as distinct from the war chiefs) were known as *royaneh,* "lords," and were treated with high respect, but they put on no airs. They were often poorer than the people about them. It was a point of honor for them to share, or give away, whatever they possessed.

The Onondaga Council had no police to enforce its wishes. It ruled by consent, the chiefs relying on the matrons who had appointed them to move public opinion. There were other channels of pressure, but this was the main one. For example, if the Onondaga Council decided to enter peace negotiations with a former enemy, such as the Catawbas, it was necessary to hold the young men back from their scheduled war raids. The chiefs consulted the matrons, and the matrons broadcast the news through the longhouses, using their personal influence to keep the young men at home. Thus we see that, as John Collier writes in *The Indians of the Americas*, "authority flowed upward, from the smallest and most organic units." Through the same channels that had put the chiefs in power, their combined wisdom was filtered back to the people.

Between the chiefs' council and the populace there were many channels of communication. There were councils at all levels, in all places, both men's councils and women's councils, family councils, councils of warriors, councils of elders. Frequently these subsidiary councils chose spokesmen to represent them before the Great Council. And the chiefs of the Great Council influenced public opinion by reversing the process and letting their advice percolate through these lesser councils to the level of the family and the individual.

"From family council to town, to tribe, to confederacy and down again there were regular steps in a chain of administration," writes Dr. William N. Fenton. "Their confederacy was but a League of ragged villages, . . . but it worked better than any other in the colonies."

The member nations of the Confederacy, in their official relations with one another, adopted the familiar terms of a matrilineal society founded on ties of kinship. There were three Elder Brothers: the Mohawks, Senecas, and Onondagas. The Mohawks were known as Keepers of the Eastern Door, the Senecas as Keepers of the Western Door, and the Onondagas tended the council fire in the middle, the Fire That Never Dies. The Younger Brothers were the Oneidas, affiliated with the Mohawks, and the Cayugas, affiliated with the Senecas. Two more Younger Brothers were added later, the Tuscaroras and the Delawares, who were adopted "on the cradleboard."

THE FOUNDING LEGEND

The Five Nations were united in reverence for two culture heroes, Deganawidah and Hiawatha, the traditional founders of the Confederacy, whose words were treasured as revelations from the Creator.

There is no explicit record of the founding of the Confederacy. The "Hiawatha Belt," now in the custody of the New York State Museum at Albany, has been traditionally regarded as a contemporary record of the founding. Scientific examination has shown, however, that its beads were strung together in their present form, probably in the eighteenth century, from several earlier wampum belts. The design is interesting as an ancient symbol of the League, but the belt itself is not so old.

The coming together of these five nations in the Iroquois Confederacy was not a single act of creation at a determinable moment in time. The "completed cabin" (the Longhouse) was probably the culmination of a long process of development during which smaller leagues had been formed. A committee of Iroquois chiefs in 1900 set the date of the final act of union as 1390. Horatio Hale, who worked for years among the Iroquois, thought the League had been founded about the middle of the fifteenth century. Some recent scholars have set the date as late as 1570 or even 1630. Such dating seems untenable, for the *Jesuit Relations* of the seventeenth century refer repeatedly to the "completed cabin" as something not only beyond the memory of man, but as "of the greatest antiquity." The Relation of 1654 quotes a Mohawk Indian as saying, "We, the five Iroquois Nations, compose but one cabin; we maintain but one fire; and we have, from time immemorial [*de tout temps*], dwelt under one and the same roof."

The founding of the Confederacy was described in a powerful and beautiful legend which they held sacred. It was their Bible. Although it is in part a product of the popular imagination, it is important historically both for the core of truth contained in it and for the influence it exerted on later Iroquois history. The ideal it contained of a peaceful world and the practical means it proposed to attain that end inspired men with a depth of devotion that, even in these days of fervid nationalism, can hardly be equaled. It gave to their wars something of the complexion of religious crusades. "The Master of Life fights for us," they said to the Eries.

The Iroquois believed in the divine origin of their League. As the legend runs, Deganawidah's mother was a virgin through whom the Great Spirit, in compassion for mankind, became incarnate, bringing to earth a message of "Peace and Power": peace, that is, based on law and justice, and backed by sufficient military power to make such a peace prevail.

In the beginning, it is said, Deganawidah won Hiawatha (from whom [poet Henry Wadsworth] Longfellow got the name, though not the adventures, of his hero) as his first disciple and sent him out to announce the Good News of Peace and

Power among the neighboring Iroquois. There followed a long political campaign. The principal obstacle was Atotarho, according to legend a tyrant whose body had seven crooks in it and whose head was covered with snakes instead of hair. In the end, Hiawatha (whose name means "He Who Combs") combed the snakes out of Atotarho's hair, and the union was completed on the shore of Onondaga Lake. Deganawidah there planted the Tree of Peace and presented to his people (according to the legend) a body of laws, which are sometimes known as the "Constitution of the Five Nations." In its legal aspect, the Confederacy became known as *Kayenerenkhowa*, the Great Peace.

The legend is full of familiar but unforgettable images, symbols of man's hope for a world in which, as a later Iroquois expressed it, "The land shall be beautiful, the river shall have no more waves, one may go everywhere without fear." The Tree of Peace was seen as a great white pine "rising to meet the sun" (the Eye of the Creator), with branches representing the law and white (i.e., living) roots extending to the Four Quarters of the earth so that men everywhere might be able to trace peace to its source. Above the tree was the Eagle That Sees Afar, symbol of "preparedness," watching the horizon to warn peace-loving people of approaching danger.

The population of the Five Nations was small. According to a recent estimate, it was never more than twelve or fifteen thousand men, women, and children. How can their influence over such vast areas and such large populations as acknowledged their authority be explained? The answer is to be found in a combination of circumstances, these among others:

1. They had a driving economic motive to expand, as George T. Hunt has shown in *The Wars of the Iroquois*, once the fur trade had made their survival dependent on gaining access to territories not yet denuded of beaver.
2. They held a strategic military position among the mountains flanking the St. Lawrence River and Lake Ontario.
3. They had the advantage of a strong political organization, which enabled them to act together when necessary and to take the long view in their plans.
4. They had a highly-developed agriculture, with large corn surpluses which they stored to carry them over emergencies.
5. They were wise enough to know when to bury the hatchet and turn to negotiations.

6. Holding the balance of power in America between the English and the French, they made good use of their bargaining power.
7. Their religion gave them unity and a purpose: to make the Great Peace prevail.

Whether there was an element of self-deception in their warring for peace is not the question here. We note merely that the Iroquois had a sense of mission which nerved them . . . to win victories.

It is easy to see that not all the actions of the Five Nations were in harmony with Deganawidah's ideal. But the ideal was nevertheless there, and the course of early American history bears frequent witness to it.

IMMIGRATION FROM THE ENGLISH BORDERLANDS

David Hackett Fischer

Migration to the English colonies in the New World came in identifiable waves. Each wave tended to come from the same region of Britain and tended to settle in the same region of the new colonies. Prior to the revolutionary period three waves of immigrants had already arrived: the East Anglian Puritans, who settled in New England, the southern English Episcopalians, who settled mostly in Virginia, and the central English Quakers, who settled mostly in Pennsylvania. During the revolutionary period a fourth wave arrived. These people came from northern England, southern Scotland, and northeastern Ireland—a region called the borderlands. They tended to settle in the backwoods regions of the New World, in the western forests near the Appalachian Mountains. It was their leather leggings, buckskin, and fierce independence that later came to be thought of as quintessentially American.

David Hackett Fischer teaches American history at Brandeis University. Besides *Albion's Seed*, he is also the author of *Paul Revere's Ride* and *Growing Old in America*. In this selection he argues that much of the characteristically "American" culture of the frontier immigrants was actually brought over with them from the British borderlands.

David Hackett Fischer, *Albion's Seed: Four British Folkways in America*, New York: Oxford University Press, 1989. Copyright © 1989 by David Hackett Fischer. Reproduced by permission.

E arly in the summer of 1717, the Quaker merchants of Philadelphia observed that immigrant ships were arriving in more than their usual numbers. By September, as the first hint of autumn was in the air, the Delaware River was crowded with vessels. They came not only from London and Bristol, but from Liverpool and Belfast, and small northern outports with strange-sounding names—Londonderry and Carrickfergus in northern Ireland, Kirkcudbright and Wigtown in Scotland, Whitehaven and Morecambe on the northern border of England.

In October of the same year, a Philadelphia Quaker named Jonathan Dickinson complained that the streets of his city were teeming with "a swarm of people . . . strangers to our Laws and Customs, and even to our language." These new immigrants dressed in outlandish ways. The men were tall and lean, with hard, weather-beaten faces. They wore felt hats, loose sackcloth shirts close-belted at the waist, baggy trousers, thick yarn stockings and wooden shoes "shod like a horse's feet with iron." The young women startled Quaker Philadelphia by the sensuous appearance of their full bodices, tight waists, bare legs and skirts as scandalously short as an English undershift. The older women came ashore in long dresses of a curious cut. Some buried their faces in full-sided bonnets; others folded handkerchiefs over their heads in quaint and foreign patterns.

MIGRATION FROM THE BORDERLANDS

The speech of these people was English, but they spoke with a lilting cadence that rang strangely in the ear. Many were desperately poor. But even in their poverty they carried themselves with a fierce and stubborn pride that warned others to treat them with respect.

The appearance of these immigrants in the streets of Philadelphia marked the start of yet another great folk migration from Britain to America. The magnitude of this movement was very large—more than a quarter-million people altogether. This was truly a mass migration, on a scale altogether different from the movements that had preceded it. Its rhythm was different too—not a single migration but a series of wavelike movements that continued through much of the eighteenth century. It also drew from a different part of Britain. Many of these people came from territories that bordered the Irish Sea—the north of Ireland, the lowlands of Scotland, and the northern counties of England. Together they introduced still another variety of British culture to the New World.

The first slow trickle of emigration from North Britain to America had actually begun much earlier, in the seventeenth century. In Virginia, headrights had been granted for Irish servants before 1630. In New England, a group of 140 Irish Calvinists had arrived from Belfast as early as the year 1636, on board an immigrant ship nicely named *Eagle's Wing*. A small flow of population continued through the seventeenth century. Then, after the end of Queen Anne's War in 1713, this movement began to accelerate in a strong wavelike rhythm that continued to the outbreak of the American Revolution. Peak periods occurred in the years 1718, 1729, 1741, 1755, 1767 and 1774. Two-thirds of this traffic was concentrated in the decade from 1765 to 1775. As much as one-third of it may have occurred in the four years preceding American Independence. . . .

BACKCOUNTRY SETTLERS

The borderers entered America principally through the ports of Philadelphia and Newcastle. They moved quickly into the surrounding countryside, and in the words of one official, simply squatted wherever they found "a spot of vacant land." The Quakers were not happy about this invasion. "Our people are in pain," wrote Jonathan Dickinson in 1717, "From the north of Ireland many hundreds [have come]." The North Britons brought with them the ancient border habit of belligerence toward other ethnic groups. As early as 1730, Pennsylvania officials were complaining of their "audacious and disorderly manner." One of them wrote, "I must own from my own experience in the land office that the settlement of five families from Ireland gives me more trouble than fifty of any other people. Before we were now broke in upon, ancient Friends and first settlers lived happily; but now the case is quite altered."

Among Quakers there was talk of restricting immigration as early as 1718, by "laying a Duty of £5 a head on some sorts and double on others." But this idea cut against the grain of [colony founder] William Penn's holy experiment, and was not adopted. Instead, the Quakers decided to deal with the problem in a different way, by encouraging the borderers to settle in the "back parts" of the colony. In 1731, James Logan informed the Penns in England that he was deliberately planting the North Britons in the west, "as a *frontier* in case of any disturbance." Logan argued that these people might usefully become a buffer population between the Indians and the Quakers. At the same time, he frankly hoped to rid the east of them.

With much encouragement from Quaker leaders, the North Britons moved rapidly westward from Philadelphia into the rolling hills of the interior. Many drifted south and west along the mountains of Maryland, Virginia and the Carolinas. They gradually became the dominant English-speaking culture in a broad belt of territory that extended from the highlands of Appalachia through much of the Old Southwest. . . .

THE ORIGINS OF SOUTHERN COOKING

In regard to diet, the southern back settlements differed fundamentally from other regions of British America. Samuel Kercheval recalled that the "standard" supper dish in the mid–eighteenth century was a wooden bowl of milk and mush—seasoned with a splash of bear oil. The Anglican missionary Charles Woodmason regarded these backcountry meals with horror, and complained incessantly about what he was expected to eat. "Clabber, butter, fat mushy bacon, cornbread," he wrote, "as for tea and coffee they know it not . . . neither beef nor mutton nor beer, cyder or anything better than water." When he visited a community of Ulster emigrants, Woodmason noted that "the people are all from Ireland, and live wholly on butter, milk, clabber and what in England is given to hogs."

Many visitors remarked that backsettlers ate food which other English-speaking people fed to their animals. This observation was repeated so often that it became a cliché of travel literature in the southern highlands. It is interesting to discover that precisely the same statements were made by English travelers in the borderlands of North Britain.

Backcountry food ways are sometimes thought to be the product of frontier conditions. So they were, in some degree. But mainly they were an expression of the folk customs that had been carried from the borders of North Britain. Strong continuities appeared in favored foodstuffs, in methods of cooking and also in the manner of eating.

One important staple of this diet was clabber, a dish of sour milk, curds and whey which was eaten by youngsters and adults throughout the backcountry, as it had been in North Britain for many centuries. In southern England it was called "spoiled milk" and fed to animals; in the borderlands it was "bonny clabber" and served to people. Travelers found this dish so repellent that some preferred to go hungry.

Another important foodstuff in the borderlands and the back settlements was the potato. This American vegetable had been widely introduced to western Europe during the seventeenth and eighteenth centuries, and became especially popular in Ireland, Scotland and the north of England. Despite its American origins, the potato had been uncommon in the English colonies until the North Britons arrived during the eighteenth century, and made it an important part of backcountry diet.

Yet another staple was a family of breadstuffs variously called "clapbread," "haverbread," "hearth bread," "griddle cakes," and "pancakes." Sometimes they were also called scones, after an old Norse word for crust. Ingredients varied, but methods of cooking were often the same: small cakes of unleavened dough were baked on a flat bakestone or a circular griddle in an open hearth. These breadstuffs were brought from the borderlands to the backcountry, where they remained a major part of regional cuisine for many generations.

ADAPTING TO THE NEW WORLD

In other respects, backcountry food ways necessarily departed from the customs of North Britain. Oats yielded to maize, which was pounded into cornmeal and cooked by boiling. But this was merely a change from oatmeal mush to cornmeal mush, or "grits" as it was called in the southern highlands. The ingredients changed, but the texture of the dish remained the same.

Another change occurred in the consumption of meat. The people of North Britain had rarely eaten pork at home. Pigs' flesh was as loathesome to the borderers as it had been to the children of Abraham and Allah. But that taboo did not survive in the New World, where sheep were difficult to maintain and swine multiplied even more rapidly than the humans who fed upon them. Pork rapidly replaced mutton on backcountry tables, but it continued to be boiled and fried in traditional border ways.

New American vegetables also appeared on backcountry tables. Most families kept a "truck-patch," in which they raised squashes, cushaws (a relative of squash), pumpkins, gourds, beans and sweet roasting ears of Indian corn. Many families also raised "sallet" greens, cress, poke and bear's lettuce. Here again, the ingredients were new, but the consumption of "sallet" and "greens" was much the same as in the old country.

The distinctive backcountry beverage was whiskey. A taste for liquor distilled from grain was uncommon in the south and east of England. But it was highly developed in north Britain, and was brought to the American backcountry by the people of that region. "'Wheyski,'" the Marquis de Chastelleux wrote in backcountry Virginia, "was our only drink, as it was on the three days following. We managed however to make a tolerable towdy [toddy] of it."

A change of ingredients was made necessary by the new environment. In the back settlements Scotch whiskey (which had been distilled from barley) yielded to Bourbon whiskey (which was made mainly from corn and rye). But there was no other change from the borders, except perhaps in the quantity of consumption. Whiskey became a common table drink in the backcountry. Even little children were served whiskey at table, with a little sugar to sweeten its bitter taste. Temperance took on a special meaning in this society. Appalachia's idea of a moderate drinker was the mountain man who limited himself to a single quart at a sitting, explaining that more "might fly to my head."

Other beverages were regarded with contempt in the backcountry. "Tea and coffee were only slops," [early Virginia historian Samuel] Kercheval remembered, "they were designated only for persons of quality who did not labor, or the sick. A genuine backwoodsman would have thought himself disgraced by showing a fondness for these slops. Indeed many of them have to this day very little respect for them."

METHODS OF COOKING

Methods of food preparation also showed strong continuities from the borderlands to the back settlements. In the southern highlands, backcountry cooking ran more to boiling than to baking or roasting. This had also been the case in North Britain. Studies of regional cooking methods in Britain, as we have seen, find that the south and west of England had a taste for frying; East Anglia, a preference for baking; and the North, a penchant for boiling. The "simmering pot" became a cliché of border poets and antiquarians. John Gough observed that border breakfasts consisted "chiefly of porridge . . . boiled in milk." Many travelers to the backcountry noted the taste for "mush boiled in milk." Both borderers and backcountry people also consumed soups, stews and potpies for their second meal.

Backcountry cuisine was less fastidious than that of other Anglo-American cultures—"all the cooking of these people being exceedingly filthy and most execrable," Woodmason grumbled. This observation was made by many travelers in the American back settlements, and in the British borderlands. One visitor was astonished when his hostess proceeded to wash her feet in the cookpot. Another was given the tablecloth for a bedsheet. The folklore of that region actively discouraged cleanliness. To wash a milk churn was thought to be unlucky. Frogs were dropped into the milk to make it thicken. The quality of butter was believed to be improved in proportion to the number of human hairs embedded in it. "The mair dirt the less hurt," Appalachian housewives liked to say.

The backsettlers also differed from other cultures in their eating habits. They tended to take only two meals a day—a plain breakfast and a hearty meal in mid-afternoon. "These people eat twice a day only," Woodmason declared, and complained that he was unable to find a proper English breakfast, lunch and dinner. The rhythm of two daily meals was a North British custom, carried to the interior of America by the border people.

Tables were set with trenchers and noggins of wood and pewter. The utensils were two-tonged forks, heavy spoons and hunting knives. Kercheval remembered that the use of china was actively opposed. "The introduction of delft ware was considered by many of the backwoods people as a culpable innovation," he wrote. "It was too easily broken, and the plates of that ware dulled their scalping and clasp knives."

There was much feasting in the back settlements. On these grand occasions, the major dishes were not baked as in New England, or roasted as in Virginia, but boiled in black-iron cooking pots which hung over backcountry hearths. Kercheval remembered that "the standard dinner dish" for a "log-rolling, or house-raising and harvest-day" was a "pot-pie, or what in other countries is called sea-pie." There was little of the dietary asceticism that marked the food ways of Puritans and Quakers. When backsettlers and borderers could eat and drink abundantly they did so with high enthusiasm. Altogether, the food ways of these people were the product of a cultural tradition which had a long past in the British borderlands, and a long future in America's southern highlands.

Travelers also expressed surprise at the costume of the backsettlers. Men, women and even children tended to adorn themselves in a manner that seemed fundamentally alien to other English-speaking people.

Backcountry women dressed in what Anglican clergyman Charles Woodmason called "shift and petticoat," which were its nearest equivalents in the south of England. But in fact it was a different style of clothing altogether—a full bodice with deep décolletage, tight-fitted waist, short full skirt and a hem worn high above the ankle. The Anglican missionary thought it scandalously revealing.

Married women covered themselves more modestly in long dresses, with heavy woolen shawls draped across their head and shoulders. Elderly women wore heavy-hooded bonnets made of what was called "six or seven hundred" linen, and covered their feet with coarse shoes or heavy "shoepacks" as they were called in the eighteenth century.

Backcountry women of all ages normally wore homespun linsey-woolsey garments, often of exquisite beauty and refinement. Even the acidulous Anglican Charles Woodmason was moved to admiration by the sight of fifty Presbyterian ladies, "all dressed in white of their own spinning." These dresses were not shut away in closets but draped upon the cabin walls as a form of decoration. A backcountry writer remembered that in the eighteenth century:

> The coats and bedgowns of the women . . . were hung in full display on wooden pegs around the walls of their cabins, so that while they answered in some degree the place of paper hangings or tapestry, they announced to the stranger as well as neighbor the wealth or poverty of the family in the articles of clothing. This practice has not yet been laid aside among the backwoods families.

Male backsettlers also had a style of dress that startled strangers. They commonly wore shirts of linen in the summer and deerskin in the wintertime. Kercheval recalled,

> The hunting shirt was universally worn. This was a kind of loose frock, reaching halfway down the thighs, with large sleeves open before, and so wide as to lap over a foot or more when belted. The cape was large, and sometimes handsomely fringed with a raveled piece of cloth of a different color. The bosom of this dress served as a wallet to hold a chunk of bread, cakes,

> jerk, tow for wiping the barrel of the rifle, or any other
> necessary for the hunter or warrior. The belt, which was
> always tied behind, answered for several purposes. . . .
> The hunting shirt was generally made of linsey, some-
> times of coarse linen and a few of dressed deerskins.

This upper garment was cut full in the chest and shoulders,
with broad seams that ran horizontally across the front and
back, and was drawn or "cinched" tightly at the waist. The effect was to enlarge the shoulders and the chest. Much as female
costume created an exceptionally strong sense of femininity,
male dress in the backcountry put equally heavy stress on masculinity. The dress ways of the backcountry were designed to
magnify sexual differences.

The men of the backcountry also wore loose, flowing trousers
or breeches or "drawers" as Kercheval called them. The lower
legs were sometimes sheathed in gaiters called "leather stockings," which writers such as James Fenimore Cooper in his
Leatherstocking Tales made the hallmark of the backcountryman.

Children in the backcountry also dressed differently from
youngsters in other parts of British America. They were allowed
great freedom in articles of clothing. "No shoes or stockings,"
Charles Woodmason wrote, with his accustomed air of disap-
proval. "Children run half-naked. The Indians are better
cloathed and lodged."

These backcountry dress ways were often compared with
those of the Indians. But in fact the costume of adult back-
woodsmen and women was very different from the breech-
clouts, tight leggings, and matchcoats of the eastern tribes. It
was also highly impractical in the eastern woodlands—"very
cold and uncomfortable in bad weather," Kercheval remembered, and was put aside in time of military campaigning, when
according to Kercheval young Europeans tended to copy the
more functional clothing of their Indian counterparts.

Later generations remembered this backcountry costume as
aboriginally American—the pioneer dress of the frontier. But it
was not worn on most frontiers, and was not invented in America. It was similar to dress ways described by travelers in the
north of England, the lowlands of Scotland and northern Ireland. This male costume in the British border country was very
similar to that which would be worn in the American backcountry—the same linsey or leather shirts, the same broad cut
across the shoulders and chest, the same horizontal seams, the

same heavy stress on masculinity, the same "drawers" and trowsers, the same leather stockings. Leather shirts and leggings were not frontier inventions. They were commonly worn throughout the borders in the eighteenth century. The account books of one Cumbrian yeoman recorded the cost of covering his legs in sheepskin leggings. Another bought gaiters which he called "leather stockings" at Carlisle in 1742. That phrase, which American writers such as Cooper tied to the frontier, was in fact a common north border expression. The distinctive dress of the American frontiersman was adapted from the customs of the British borderlands in all respects except the moccasins and coonskin cap.

CRIME AND PUNISHMENT IN COLONIAL AMERICA

ARTHUR M. SCHLESINGER

Among the profound social changes in eighteenth-century America was the development of cities. Boston, Philadelphia, New York, and Charleston grew into cities as large and imposing as many in Europe. With the growth of these urban centers came an increase in urban problems, including crime. Urban crime in the English colonies was not as severe a problem as it was in some European cities, but it was not nonexistent. The philosophy of punishment and the methods employed during this period are strikingly different than the philosophy and methods common to our own time.

Arthur M. Schlesinger (1888–1965) served as Francis Lee Higginson Professor of History at Harvard University and as president of the American Historical Association. He is the author of numerous books on American history, including the thirteen-volume *History of American Life*. In this selection he gives a description of crime and punishment in early America, including an account of some of the notorious criminals.

D uring most of the seventeenth century every adult male had taken his turn at being a day constable or night watchman without compensation, on pain of supplying a substitute or paying a fine. The watches, carrying lanterns on their rounds, would reassure the townsfolk that they were be-

Arthur M. Schlesinger, *The Birth of a Nation: A Portrait of the American People on the Eve of Independence*, New York: Alfred A. Knopf, 1968. Copyright © 1968 by Arthur M. Schlesinger Jr. and Thomas B. Schlesinger. Reproduced by permission.

ing well guarded by calling out the hours and the state of the weather. But, as the difficulties of maintaining order increased, the principal communities found it necessary to organize paid forces with relatively fixed personnel. Something resembling a police department thus emerged. Even so, newspaper critics found occasion to complain. When some "malicious and evil minded Persons" one night in 1742 stole the door off a Boston watchhouse, a newspaper writer commented sarcastically that "the Watch-Men ought at least to take Care of their own Lodgings"; and ten years later a New Yorker disparaged the patrols of that place as being mostly "idle, drinking, vigilant Snorers, who never quell'd any nocturnal Tumult in their Lives." Nevertheless the evidence indicates that the preservation of law and order in American towns was more effective than in comparable Old World ones.

DETERRING URBAN CRIME

Evildoing flourishes in the dark, and one obstacle to better enforcement was the fact that until the close of the colonial period the streets were lighted only with lanterns hung from the windows of private houses. A writer in the *Massachusetts Gazette and Boston News-Letter*, February 27, 1772, perhaps knowing what had already been done elsewhere, pleaded for the "introduction of public Lamps" as tending "both to secure our persons from insult and abuse and our property from robbery and violence." The idea had some time before taken hold in Philadelphia, which in 1751 established a municipal system of whale-oil lights mounted on wooden posts, with provision for lamplighters and for the fining of persons who broke the lamps. New York followed in 1761, Charleston in 1770, and Boston in 1774; Newport alone of the major centers clung to the older method. Indeed, Philadelphia's 320 lamps in 1767 made it the best lit city in the British Empire.

Urban crime, though alarming enough to the colonists, never attained serious proportions. As long as the towns were small enough for everybody to know everybody else, community opinion acted as a deterrent; and, even when expanding populations altered this, the easy economic conditions rendered life and property safer than in Old World cities. In Pennsylvania, for instance, according to fairly complete statistics, only thirty-eight persons were convicted of murder from the first days of settlement to September 1775, or a little more than one every three years, while the corresponding figure for burglaries was less than one a year, a record all the more surprising in view of that province's great mixture of nationalities, the continuing frontier disorders, the presence of British-deported felons, and the temptations to criminality presented by the wealth centered in Philadelphia. The most frequent offenses there, as in the other colonies, were of a different order—petty thievery, drunkenness, assault and battery, and sexual irregularities.

Prostitution throve in the leading ports, fostered by the undersupply of marriageable women as well as by the habits of sailors on shore leave. In an attack on the problem the Massachusetts legislature as early as 1672 prohibited under stiff penalties the erection in Boston of "a stews, whore house or brothel house," but with what result is suggested by the fact that a hundred years later, in 1771, the Boston press carried an obituary of "Man of War Nance," described as a "likely looking Woman" with "a bad Character for Chastity and Sobriety." In 1734, 1737 and again in 1771 mobs broke up particularly flagrant bagnios [brothels]; and conditions in the other cities were little if any better. In 1744 a Philadelphia grand jury protested that "disorderly Houses" had so multiplied as to give one neighborhood "the shocking name of Hell Town"; and twenty years later a Charleston grand jury remonstrated against the "bawds, strumpets, drunkards, and idle persons" infesting its streets. Nor were masculine offenders against chastity always of humble station. The Massachusetts patriots, for example, discovered in 1775 the treachery of their trusted associate Dr. Benjamin Church from a letter he had indiscreetly confided to his mistress for delivery to the British army. "There is seldom an Instance of a Man guilty of betraying his Country," sententiously declared Samuel Adams, "who had not before lost the feeling of moral Obligation in his private Connections."

NOTORIOUS CRIMINALS

With the major towns geographically isolated from one another, it is strange that a greater number of lawbreakers did not simply move on to other places when conditions became too hot for them in their local communities. One who did so was "the famous and Notorious Villain," Tom Bell, son of a respectable Boston shipwright, who embarked on his nefarious career while a student at Harvard. Expelled in 1733 for "scandalous neglect" of his studies, petty thievery, and "complicated lying," he turned to greener fields, wandering up and down the coast for the next decade or so, at times lining his purse with funds obtained by posing as a temporarily straitened member of the Winthrop, De Lancey, Fairfax, or some other eminent family, at times employing his talents as a forger, counterfeiter, or horse thief. The *New-York Post-Boy*, November 5, 1744, warned its readers that Tom was at the moment believed to be "walking about this city with a large Patch on his face and wrapt up in a Great Coat, and is supposed to be still lurking." Whenever the law caught up with him, he usually managed to break jail or to escape punishment by some "cunning Stratagem." Then, surprisingly, in 1750, at the age of thirty-seven, the versatile rascal took up schoolteaching in [revolutionary leader] Patrick Henry's county of Hanover, determined, so he informed Hunter's *Virginia Gazette*, to "wipe off the Odium that his former Manner of Life had fix'd on him." When last mentioned in the press a few years later, he was plying that pedestrian occupation in Charleston, South Carolina, and soliciting subscriptions for his memoirs, which, unfortunately for a curious posterity, never seem to have materialized.

Hardly less colorful but with overtones of comedy was the Cinderella-like story of Sarah Wilson, who had begun her erring career in England by stealing some of her mistress's jewels. Deported for the offense to Maryland in 1771 as an indentured servant and soon escaping from her owner, she miraculously turned up in Charleston early in July of the next year, elegantly arrayed and feigning to be none other than Sophia Carolina Mathilda, Marchioness de Waldegrave and sister to Queen Charlotte, whose picture she displayed as a sort of passport. To what was doubtless her cynical amusement, all doors were immediately opened to her, as were also all purses when she assured her hosts of offices and other royal favors at her disposal. After living off the fat of the land for four months she then made her way northward, repeating her triumphs in Philadelphia, New York, Newport, Boston, and Portsmouth. An offer of a reward by her master in mid-1773, though widely copied in the press, failed for some reason to end the masquerade. As late as July 17, 1775, the *Newport Mercury* reported the fictitious peeress as returning from that place to New York. Therewith she vanishes from history. . . .

PUBLIC DISTURBANCES

Urban mass violence reflected in part the lack of more wholesome outlets for animal spirits. The mob assaults on the broth-

els in Boston were one example; and regularly on the night of
November 5 gangs from the north and south ends of the town
celebrated Guy Fawkes day by engaging in anti-Catholic
demonstrations. Increasingly, too, mobs in Boston and elsewhere sprang up to resist navy impressments and to attack revenue officers and informers seeking to enforce the Acts of Trade.
But it was not until the Stamp Act that the outbreaks became
epidemic. Even the hoodlums from Boston's north and south
ends buried their differences to unite in the demonstrations; and
better-class citizens often encouraged them to express the resentment of the populace toward the ministerial measures. Although the proceedings were criminal conspiracies in British
eyes, no American jury ever convicted a participant.

The disorders reached crisis proportions in clashes with
British garrisons at New York and Boston in 1770—magnified
by the colonists as the Battle of Golden Hill and the Boston Massacre—and again in the Boston Tea Party three years later. It was
this last disturbance, engineered by the patriots after the royal
governor declined to send away the East India Company without payment of the obnoxious tax, which goaded Parliament
into altering the democratic features of the Massachusetts charter and closing the port of Boston. But the Ministry had acted
too harshly and too late. A people accustomed to taking the law
into their hands now responded with armed rebellion.

FORMS OF PUNISHMENT FOR SERIOUS CRIMES

The punishments prescribed for lawbreakers were for the most
part excessive or bizarre by modern standards, when not both.
For example, New York in 1776 provided death for sixteen acts
when committed the first time—including counterfeiting,
forgery, burglary, horse stealing, and arson—and for as many
more upon a second conviction. Delaware demanded the extreme penalty in twenty instances, Pennsylvania in eighteen,
Connecticut in fifteen. Colonial law, after the Old World fashion, sought to safeguard the community against what it ranked
as major crimes by terrifying and irrevocable retribution. The
codes made no allowance for the relative gravity of the transgressions, extenuating circumstances, or the possibility of re-
forming the convicted. Every individual was presumed to be a
free moral agent who had willfully chosen to go wrong.

Even so, the number of capital offenses was far less than in
England and the treatment of malefactors more lenient. For one

thing, the comparative smallness and amiability of the colonial town made the problem less formidable. For another, the spectacle of felons expelled from Britain turning into useful members of society contributed to a more humane attitude. In practice, moreover, the letter of the law was often nullified by juries refusing to convict when the penalty seemed disproportionate, while other mitigations came about through the exercise of the pardoning power or the commuting of the death sentence to banishment. And, increasingly, evildoers saved their lives by pleading benefit of clergy.

This curious usage had arisen in medieval England to enable churchmen charged with major crimes—murder, arson, treason, and the like—to be tried in ecclesiastical courts, which did not administer capital punishment, instead of secular ones, which did. Over the years the practice spread in somewhat modified form to the temporal courts. It was at first made available to all persons who read Latin, then to all who read English, and finally, in 1707, to the illiterate as well. However, to prevent their claiming the privilege a second time, the culprits, in a crude anticipation of modern fingerprinting, were branded on the thumb.

The judges in all the colonies but Connecticut followed the English example, granting the exemption for all crimes except murder, treason, and piracy. In New York alone the concession was invoked no fewer than seventy-three times between 1750 and 1775. To cite a Massachusetts example, the Boston printer John Boyle laconically noted in his diary on February 25, 1773: "James Bell, Shoemaker, tryed for the Murder of his Wife on the 5th. Jany last, and found Guilty of Manslaughter; but pleading the Benefit of ye Clergy was burnt in the hand and discharged." The occasion that lives in history books took place a few years before when the two soldiers convicted of manslaughter in the Boston Massacre were let off with the lesser punishment. This deep-rooted but archaic method of tempering justice with mercy persisted until after Independence; Massachusetts gave it up in 1785, and by 1800 the other Northern states and Virginia, as well as the new federal government, followed suit. The rest of the original thirteen acted more slowly, South Carolina delaying till 1869. Great Britain itself did not cease the practice until 1827.

FORMS OF PUNISHMENT FOR LESSER CRIMES

For lesser breaches of the law the colonial wrongdoer, also after the English fashion, underwent a variety of picturesque and degrading punishments, such as being whipped at successive street corners, or confined for long hours with his feet in the stocks or his head and hands in the pillory, or exposed on the gallows with his neck in the noose. A delinquent was lucky to escape with a mere fine. As especially fitting the misdeed, a malicious gossip or common scold—seemingly always a feminine offender—was required to stand gagged before her house or with a cleft stick on her tongue and, in aggravated instances, to endure the ordeal of the ducking stool. For graver transgressions short of capital crimes the unfortunate might suffer the lifelong stigma of having his ears cropped or cut off or of being branded on the hand or face with a letter telling the nature of his guilt. In accordance with a roughly alphabetical plan, "A" signified adultery, "B" burglary or blasphemy, "C" counterfeiting, "D" drunkenness, "F" forgery. A humane substitute in cases of adultery was to stitch the symbol onto the female offender's clothing, which was the fate of Hester in [author Nathaniel] Hawthorne's *The Scarlet Letter*. For cumulative effect the penalties might be combined, as when "one Lindsay," convicted of forgery in Worcester in 1769, was sentenced to the pillory for an hour, then thirty lashes, and finally, to being seared on the hand.

Public humiliation was regarded not only as heightening the punishment but also as a means of identifying the culprits to the community at large. The townsfolk, for their part, found the sight a welcome relief from the daily routine. The whipping post, the stocks, the pillory, the ducking stool, and the gibbet all served as agencies of gruesome entertainment, with a constantly changing plot and cast of characters. Some five or six thousand persons, many from the countryside, witnessed the hanging of . . . two pirates in Newport in 1760, and the entire population of Charleston turned out in 1767 for the hanging of two horse thieves. To cash in on such occasions, enterprising printers struck off handbills and leaflets spiced with lurid woodcuts and the alleged dying words of the departed. Young Benjamin Franklin hawked about the streets of Boston a ballad of his own composition celebrating the downfall of the redoubtable [pirate] Blackbeard—an effusion which he ruefully characterized in his old age as "wretched Stuff, in the Grubstreet Ballad Stile." The *Life and Confessions* of Herman Rosencrantz, executed in Philadelphia in 1770, ran through two editions of two thousand each in a single month.

Conspicuously absent from the round of punishments was

the familiar modern method: imprisonment. The colonists held that a wrongdoer should settle his debt to society by a single quick payment, whether it be death, mutilation, or some lesser atonement. Locking up the offender meant the withdrawal of needed labor from the community, and, besides, it would create a tax burden that might be aggravated if his dependents became public charges. To be sure, "gaols" were to be found in all the colonies, but these buildings, typically of flimsy construction and unheated in winter, served almost exclusively for detaining prisoners until they were tried or the penalties inflicted. The inmates had to provide their own food or depend for their fare on kind-hearted outsiders, with the result that they sometimes perished of starvation, as did three of those in custody in Philadelphia in 1772.

The principal exception to the rule against imprisonment was the treatment of delinquent debtors, whose sentences ran until their obligations were discharged. Here all other considerations gave way to the fear of their fleeing to parts unknown and the related hope that confinement would either make them disclose any hidden resources or bring their friends to their rescue. The law ordinarily drew no line between large and small debtors or between fraudulent and honest ones, nor did it usually assure an equitable distribution of the assets among several creditors. The first to prosecute was the first to collect. Because of society's need for labor, however, the system differed from that in England by allowing the indebtedness to be commuted into a term of service to the creditor or some other master, but this option was not often resorted to. Instead, the unfortunates languished in jail without means of earning their release. An anonymous Newport pamphlet in 1754 dwelt at length on *The Ill Policy and Inhumanity of Imprisoning Insolvent Debtors,* and newspaper writers worried the theme on occasion; but it was difficult for the people of the time to envisage any rational alternative. In fact, it was not until many years after the Revolution, with the rise of wage earners as a force in political life, that imprisonment for debt was finally abandoned.

The Seven Years' War, 1756–1763

CHAPTER 2

THE AMERICAN ORIGINS OF THE SEVEN YEARS' WAR

T.R. CLAYTON

The Seven Years' War between France and England began as a territorial dispute in North America. According to an accepted version of history, the British stumbled into the war through a combination of greed and incompetence. Robert Dinwiddie, the governor of Virginia, was an investor in the Ohio Company, which brokered the sale of land to settlers in the Ohio River Valley. When the French attempted to consolidate their hold on the Ohio River, Ohio Company interests were threatened. Concerned about his investments, Dinwiddie complained to the British Board of Trade, which passed his concerns on to Thomas Pelham-Holles, duke of Newcastle. According to this version of history, the duke of Newcastle was an ineffective and incompetent secretary of state who was easily stampeded into war with France because of his ignorance of North American geography and of British claims in North America.

In this selection, British historian T.R. Clayton, a professor of history at the University of Cambridge, challenges this version of history, arguing instead that the duke of Newcastle was well informed about British claims in the Ohio River Valley, and that, far from hastily rushing into an ill-advised war, he was acting on long-standing concerns about French expansion. Dinwiddie may have had financial interests at stake, but even governors without financial concerns shared his opinion. According to Clayton, the duke of Newcastle's only mistake was in believing

T.R. Clayton, "The Duke of Newcastle, the Earl of Halifax, and the American Origins of the Seven Years' War," *The Historical Journal*, vol. 24, 1981. Copyright © 1981 by *The Historical Journal*. Reproduced by permission.

that he could contain the French in North America without sparking a general war in Europe.

O n the fourth of July 1754 a garrison of Virginians, under the command of the young George Washington, marched its British colours out of a small log fort in an isolated valley of the Appalachian mountains, where it had capitulated to a French detachment the previous evening. Washington's defeat had an impact upon world history no less significant than did his more famous victories subsequent to a more dramatic removal of British colours, on another fourth of July twenty-two years later. The French expulsion of British colonials from the Ohio valley led to nine years of war in America and quickly escalated into seven years of general war, so wide in its geographical extent that [British prime minister Winston] Churchill called it the first world war. At the end of hostilities in 1763 the acquisition from France of Canada and a number of West Indian islands laid the foundations of the nineteenth-century British empire.

The question of why the events in a remote part of the Ohio valley escalated into a general war is an important one, but the American origins of the war have been surprisingly neglected by historians. The most notable study of those origins, which has remained unchallenged since its publication in 1968, makes it even more difficult to understand why the Newcastle ministry was so alarmed when it heard the news of Washington's defeat. According to Professor [Patrice Louis-René] Higonnet, the duke of Newcastle, secretary of state for the northern department until March 1754 and first minister thereafter, expressed no real concern about the Anglo-French skirmishes in America before May 1754: indeed all British ministers did not really care about the Ohio valley until they were persuaded of its importance by the lieutenant-governor of Virginia, Robert Dinwiddie. The British claim to the Ohio region was, Higonnet claims, really a very thin one. Dinwiddie is said to have convinced Whitehall [a synonym for British government derived from the fact that many government buildings are located on Whitehall Street in London], particularly the Board of Trade under its industrious new president [George Montagu Dunk,] the earl of Halifax, that the British claim to the Ohio was, however, indisputable. Dinwiddie's motives were allegedly those of 'greed, incompetence, or imperialism, but in any case from pri-

vate motive'. This is said to have been important because 'Had
Halifax not backed Dinwiddie, and Dinwiddie not backed the
Ohio Company [a company involved in the sale of land in the
Ohio River Valley], Newcastle might never have had to fight
over Fort Necessity, for it would not have existed'. But this now
conventional interpretation is both misleading and in many
ways erroneous. . . .

Governor Dinwiddie's Concerns

After his appointment as lieutenant-governor of Virginia in 1751
Dinwiddie sent a series of letters to London emphasizing the
threat of French encirclement of the British American colonies.
It has been implied in the most notable study of the origins of
the Seven Years' War that Dinwiddie deliberately spoke in this
way in order to mask the activities of the Ohio Company, of
which he was a leading shareholder. With his private interests
in mind Dinwiddie is said to have found a 'very thin' British
claim to the Ohio Valley. 'London', it is claimed, did 'not much
care about the Ohio Valley' and Halifax only 'began' to believe
that French penetration of the Ohio region was the beginning
of a full-fledged attack on English possessions in America after
he received a letter from Dinwiddie in August 1753.

In fact Dinwiddie was only one of many colonial governors
who were convinced of that threat. The governors of New York,
Pennsylvania, and also the proprietors of that colony, did not
have vested interests in the Ohio Company: but they all expressed grave concern about the threat which French encroachments posed to the security of their provinces. Governor
[James] Glen of South Carolina disagreed with Dinwiddie on
minor points of detail about the Virginian claim to the Ohio valley. But he insisted that the British right to all that region was
an 'undoubted' one, and 'France neither had or pretended to
have the least Right'. Glen wrote letters about French encroachments similar to those of Dinwiddie. He claimed to have
been watching French designs for some years by June 1753, but
the French had now 'thrown off the mask' by a barefaced attack
on His Majesty's dominions.

The Board of Trade had been collecting information about the
boundaries of the American colonies since 1750, and a very
strong British claim to the Ohio valley had been ascertained
without the help of Dinwiddie. A circular letter to all governors
in July 1750 requested the sending to London of a map and an

exact account of the boundaries of their respective colonies. This should indicate in particular 'the History of whatever Encroachments have been made.' A Virginian living in London, Dr. John Mitchell, had come to the attention of Halifax in 1750 by virtue of his having drawn a map illustrating French encroachments in America. Mitchell helped the Board of Trade to interpret for themselves the maps sent by governors. The map from Virginia, drawn up by Joshua Fry and Peter Jefferson in 1751, led Mitchell to write a lengthy documentation of British claims beyond the Appalachian mountains in which he indicated areas where the Virginians had not perceived the full extent of the British claim. This list of 'Additions', and Mitchell's comments on the threat of French encirclement, were read before the Board of Trade on 15 April 1752.

London's Francophobic geographers probably also exerted some influence on the formulation of Board of Trade policy. But even before Halifax had become the Board's president, the lords had stressed the importance of the Ohio valley. They believed that settlements there 'may likewise be a proper step towards disappointing the views and checking the encroachments of the French, by interrupting part of the communication from their lodgements upon the Great Lakes to the Mississippi'. After 1748 Halifax enthusiastically supported his fellow lords of trade in this view. If Dinwiddie supported the Ohio Company for private reasons, his support of that company was in no way contrary to British policy. The Governor's letters to London were a reasonable response to the information he was receiving about French encroachments, and he did nothing without the prior approval of his superiors in London.

Although French activities in the Ohio valley were a cause for concern in London, their actions had not been overtly provocative until they organized the sending of an expedition to the Ohio in 1753. Appropriate defensive, yet also unprovocative, measures had therefore been authorized in London before that date. But Dinwiddie's letter of 16 June 1753, which was received in London on 11 August, confirmed that the French were now actually building a fort in the Ohio valley and that English traders had left the region 'in a great panick'. Halifax wrote a private letter to Newcastle and waited upon him at Newcastle House. On 15 August the first lord of trade circulated a long memorandum which listed all instances of French aggression in Nova Scotia and the West Indies since 1748, and which condemned all French forts and settlements from the Great Lakes to the Ohio valley as incursions upon the lands of the six nations [the Iroquois Confederacy], who had been recognized as English subjects. . . . Halifax concluded that if Britain did not soon vigorously oppose the French attempts at encirclement, she would lose nearly half of the territory to which she was 'indisputably entitled', and in the event of war would find it extremely difficult to retain the other half. But with a wide selection of information at his disposal Halifax had not simply 'begun' to follow the 'Dinwiddie line', because there was nothing unique about that Governor's opinions. The official Board of Trade representation on these matters of 16 August was not drawn up by a 'sly' first lord of trade and was not embellished with 'fictitious and ambiguous details', as two historians [Higonnet and Steven G. Greiert] have argued, in order to stampede the cabinet into aggressive measures. Moreover [according to Greiert] the time had not come for Halifax 'to force the pacific Newcastle into adopting a more belligerent attitude towards the French'. The time had come for Halifax and Newcastle to impress the wisdom of their long-held views of French ambitions upon members of the cabinet who had often underestimated the French threat.

THE WAR BEGINS

The cabinet now agreed that recent intelligence from the Ohio and the West Indies warranted the sending of orders to all American governors 'to prevent, by Force, These and any such attempts that may be made by the French, or by the Indians in the French interest'. However [British secretary of state for the southern department Robert D'Arcy, earl of] Holdernesse sent a circular instruction to all American governors on 28 August 1753 without the assistance of either the Board of Trade or Newcastle, who was on his way to Hanover with the king. That instruction authorized governors to 'repel Force by Force' within 'the undoubted limits of His Majesty's Dominions'. But Holdernesse made no attempt to stipulate what those limits actually were. In the event the instructions were only used as the authority for a use of military force against the French in Virginia, and, since that colony was the most directly affected, special instructions had been sent to Dinwiddie which explicitly defined as acts of aggression any attempts to build forts in the Ohio valley, or attempts to prevent the erection of the forts which the Ohio Company had been given royal permission to erect since 1749.

In accordance with his instructions to require the French 'peaceably to depart' before the use of force, Dinwiddie sent Adjutant George Washington to deliver a stern warning to the French commander at Fort Le Boeuf. A defiant reply from the French commander gave the Virginia Council no alternative but to send Washington back to the Ohio with two hundred men 'to protect and assist those already there in building the fort'. However, on 17 April 1754 a large French force . . . captured the fort [Fort Duquesne] built by Captain William Trent at the forks of the Ohio and Monongahela. On 28 May a French commander, Ensign Jumonville, was accidentally shot by one of Washington's men, and on 5 July Jumonville's brother, de Villiers, captured Fort Necessity.

Braddock's Defeat at Fort Duquesne

Benjamin Franklin

The war with France created a moral dilemma for the Quakers who controlled the Pennsylvania Assembly. They needed protection from French and Native American attacks, but their pacifist principles prevented them from openly supporting the British cause. Benjamin Franklin tried to set an example for his fellow Pennsylvanians by using his own fortune to outfit General Edward Braddock's expedition to take Fort Duquesne. The disastrous defeat of Braddock's army was a personal embarrassment for Franklin. However, Braddock's defeat also convinced many Pennsylvanians that pacifism was unsuitable as a principle of government. After 1755 Quakers withdrew from government positions, preferring to make their pacifism solely a matter of personal principle. This left more militant patriots, such as Franklin, who had been elected to the assembly in 1751, in control of Pennsylvania's government.

In this selection Franklin recounts, with the clarity of hindsight, his doubts concerning Braddock's ability to lead his army safely through the dangerous Pennsylvania wilderness. Benjamin Franklin is, of course, one of the most important figures of the revolutionary period. When he arrived in Philadelphia he was a penniless seventeen-year-old. He quickly learned the printer's trade, bought his own press, and by 1748, at the age of forty-two, was the first American to have made a fortune in the publishing industry. He became an important scientist and inventor, and he then turned to politics. After serving in the Pennsylvania Assembly, he represented Pennsylvania in the Continental Congress, at which he signed the Declaration of In-

Benjamin Franklin, *The Autobiography of Benjamin Franklin*, Boston: Little, Brown & Company, 1941.

dependence. He then served as ambassador to France, helped negotiate the Treaty of Paris of 1783, and finally, at the age of eighty-one, helped write the Constitution of the United States. Few individuals have had a more profound effect on the course of history.

I n Conversation with [General Edward Braddock] one day he was giving me some account of his intended progress. "After taking Fort Duquesne," says he, "I am to proceed to Niagara; and, having taken that, to Frontenac, if the season will allow time, and I suppose it will, for Duquesne can hardly detain me above three or four days; and then I see nothing that can obstruct my march to Niagara." Having before revolved in my mind the long line his army must make in their march by a very narrow road, to be cut for them through the woods and bushes, and also what I had read of a former defeat of fifteen hundred French, who invaded the Iroquois country, I had conceived some doubts and some fears for the event of the campaign. But I ventured only to say: "To be sure, sir, if you arrive well before Duquesne with these fine troops, so well provided with artillery, that place, not yet completely fortified, and, as we hear, with no very strong garrison, can probably make but a short resistance. The only danger I apprehend of obstruction to your march is from ambuscades of Indians, who, by constant practice, are dexterous in laying and executing them; and the slender line, near four miles long,

Benjamin Franklin

which your army must make, may expose it to be attacked by surprise in its flanks, and to be cut like a thread into several pieces, which, from their distance, cannot come up in time to support each other."

GENERAL BRADDOCK'S ARROGANCE

He smiled at my ignorance, and replied: "These savages may, indeed, be a formidable enemy to your raw American militia, but upon the King's regular and disciplined troops, sir, it is impossible they should make any impression." I was conscious of an impropriety in my disputing with a military man in matters of his profession, and said no more. The enemy, however, did not take the advantage of his army which I apprehended its long line of march exposed it to, but let it advance without interruption till within nine miles of the place; and then, when more in a body (for it had just passed a river where the front had halted till all had come over), and in a more open part of the woods than any it had passed, attacked its advance guard by a heavy fire from behind trees and bushes, which was the first intelligence the general had of an enemy's being near him. This guard being disordered, the general hurried the troops up to their assistance, which was done in great confusion, through wagons, baggage, and cattle; and presently the fire came upon their flank. The officers, being on horseback, were more easily distinguished, picked out as marks, and fell very fast; and the soldiers were crowded together in a huddle, having or hearing no orders, and standing to be shot at till two-thirds of them were killed; and then, being seized with a panic, the whole fled with precipitation.

The wagoners took each a horse out of his team, and scampered; their example was immediately followed by others, so that all the wagons, provisions, artillery, and stores were left to the enemy. The general, being wounded, was brought off with difficulty; his secretary . . . was killed by his side; and out of eighty-six officers, sixty-three were killed or wounded, and seven hundred and fourteen men killed out of eleven hundred. These eleven hundred had been picked men from the whole army; the rest had been left behind with Colonel [Thomas] Dunbar, who was to follow with the heavier part of the stores, provisions, and baggage. The flyers, not being pursued, arrived at Dunbar's camp, and the panic they brought with them instantly seized him and all his people; and though he had now above one thousand men, and the enemy who had beaten Braddock did not at most exceed four hundred Indians and French together, instead of proceeding and endeavoring to recover some of the lost honor, he ordered all the stores, ammunition, etc., to be destroyed, that he might have more horses to assist his flight toward the settlements and less lumber to remove. He was there met with requests from the governors of Virginia, Maryland, and Pennsylvania, that he would post his troops on the frontiers so as to afford some protection to the inhabitants; but he continued his hasty march through all the country, not thinking himself safe till he arrived at Philadelphia, where the inhabitants could protect him. This whole transaction gave us Americans the first suspicion that our exalted ideas of the prowess of British regulars had not been well founded.

THE ROAD TO BRITISH VICTORY

JAMES P. MYERS JR.

The winning of wars often has more to do with supply routes than with battle tactics. As Napoléon once said, "An army travels on its stomach." Hence, the building of roads is often an essential part of a military campaign. However, roads built for military purposes continue to exist even after the war is over and can be used by settlers and explorers as well as by armies. The road built by General John Forbes was an important turning point in the Seven Years' War since it gave the British a reliable supply line to the Great Lakes and the Ohio River Valley. It was also a turning point in western expansion. Prior to the building of the road, the best access to the fertile Ohio River Valley was from Virginia in the south. Once the road was built, the best access was from Massachusetts, Pennsylvania, and New York to the east. The road dramatically altered the pattern of western migration by Americans.

In this selection James P. Myers Jr., a professor of English and Irish literature at Gettysburg College, recounts the heroic efforts that went into the building of the road to Fort Duquesne. Myers has been attempting to reconstruct the route of the military road and to locate sections of the road that may still survive.

On November 11, 1758, Brigadier General John Forbes convened a council of war at his headquarters in Fort Ligonier, about 40 miles east of the French stronghold of Fort Duquesne. His staff represented a distinguished collection of experienced and battle-hardened colonels. Sir John St.

James P. Myers Jr., "General Forbes' Road to War," *Military History*, vol. 18, December 2001. Copyright © 2001 by Cowles Enthusiast Media 2001. Reproduced by permission.

Clair, his deputy quartermaster general, was a veteran of Major General Edward Braddock's ill-starred expedition to take Fort Duquesne in 1755. Swiss-born Henry Bouquet of the 60th Regiment of Foot (the Royal Americans) served as his second-in-command. Also present were Archibald Montgomery of the 77th Highland Regiment of Foot ([Richard] Montgomery's Highlanders); George Washington and William Byrd, commanding the two Virginia Regiments; and John Armstrong (the "Hero of Kittanning"), James Burd and Hugh Mercer of the Pennsylvania Regiment. With what was left of his 6,000-man army poised to strike at Fort Duquesne, and with winter about to trap his army in the Allegheny Mountains, Forbes had to decide whether to advance on the French fortress or to settle into winter quarters until the spring.

Rationally, the decision was an easy one. His troops, having struggled through the wilderness of central Pennsylvania, were poorly fed, sick and deserting in alarming numbers. Provisions were difficult to transport by way of the crude road cut through virgin forests and over the four wall-like rides of the Alleghenies that lay between Ligonier and Forbes' supply base in Carlisle; in winter they would be impossible to obtain. The number of hostile Indians encamped at Fort Duquesne was difficult to determine. Unclear, too, was the precise size of the French garrison. Moreover, even if the British and Americans reduced the fort, they were uncertain of holding it throughout the winter. In the laconic conclusion of Lt. Col. Bouquet, "The risks being so obviously greater than the advantages, there is no doubt as to the sole course that prudence dictates." Forbes and his officers agreed to delay the attack on Fort Duquesne until early the following year.

Within two weeks, however, the circumstances besetting Forbes' army underwent so dramatic a change that his expedition would stand out, in the words of historian Lewis C. Walkinshaw, as "one of the greatest in American history." Appreciating this paradox may be counted among the essential challenges confronting scholars of the French and Indian War.

THE STRATEGIC IMPORTANCE OF FORT DUQUESNE

The campaign to seize Fort Duquesne had its origins in the French and British struggle for control of the fertile Ohio River valley. Erected at the junction of the Allegheny and Monongahela Rivers—the "Forks of the Ohio," site of today's Pitts-burgh—Fort Duquesne revealed its strategic importance soon after its construction. At Great Meadows, Lt. Col. George Washington's attempt to secure a foothold for Virginia in western Pennsylvania was checked on July 4, 1754, when a French force based at Duquesne forced him to surrender the poorly situated Fort Necessity.

During the summer of 1755, a British expeditionary force commanded by General Braddock set out to seize Fort Duquesne. As nearly every schoolchild has learned since, Braddock's army, advancing north along the Monongahela, was ambushed and routed, and its commanding officer mortally wounded on July 9. A disaster for Braddock's combined colonial and royal army, the defeat also allowed the French and their Delaware and Shawnee allies to use Fort Duquesne as a base from which to raid with impunity the British settlements recently established on the western margin of the Susquehanna River.

British colonials on the Pennsylvania frontier panicked and began directing a stream of letters to Philadelphia, as well as to one another, recording the terror that swept through Cumberland and western York counties like a wildfire, and urging their provincial leaders to send soldiers and to build forts. Pennsylvania Governor Robert Hunter Morris could do little, however. Thwarted by a legislature that was dominated by the pacifist Quaker faction, he could not immediately obtain the militia and supply bills needed to meet the emergency. Morris did find a way around the assembly's stubbornness, though. Invoking powers he enjoyed under royal charter, he raised volunteer units of militia known as "associated companies." He also initiated the building of a defensive chain of fortifications beginning at the Delaware River and running west and southwest to the Maryland border.

Notwithstanding Colonel John Armstrong's destruction of the Delaware staging point of Kittanning in the autumn of 1756—a great morale-booster to the people of the Pennsylvania frontier—the French and their allies continued to harass the frontier with lightning guerrilla raids. They also launched several well-organized military operations in the latter part of 1757 and early 1758. The British colonists soon reported "a large Body of Troops . . . with a Number of Waggons and a Train of Artillery," in the words of John Dagworthy, marching south along the Braddock road toward Fort Cumberland in Maryland.

Even as they threatened the southern access into the Ohio Valley, the French also began advancing east along a northerly route from Forts Niagara and Duquesne toward Fort Augusta on the Susquehanna (today's Sunbury), Pennsylvania's most powerful frontier outpost. At one point, Colonel Conrad Weiser reported that the French had actually cut a road to within 10 miles of Augusta.

Late in 1758, the British finally countered with a grand strategy for reversing the tide. In a three-pronged offensive, they would attack the French at their stronghold in Louisbourg, Nova Scotia; drive them from the Champlain–Lake George valley of New York by taking Fort Carillon; and eliminate the small chain of forts extending south from Lake Erie to Fort Duquesne. To accomplish that third objective, the War Office appointed Brig. Gen. John Forbes to command a combined provincial and Regular British expeditionary force.

Instead of using the old Nemacolin Indian trail that ran west then northerly from Fort Cumberland in Maryland as Braddock's army had done, Forbes decided to blaze a new trail to the west. Besides its association with his predecessor's disastrous campaign, the old road required several river crossings over the treacherous Monongahela and Youghiogheny. Forbes wanted to take a shorter route, using only one easy crossing (of the Juniata), which could also give him easier access to Pennsylvania's fertile eastern farmlands and its busy port.

Forbes did not completely abandon the old Braddock road, however, and even had work parties clearing and grading it. He believed that by not irretrievably rejecting the Braddock road, while simultaneously advancing on Duquesne over a route even he had not worked out completely, he would have a ready alternative route should he change his mind and keep the French uncertain of his movements, thus compelling them to widely disperse their reconnaissance elements. In this he succeeded, for by the time Duquesne's commandant, Francis-Marie Le Marchal de Lignery (Ligneris), had obtained unambiguous intelligence regarding the route of Forbes' advance, the British had virtually secured their foothold at Fort Ligonier.

OBSTACLES TO BUILDING A ROAD

Building his road involved Forbes in two significant difficulties. First, nobody was certain how to penetrate Pennsylvania's largely uncharted western forests, nor where or how to clear an adequate way over four or five steep ridges of the Alleghenies that could carry not only 6,000 soldiers but also the continuous supply columns and wagons required to sustain that army.

Second, the Virginians, led by Colonel George Washington, did not want Pennsylvania to open a route into the Ohio territories, which both provinces claimed. Virginia's own interests lay in repairing the Braddock road that already gave it direct access to the Forks of the Ohio. This resistance by Virginia burgeoned into a major dispute within Forbes' command and threatened to undermine his campaign.

Before the new road could be cut, its route had to be determined. In 1755, Pennsylvania's James Burd had already started to open a road part of the way in order to provide Braddock with supplies from eastern Pennsylvania. The older Burd road thus solved the problem of getting Forbes' army from Shippensburg to a point somewhat west of Raystown (today's Bedford). Forbes and his engineers decided to strike northwest from the point where Burd's unfinished route turned southwest. The principal obstacle to determining how to proceed involved discovering suitable passes through the Allegheny and Laurel Ridges. A great deal of time was lost in reconnoitering a feasible route.

Forbes, however, was not content merely to survey and construct a new road. Determined to avoid Braddock's mistakes, he carefully laid down a network of fortified supply depots and encampments along the new road within convenient distance of one another. In addition, therefore, to having some 1,000 men felling trees, moving boulders and crudely grading the roadbed, and to the hundreds standing guard against attack, he had to divert sorely needed manpower to erect and then garrison his storehouses and stockades.

Nature withheld its benediction of Forbes' enterprise throughout that summer and fall of 1758, with one of the rainiest seasons in anyone's memory. The road flooded repeatedly, its clay and rocky bed becoming impassable. Landslides blocked passage and torrents often washed away the road where it traversed the mountain passes. Great numbers of wagons, bearing between 1,600 and 2,000 pounds of supplies, simply became marooned; worse, the stumps and boulders left on the road destroyed them by the hundreds.

Never fed adequately, hundreds of soldiers became ill with respiratory and intestinal infections. Surviving letters reveal that many of Forbes' officers became bedridden for long periods of time. Forbes himself was extremely ill throughout the campaign. In fact, Forbes, trained for a profession in medicine probably at the University of Edinburgh, realized he was a dying man (he survived until March 11, 1759). Although he identified his fatal disease as the "bloody flux," he seems to have suffered from more than one affliction. Blinded by migraines, dehydrated, brutally constipated, barely able to walk at times of severest attack, he could find no rest, nor could he get out of bed. One of the sad spectacles the soldiers often witnessed was that of their commanding officer being carried along the road in a litter slung between two horses as he struggled heroically to catch up with the advance companies, from Carlisle to Shippensburg, to Fort London, to Fort Bedford, over the tortuous mountains, to Fort Ligonier on Loyalhanna Creek. Yet, even though he could not even write out his communiques on certain days, his mind remained acute, his perseverance undiminished.

As if Forbes' physical infirmities were not torment enough, there is strong indication in the extant documents that he had been virtually abandoned to his own resources by his commanding officer, Maj. Gen. James Abercromby, and the Crown's agent for Indian affairs, northern district, Sir William Johnson. Still, Forbes refused to quit. As he wrote on October 25 to his second-in-command, Bouquet, "Whatever you and I may suffer in our minds, pray let us put the best face upon matters, and keep every body in Spirits."

RIVALRY AND DISSENSION

At least part of what Forbes alluded to in his phrase "suffer in our minds" points to the demoralizing effects of the shortages and the rivalrous conflicts undermining his command structure. During the planning stage, moreover, the British sought participation by the southern Indians. Mortal enemies of the Iroquois, "protectors" of the Shawnee and the Delaware, the Cherokees and Catawbas would provide Forbes with invaluable support in reconnaissance and guerrilla operations against the French and their own Indian allies. In May 1758, about 650 southern Indians had gathered at Winchester, Va., with 400 more expected. Unfortunately for Forbes and his staff, he noted that the Cherokees and Catawbas came "almost naked, and without arms." They required provisioning and a constant supply of gifts. Accordingly, an enormous sum of 8,000 pounds was allotted to keeping Forbes' Indian allies equipped and content. They also required activities to sustain their interest, having little patience with the slow, meticulous advance executed by Forbes.

By June, the southern Indian allies had begun deserting in large numbers. Forbes himself wrote Abercromby that "we shall not be able to keep the Cherokees notwithstanding all the pains and expenses that they have cost us." All but about 160 had abandoned the army by July. To make matters worse, word came back to Forbes that the bored Cherokees encamped in Virginia had started attacking and scalping the settlers.

As the Indians continued to desert and became more difficult to manage, Forbes complained to Bouquet about their "bullying" behavior and "most sordid and avaritious [sic] demands." Bouquet, who had to deal with them directly and daily, summarized what must surely have been the army's prevailing feeling: "Our Indians are rascals who are worth neither the trouble nor the expense they have cost."

Of more serious concern was the composition of Forbes' 6,000-man force, a polyglot collection of competing ethnic and political interests. The principal British contingent was the 77th Highland Regiment of Foot, Montgomery's Highlanders. To this were added several companies of the 60th Regiment of Foot, the Royal Americans, whose ranks consisted mainly of Germans from the middle colonies and whose officers included European, some British, but mostly Swiss German and Swiss French. The 60th was commanded by Colonel Bouquet, a professional soldier from Switzerland who, in 1763, would win a two-day battle at Bushy Run and go on to suppress the bloody war initiated by Chief Pontiac [of the Ottawa tribe].

Although several other smaller units from Maryland and the Carolinas participated, the principal provincial contribution came in the form of three battalions of the Pennsylvania Regiment, who were mostly Scots-Irish, and the two Virginia Regiments commanded by William Byrd and George Washington. Although the Pennsylvania Regiment was riddled by contentiousness, desertion, some drunkenness, and other behavior Bouquet and Forbes often regarded as unprofessional, the Virginians—Washington, particularly—at times actively conspired against Forbes' decision to open the new road. That involved actions and attitudes beyond mere foot-dragging, even to the point of trying to get rid of the general himself.

Several of Washington's letters reveal his anger over Forbes' and Bouquet's refusal to yield to his incessant arguments—he had converted Deputy Quartermaster General Sir John St. Clair—but none speaks so unambiguously as his September 1 communication to John Robinson. In it, Washington complained of how "our time has been misspent." He wondered whether Forbes could actually "have Orders for this," and then answered his own question: "Impossible." If necessary, Washington wrote, he would journey with the upcoming Virginia mission to England, there to apprise the king "how grossly his [Honor] and the Publick money have been prostituted." Not mincing words, he concluded that he "could set the Conduct of the Expedition in its true colours, having taken some pains, perhaps more than any other to dive into the bottom of it."

When he discovered that Washington was engaged in an effort behind his back to have him declared unfit for command, Forbes was understandably furious. Notwithstanding his anger, though, he saw Washington's plot for what it was, a maneuver to advance Virginia's claim to the western territory and to prevent Pennsylvania from asserting its own. Writing to Bouquet, he remarked on "a very unguarded letter of Col. Washington's" that had fallen into his hands, one that allowed him to see to "the bottom of their Scheme against this new road, A Scheme that I think was a shame for any officer to be Concerned in." Those were hard words for the future commander in chief of the United States.

Washington evidently attempted to learn from his indiscretion. Though he continued to exult in the expedition's imminent failure because Forbes ignored his arguments for using the Braddock road, evidence suggests that he executed his orders with professional diligence. . . .

MILITARY REVERSAL

That the entire command teetered on the edge of disaster was emphasized by a significant military reversal. As the army inched closer to the Forks of the Ohio, Forbes and Bouquet desperately required concrete intelligence concerning exact distances to the fort, the extent and state of its fortifications, the morale of its garrison, and the number of Shawnees and Delawares encamped about the stockade. At the head of about 800 men, Major James Grant was sent to reconnoiter Fort Duquesne and its environs. Instead of strictly following his orders to conduct his reconnaissance in secret, however, Grant split his force in two, then baited the French by literally beating his drums. The French obliged. Marching out of Duquesne on September 14, they destroyed Grant's forces in pitched battle, killing and capturing hundreds.

By November, it had become fairly evident that the British could not hope to reduce Fort Duquesne before the winter set in. Forbes and his staff concluded as much at the war council held on the 11th of that month. The next day, the French again attacked, this time nearer the main British base camp at Ligonier, and though they were driven back, events occurred that in a way epitomized how lost Forbes' army had become.

The French struck at advance positions commanded by Colonel Washington. Military records of this skirmish are remarkably few and terse, but more details appeared in an anonymous account in the November 30, 1758, edition of the *Pennsylvania Gazette*. The writer reported that during the engagement another element of Forbes' army, hearing the attack, hurried through the dusk to Washington's assistance. But they were soon fired upon by the very soldiers they had come to assist. Before the confusion was sorted out, some 14 Virginians had been killed by friendly fire. Much later, in 1818, William Findley set down a recollection of Washington's own account, told to him years earlier. Findley wrote that "the parties met in the dark and fired upon each other till they killed thirty of their own number; nor could they be stopped till he [Washington] had to go in between the fires and threw up the muzzles of their guns with his sword." Two units of Forbes' army shooting at each other by night on the shores of the Loyalhanna must have brought Forbes' expedition to its nadir. Stalled at the boundary between the wilderness and civilization, the British resigned themselves to a depressing and possibly fatal delay, within marching distance of their ultimate goal. Yet, at that darkest moment, everything turned around.

During the French attack, the British had taken several prisoners who revealed that the French soldiers at Duquesne were extremely weak, hardly fit to defend the fort. The French had drastically reduced the garrison; their Delaware and Shawnee allies were leaving. Provisions were almost gone—in fact, the British later discovered that the French had begun eating their horses. The defending garrison was actually far worse off than the attacking army.

How had the French at Duquesne, recently powerful enough

to launch, if not execute, two expeditions, against Fort Cumberland in Maryland and Fort Augusta in Pennsylvania, come to this pass? Generally speaking, they lacked the resources—great numbers of men and great quantities of materiel—that the British could rely on. Add the fact that their outposts were situated too far from their sources of supply, and the advantage they had won and come to enjoy became precarious indeed. Nova Scotian Lt. Col. John Bradstreet of the Royal Americans demonstrated how vulnerable Duquesne's supply line was on August 27, 1758. On that date, he captured the principal French supply depot at Fort Frontenac (Cadaraqui) on Lake Ontario and destroyed vast amounts of provisions destined for Forts Niagara, Detroit and Duquesne, together with the boats that were to deliver them.

Cut off completely from Quebec and Montreal, Commandant Lignery also lost the diplomatic war being waged to obtain and preserve Indian support. By means of Forbes' behind-the-scenes maneuvering with the Philadelphia Quakers to obtain the crucial Treaty of Easton (October 1758), and through the heroic efforts of the Moravian missionary Christian Frederick Post, who negotiated with the Indians virtually within the shadow of Fort Duquesne, the formerly hostile Delawares and Shawnees had agreed to make peace with the British and began returning to their homes.

Immediately upon hearing the new intelligence regarding the French weaknesses, Forbes ordered units of the Pennsylvania Regiment, 1,000 strong and commanded by Colonel Armstrong, to march on Duquesne the next day. A few days later, he followed with the main body of the army, 4,300 effective men.

With his garrison starving and his Indian allies deserting, Lignery had no choice but to send his French militia back to Illinois and Louisiana. After obtaining undisputable evidence that Forbes' army was resolutely marching on his remaining garrison of about 400 men, he decided to cut his losses and retreat, after destroying what he could. On November 24, scouts brought news to Forbes' advance road cutters that Fort Duquesne was on fire. The army heard a tremendous explosion about midnight.

On the following morning, the entire force advanced along the trail, where they discovered the corpses of those killed at Grant's defeat. They also saw with horror and rage the corpses of numerous captured comrades fastened on stakes, where they had been tortured and murdered—"so many Monuments of French Humanity," in the words of one writer.

The Road as Symbol

That day, Forbes' expeditionary force took possession of the Forks of the Ohio and renamed the burned stronghold after British Prime Minister William Pitt. The same men who had only days earlier perceived themselves trapped, as it were, just below the summit of their goal now experienced jubilation that admitted almost no limits. They had suffered, but they had persevered and had been rewarded, as if by the gift of grace. Several letters announcing the investment of Duquesne expressed the army's elation, but none so unequivocally as an anonymous notice that appeared in the *Pennsylvania Gazette:* Blessed be God, the long look'd for Day is arrived, that has now fixed us on the Banks of the Ohio! with great Propriety called La Belle Riviere.
. . . These Advantages have been procured for us by the Prudence and Abilities of General FORBES, without Stroke of Sword. . . . The Difficulties he had to struggle with were great. To maintain Armies in a Wilderness, Hundreds of Miles from the Settlements; to march them by untrodden Paths, over almost impassable Mountains, thro' thick Woods and dangerous Defiles, required both Foresight and Experience . . . consider . . . his long and dangerous Sickness, under which a Man of less Spirits must have sunk; and the advanced Season, which would have deterred a less determined Leader, and think that he has surmounted all these Difficulties, that he has conquered all this Country, has driven the French from the Ohio, and obliged them to blow up their Fort. . . . Thanks to Heaven, their Reign on this Continent promises no long Duration!"

In the surviving written record of the Forbes campaign—in the Pennsylvania and Virginia archives, and particularly in the letters of officers Forbes, Bouquet and Washington—present-day scholars can detect intimations that the new way west was, if only subconsciously, often viewed as something other than merely a military road. It led toward the setting sun, backward in time, into barbarism and a wilderness where no other roads existed and where the blood-edged tomahawk reigned supreme. At times, the march invited comparison with Biblical and classical descriptions of hell, as it certainly did for Colonel Stephen when he wrote, "a dismal place! [it] wants only a Cerebus to represent Virgil's gloomy description of Aeneas' entering the Infernal Regions."

Yet, this transit through nightmare, despair and the dark

night of the soul was an essential prelude to the miraculous reversal. Snaking its way slowly through a gloomy, forsaken no man's land, Forbes' army finally ascended, in the words of the anonymous report to the *Pennsylvania Gazette*, into "the finest and most fertile Country of America, lying in the happiest Climate in the Universe," a vast fabled garden watered by the fairest and loveliest of all rivers—La Belle Riviere.

In its own unwitting way, the Forbes expedition of 1758 anticipated in miniature the myth inspiring the pioneers' movement westward as they struggled, blindly at times, to take possession of the North American continent.

THE BATTLE OF QUEBEC

FRED ANDERSON

The most legendary hero of the Seven Years' War was Major General James Wolfe, who succeeded in taking the city of Quebec from the French at the cost of his own life. Years later a painting by Benjamin West of General Wolfe's death at the Battle of Quebec sparked a revolutionary new art movement, and established a distinctively American school of art.

Naturally, General Wolfe's victory was thought, at the time, to be a brilliant and daring tactical stroke. Unable to take the city from the north, Wolfe surprised the French by suddenly repositioning his army on the Plains of Abraham, above the city to the south. To do so he had to move the entire army along an impossibly narrow trail and up a steep cliff under the cover of darkness. General Wolfe led the advance forces himself. The following day, in the ensuing battle, Wolfe was shot and killed.

Fred Anderson, a professor of history at the University of Colorado, argues that General Wolfe did not expect, or even intend, that his maneuver would succeed. Wolfe was already dying of a fever and cough. According to Anderson, Wolfe engineered the attack hoping only to die honorably in battle. His success surprised and discomfited him almost as much as it did the French.

Québec stood on the northern shore of the St. Lawrence at the point where the river flowed into a broad basin, its channel widening from three-quarters of a mile to nearly two miles across. Atop a headland, 200 to 350 feet above

Fred Anderson, *Crucible of War: The Seven Years' War and the Fate of Empire in British North America, 1754–1766*, New York: Alfred A. Knopf, 2000. Copyright © 2000 by Fred Anderson. Reproduced by permission.

the water, the Upper Town nestled snugly within walls, looking out across the basin and down upon the houses and docks of the Lower Town as well as the suburbs of St.-Roch and Palais. Immediately below, the St. Charles River flowed into the St. Lawrence, defining the northern boundary of the city's promontory with a steep escarpment. From the confluence downriver for the next three miles or so the northern shore lay low along the basin; then, near the village of Beauport, the land began to rise. From that point onward, bluffs and increasingly steep slopes lined the shore for another three miles, until they climaxed at the spot where the Montmorency River hurled itself off a three-hundred-foot cliff in a fall so spectacular that a contemporary observer could only describe it as "a stupendous natural curiosity." Thus below the town the St. Charles and the Montmorency presented substantial obstacles to the movement of attackers overland, while the shoreline offered few promising footholds for assaults from the St. Lawrence itself. Above Québec, steep wooded slopes, naked cliffs, and bluffs lined the river's northern shore for miles. Behind them lay farmland that, west of the city, flattened into a narrow plateau between the St. Lawrence and the St. Charles, where Abraham Martin, one of [French explorer Samuel de] Champlain's pilots, had settled to farm in the early seventeenth century. There, on what has ever since been called the Plains of Abraham, the level ground swept gently upward through farms and woodlots to a broken ridge, and then on to the walls of Québec.

QUÉBEC'S DEFENSIVE POSITION

Viewed from the river, the least forbidding approach to the city lay on the eastern (downstream) side, and it was there that [Major General James] Wolfe had first probed the French defenses. But [French commander Louis-Joseph de Montcalm-Gozon] had strongly fortified the riverbank and the hillsides from the St. Charles all the way to the Montmorency Falls, and Wolfe's inability to crack this defensive barrier had frustrated him into launching his campaign of "Skirmishing Cruelty & Devastation" in August. Montcalm had stationed most of his regular troops along these so-called Beauport lines, where he expected Wolfe to concentrate his attacks. The French commander had, however, also fortified the heights west (upriver) of the city as insurance against the possibility that the British fleet would be able to ride the tides past Québec's batteries. Because the threat seemed less severe upriver, Montcalm had posted militia units to defend those lines, reinforcing them with a thousand picked men under [Montcalm's aide-de-camp, Louis-Antoine de] Bougainville—a mobile force poised to repel any effort to land above the city. Montcalm's final measure had been to send his supply ships about fifty miles upriver, to the settlement of Batiscan near Trois-Rivières. This made defenders dependent on a long supply line, which could be cut if the British managed to land above the city. But by refusing to concentrate his provisions and munitions in the city, Montcalm intended to leave himself an out: should Québec have to be abandoned, his army could retreat upriver without losing its supplies.

Montcalm's efficient, conventional disposition of his forces baffled the equally conventional Wolfe. Military operations in America so far had consisted either of sieges or raids, and thus far no full *siège en forme* [formal or traditional seige] had failed to bring an attacker victory. But the defenses of Québec were so nearly seamless that Wolfe could not gain a foothold on the north shore of the St. Lawrence from which he could open a formal siege. So long as the French remained able to resupply themselves, and so long as Montcalm could shift his forces freely from one part of the lines to another, Wolfe had little hope of even beginning a successful siege. To decide the issue he needed something that had never yet taken place in America, an open-field battle. Until Montcalm consented to give him one, he could do no more than shell the town, ravage the countryside, and issue bombastic proclamations calling upon the French to surrender. As he explained in a letter to his mother, "My antagonist has wisely shut himself up in inaccessible entrenchments, so that I can't get at him without spilling a torrent of blood, and that perhaps to little purpose. The Marquis de Montcalm is at the head of a great number of bad soldiers, and I am at the head of a small number of good ones, that wish for nothing so much as to fight him—but the wary old fellow avoids an action doubtful of the behaviour of his army." In recognition of this predicament, hoping that perhaps they would approve of an all-out assault on the Beauport lines, Wolfe at the end of August convened his three brigadiers—Robert Monckton, George Townshend, and James Murray—as a council of war, and asked their advice. He did so not because he particularly valued their opinions (indeed, he had come to such bad terms with them that he would have preferred not to deal with them at all), but because the etiquette of eighteenth-century command demanded that he consult his chief officers before ordering a major attack. Their response was categorically to deny the wisdom of making another assault on Montcalm's stoutest defenses. Instead they advised Wolfe to look for an opening upriver from Québec and sever the defenders' line of supply.

By the ordinary expectations of professional military leadership, the brigadiers' opinion was binding upon Wolfe only if he wished it to be, but he was too sick, and in too precarious a mental state, to ignore their advice. He had only recently recovered from his fever enough to leave his bed; his consumptive cough was worsening, he was weak from the bloodletting to which he had been subjected; and except for the opiates his physician prescribed, he was unable even to urinate without excruciating pain. His weakness was so apparent that when he collapsed once more on September 4, the rumor spread throughout the army that he was dying. He himself believed that he had little time left and begged his doctor only to patch him up sufficiently to do duty for a few days more. Even if he lived, Wolfe realized, he would have to abandon the campaign unless he could bring Montcalm to battle before the end of September. Thereafter the change of season meant that his naval support would have to withdraw, for although the army had supplies sufficient to survive the winter, the crews of the ships, numbering more than thirteen thousand sailors, did not.

Wolfe also knew that if he did not succeed, he alone would bear the blame for failure. His brigadiers, who had come to loathe him—especially George Townshend, a member of Parliament, heir to a viscountcy, and political ally of [William] Pitt—would see to that. Convinced that he had not long to live and fearing that inaction would bring disgrace upon his memory, with his judgment clouded by opiates and his body weakened by therapeutic bleedings no less than disease, Wolfe threw himself into planning a final desperate attack on the French lines above Québec. No one knew what he hoped to accomplish or how or where he intended to act. He consulted neither Monckton, Townshend, Murray, nor his senior naval commanders, Rear Admirals Charles Saunders and Charles Holmes, who had previously run ships past Québec and from whose vessels he surveyed the shoreline for a place to land troops. Wolfe sought the advice of only one officer, a man who knew Québec better than anyone else on the expedition, Captain Robert Stobo.

THE FOOTPATH AT FULLER'S COVE

Stobo, one of the most vivid characters in a story that has no shortage of them, had lived in the city from 1755 through the spring of 1759 as a prisoner of war. He was, in fact, one of two British prisoners of longest standing, for he and Jacob Van Braam had been the officers whom [George] Washington had given up as hostages at the surrender of Fort Necessity. Thereafter he and Van Braam had been moved from Fort Duquesne to Québec for safekeeping, but not before Stobo had drawn— and, in folly or bravado, signed—a sketch of the fort's defenses and arranged for [someone] to smuggle it out to the Pennsylvania authorities. The letter in which he described the fort turned up in [Major General Edward] Braddock's captured baggage after the Battle of the Monongahela. Before this damning document came to light, Stobo had had the run of Québec, mingling in its high society and even forming a business partnership with one of its biggest merchants. Once his role in revealing Duquesne's defenses became known, however, both he and Van Braam were arrested and tried as spies. The court acquitted Van Braam but found Stobo guilty and sentenced him to death—a punishment he escaped only when the sentence was sent to Versailles for confirmation, and ordered suspended. Thereafter he enjoyed less freedom but eventually managed to move around the city and its immediate vicinity, carefully noting (as was his habit) the disposition of its defenses. Twice in 1757 he tried to escape; twice he was caught. Finally, on May 1, 1759, he led eight other prisoners, including a woman and three children, in the attempt that finally succeeded. Descending the St. Lawrence—first in a stolen canoe, later in a schooner that he and his companions hijacked, complete with captain and crew—he had reached Louisbourg shortly after the Québec expedition had sailed. With barely a pause, he turned around and ascended the river, joining Wolfe's army in July.

Although no independent evidence survives to corroborate Stobo's own account, there is good reason to believe that it was he who told Wolfe of the footpath at L'Anse au Foulon (Fuller's Cove)—a track that angled steeply up the bluff from the riverside to the Plains of Abraham, a couple of miles west of the city. On September 5, Wolfe ordered preparations for the move upriver, and on that or the following day met with Stobo. Then, evidently feeling that he had critical secret information to communicate to [Commander Jeffrey] Amherst, he sent Stobo off with a packet of dispatches on the seventh. The next day he reconnoitered with his brigadiers above the city. He spent a good deal of time looking through a field telescope at L'Anse au Foulon but said nothing to Murray, Townshend, and Monckton about any plan to land there. They believed that the assault would be made higher up the river, at Cap Rouge, which they had recommended, or perhaps at Pointe aux Trembles. As the reconnaissance progressed, more than a score of transports and warships, bearing approximately 3,600 men, rode the flood tides upriver past Québec, anchored off Cap Rouge, and awaited Wolfe's command.

But his command did not come on the tenth—a heavy storm did, forestalling all amphibious operations. Nor did it come on the eleventh, when Wolfe ordered another thousand men upriver, stripping bare the defenses of his base camp on Île d'Orléans. At last on the twelfth he issued an order warning the army to make ready for an attack that would take place that night. Even then he did not inform his brigadiers of where he intended their forces to land; nor of when, exactly, they were to do so; nor of what objectives they were to seize. On the evening of the twelfth, nervously, they sent him a letter requesting further instructions. It was not until 8:30 that night—a half hour before the troops were to begin boarding their boats—that Wolfe wrote to inform them that the goal was "the *Foulon* distant upon 2 miles, or 2½ from Québec, where you remember [from the reconnaissance] an encampment of 12 or 13 Tents and an abbatis, below it." They and their men would wait until the signal that had been announced was given—two lanterns hoisted on the main topmast of Holmes's flagship, H.M.S. *Sutherland*—and then would ride the ebbing tide downriver, under the direction of naval officers who knew the spot at which they were to disembark.

Surprised by Success

Wolfe's partisans have interpreted his delay in informing his brigadiers of their objective as a sign of his genius. More likely than any concern for secrecy, however, it would seem that a combination of disdain for his subordinates and a highly precarious state of mind explain Wolfe's silence. When the brigadiers' letter arrived at his cabin on the *Sutherland*, he was busy making what can only be interpreted as careful preparations for his death. He had summoned a friend, Lieutenant John Jervis of the Royal Navy, in order to hand over a copy of his will, all his personal papers, and a miniature portrait of his fiancée, along with instructions on how to dispose of them. Jervis had found him dressed in a bright new uniform. The two men were talking over Wolfe's presentiments of death when a messenger brought in the brigadiers' letter, impelling him to pen his irritated reply. There is no evidence that he would otherwise have troubled to tell them where they and the army were bound. Wolfe would be in one of the first boats. Somehow, that was supposed to be enough.

Although Wolfe was more eager to court his grim muse than to anticipate what might happen when the boats reached the cove, his troops embarked without a hitch. Quietly the river's current and the ebbing tide began to carry the first wave of boats downriver, close to the north shore, at about 2:00 A.M. The night was calm. The moon, in its last quarter, gave little light. Sentries ashore could dimly make out the silent passing column, and they challenged it, but when French-speaking officers in the boats responded that they were convoying supplies down from Batiscan, the guards let them continue unimpeded. About a half hour before first light, the lead boats scraped ashore a little below the cove. Without waiting for further instructions, a detachment of light infantrymen scrambled up the 175-foot-tall bluff face, following the 58th Regiment's big, nimble lieutenant colonel, William Howe. He had just turned thirty and had served in the siege of Louisbourg. Wolfe respected him for his physical courage no less than for his distinguished family connections—he was the youngest brother of Lord Howe, killed at Ticonderoga—and had given him command of a light-infantry battalion formed from the most agile men of several regiments. Now, as the boats carrying Wolfe and the rest of the advance party ground onto the shingle in the cove, Howe proved himself worthy of Wolfe's confidence. In the last minutes of darkness he and his men mounted to the top of the cliff, fixed bayonets, and charged into the little French camp. When the brief flurry of musket fire was over, the British found among the wounded the detachment's commander, Captain Louis Du Pont Du Chambon de Vergor—an officer whose only previous distinction was that in 1755 he had surrendered Fort Beauséjour to Robert Monckton. Vergor had barely had time to dispatch a runner to warn Montcalm that the British had begun to land at L'Anse au Foulon.

It was about four o'clock when Wolfe struggled up the path from the cove to the top of the bluff. Together with Howe's party, there were perhaps two hundred men with him. The remaining troops of the first wave were disembarking from their boats in the cove and starting to labor upward under the weight of their arms and packs; a French artillery battery several hundred yards upriver had just opened fire on the transports and armed sloops of the second wave, which were now approaching the cove. Things were not going as he had expected.

Wolfe had assumed that he would come ashore with the advance guard, that there would be resistance, and (if his meticulous preparations are evidence of his expectations) that he would be killed leading his men against the French outpost. If his wish were granted, he would have risked only the advance guard, the survivors of which would be free to reembark; Monckton, the second-in-command, would be free to call off an operation of which he clearly disapproved. In the event that he escaped death, Wolfe would at least have led one last heroic attempt to land troops before Québec and could order a withdrawal from the St. Lawrence with a certain degree of honor. His maladies were sure to kill him before he reached home— and disgrace; he would merely exchange a wretched lingering death for the quick glorious one he coveted.

But now on the heights Vergor's men had fled, there was no resistance except the ineffectual fire from the battery up the river, and Howe had already led his light infantry off to silence the guns. The three brigadiers were still below, and Wolfe, alone in the gray light before dawn, had no idea what to do next. In confusion he sent word down to the officer supervising operations at the cove, Major Isaac Barré, to halt the landings. Fortunately for Wolfe's historical reputation, Barré ignored the order and rushed more men up the path. Howe's light infantry meanwhile drove off the French gunners; the landings proceeded with dispatch; and Wolfe, at length collecting himself, went off to find a position for his men. Shortly after sunrise, in weather that had turned "showery," Wolfe returned and gave the order to march for Québec.

By the full light of day, seven British battalions could be seen drawn up in battle order across the Plains of Abraham, blocking the Grande Allée—the main road into town—a little less than a mile from Québec's western wall. Behind them, five more battalions were busy improving the path, guarding the landing, and harrying Canadian and Indian skirmishers out of the woods and cornfields. At the cove a detachment of sailors manhandled a pair of brass six-pounders up the trail. More than twenty sail of ships rode at anchor in the river. Wolfe's luck, always uncommonly good, had held once more. . . .

THE FRENCH ATTACK

Nothing had prepared Montcalm for what he saw when he finally arrived on the Buttes à Neveu, overlooking the plains. To the aide who rode beside him, even the sight of the redcoats was less striking than their effect on Montcalm, who sat in the saddle as if thunderstruck, wordlessly surveying the long scarlet line: for a long moment, "it seemed as though he felt his fate upon him." Then, somberly, he set about arranging his battalions in a line of battle facing the British. Elsewhere on the field, sporadic firing was already under way, as Canadian militiamen and Indians who had moved out from the city on Vaudreuil's orders sniped from cover at the double rank of redcoats, who seemed unperturbed by the harassment. More than anything else it was the impassiveness of the British that unnerved Montcalm, for their very lack of response to the snipers bespoke a kind of discipline that he knew his own forces, so heavy with militia, lacked. With increasing anxiety he waited—for it was several miles from the east end of the Beauport defenses to the Plains of Abraham—while his men marched up and assumed the positions he indicated before the walls.

As they arrived, and as he rode up and down the line positioning them for action, Montcalm's thoughts surely eddied around the perils of his situation. Québec was almost out of provisions; Wolfe's army was standing astride the road to Batiscan; and the British ships in the river were blocking access to the supply depot by water. The walls of the city offered little protection in comparison to the trench network at Beauport and Montmorency; indeed the section of wall behind his men, around the Bastion of St. Louis, was particularly weak. At most he could position about 4,500 men on the field, a number perhaps equivalent to the force of redcoats arrayed a half mile or so ahead of him. No more reinforcements were available unless Bougainville and his flying column should appear; but although a messenger had been dispatched to Bougainville's camp at Cap Rouge at 6:45, Montcalm knew that to put two thousand men in motion and to march them in good order over the eight miles to Québec would take three hours. But did he have that much time to spare?

It was about half-past nine when Montcalm concluded that

he had no choice but to attack. To his chief of artillery he distractedly announced, "'We cannot avoid action; the enemy is entrenching, he already has two pieces of cannon. If we give him time to establish himself, we shall never be able to attack him with the sort of troops we have.' He added with a sort of shiver, 'Is it possible that Bougainville doesn't hear all that noise?'" Without waiting for a reply, he cantered off down the line to warn his officers to prepare their men to advance. . . .

All told [Montcalm's forces] numbered about 4,500 men, and they were keen for a fight. When the order came to advance, they responded with a tremendous cheer. It was almost the last thing they would do in unison that day.

In the eighteenth-century infantryman's world, everything depended upon deliberation, precision, order: the better the army, the more machinelike its maneuvers on the battlefield would be. Cohesion was all, and in order to maintain it the best soldiers of the day had been trained to march at a parade-ground pace to within hailing distance of an enemy line, halt, and fire a final volley on order before they could charge headlong, bayonets fixed, at their opponents. The fate of every infantry battle ultimately rested on the ability of soldiers to withstand the physical and psychological shock of that climactic volley. But while the white-coated regulars of Montcalm's army had the discipline to perform as their general needed them to do, the un-uniformed militiamen mixed throughout their ranks had no appreciation of the necessity of making a deliberate, dress-right-dress approach to their enemy. Accordingly, almost as soon as they heard the order to advance, the militiamen broke into a run, despite the fact that the British line was at least five hundred yards away. The loss of coherence was instantaneous. "We had not gone twenty paces," wrote one witness, before "the left was too far in [the] rear and the centre too far in front." As his efforts to restore order failed, all Montcalm could do was ride along with the adrenalized tide that surged toward the still, scarlet line of British troops. . . .

THE DEATH OF GENERAL WOLFE

The redcoats stood impassive until the first attackers were within sixty yards; then they opened fire by platoons, especially on the left and the right wings. In the center, however, the 43rd and 47th Regiments stood fast until the enemy was within forty yards. Then, according to a captain of the 43rd, they delivered as

close and heavy [a] discharge, as I ever saw performed
at a private field of exercise, insomuch that better
troops than we encountered could not possibly withstand it: and, indeed, well might the French Officers
say, that they never opposed such a shock as they received from the center of our line, for that they believed every ball took place, and such regularity and
discipline they had not experienced before; our troops
in general, and particularly the central corps, having
levelled and fired—*comme une coup de canon*. [H]ere-
upon they gave way, and fled with precipitation, so
that, by the time the cloud of smoke was vanished, our
men were again loaded, and, profiting by the advantage we had over them, pursued them almost to the
gates of the town[,] . . . redoubling our fire with great
eagerness, making many Officers and men prisoners.

As the pursuit began, the British stood in danger of losing
their discipline for the first time in the day. With hair-raising
cries, the Highlanders of the 78th Foot slung their muskets, un-
sheathed their claymores—theirs was one of the few regiments
left in which privates as well as officers carried swords—and set
off at a run after the enemy. Along the rest of the line, huzzahing
and shouting, the men of the English regiments charged forward
with bayonets fixed. At the extreme right, Wolfe himself led the
28th Foot and the Louisbourg Grenadiers in the advance.

After a morning of intermittent rain, the sun broke through
the clouds and now shone warmly over a field where blood lust
had banished caution. As the British began to chase the scatter-
ing mob helter-skelter toward the city and the St. Charles River,
Canadian and Indian skirmishers opened fire from their positions on the margins of the battlefield. They took the heaviest
toll of the day. On the left it was the Scots of the 78th, charging
along the woods that lined the northern edge of the field, who
suffered the most heavily. On the right the 28th and the Louisbourg Grenadiers fell victim to marksmen concealed in a corn-
field. It was there, as he urged the Grenadiers on, that one bul-
let tore through Wolfe's intestines and another punctured his
chest. In shock and hemorrhaging uncontrollably, he clung to
consciousness long enough to learn that the French had fallen
into a general rout. He gurgled a few words in reply. Then
James Wolfe achieved the consummation he had so long sought,
and so devoutly wished.

THE TREATY OF PARIS, FEBRUARY 10, 1763

British victory at Quebec in 1759 was followed by the surrender of Montreal in 1760. This brought an end to the war in North America. In Europe, the Seven Years' War continued for another three years, and in 1762 the Spanish were drawn into the conflict, fighting against the English. The treaty of 1763, which brought the war to an end, involved a complex trading of territories among the three countries. France lost all of its North American possessions, except a few islands. England took possession of French territory in the Northeast (i.e., Canada). However, England ceded New Orleans and French territory west of the Mississippi River, to Spain in exchange for British control of Florida.

The treaty gave England effective control of North America. French power in North America had been brought to an end; and, while the Spanish were nominally in control of the wilderness west of the Mississippi, they were not really in a position to begin developing the region. (Eventually it was returned to the French.) It appeared that the English colonies could look forward to a long period of uninterrupted peace.

This excerpt from the Treaty of Paris of 1763 includes the articles that provide for the swapping between Britain, France, and Spain of New World colonial possessions.

IV. His most Christian Majesty [the king of France] renounces all pretensions, which he has heretofore formed, or might form, to Nova Scotia or Acadia, in all its parts, and guaranties the whole of it, and with all its dependencies, to the King of Great Britain: moreover, his most Christian Majesty cedes and guaranties to his said Britannic

"Treaty of Paris, February 10, 1763," *Documentary Source Book of American History, 1606–1926*, 3rd edition, edited by William MacDonald, New York: The Macmillan Company, 1926.

Majesty, in full right, Canada, with all its dependencies, as well as the Island of Cape Breton, and all the other islands and coasts in the gulph and river St. Laurence, and, in general, every thing that depends on the said countries, lands, islands, and coasts, with the sovereignty, property, possession, and all rights, acquired by treaty or otherwise, which the most Christian King, and the crown of France, have had till now over the said countries, islands, lands, places, coasts, and their inhabitants. . . . His Britannic Majesty, on his side, agrees to grant the liberty of the Catholic religion to the inhabitants of Canada: he will consequently give the most precise and most effectual orders, that his new Roman Catholic subjects may profess the worship of their religion, according to the rites of the Romish church, as far as the laws of Great Britain permit. His Britannic Majesty further agrees, that the French inhabitants, or others who had been subjects of the most Christian King in Canada, may retire, with all safety and freedom, wherever they shall think proper, and may sell their estates, provided it be to subjects of his Britannic Majesty, and bring away their effects, as well as their persons, without being restrained in their emigration, under any pretence whatsoever, except that of debts, or of criminal prosecutions: the term limited for this emigration shall be fixed to the space of eighteen months, to be computed from the day of the exchange of the ratifications of the present treaty.

Concessions to France

V. The subjects of France shall have the liberty of fishing and drying, on a part of the coasts of the Island of Newfoundland, such as it is specified in the XIIIth article of the treaty of Utrecht; which article is renewed and confirmed by the present treaty (except what relates to the island of Cape Breton, as well as to the other islands and coasts in the mouth and in the gulph of St. Laurence:) and his Britannic Majesty consents to leave to the subjects of the most Christian King the liberty of fishing in the gulph St. Laurence, on condition that the subjects of France do not exercise the said fishery but at the distance of three leagues from all the coasts belonging to Great Britain, as well those of the continent, as those of the islands situated in the said gulph of St. Laurence. And as to what relates to the fishery on the coasts of the island of Cape Breton out of the said gulph; the subjects of the most Christian King shall not be permitted to exercise the said fishery but at the distance of fifteen leagues from the coasts of the island of Cape Breton; and the fishery on the coasts of Nova Scotia or Acadia, and every where else out of the said gulph, shall remain on the foot of former treaties.

VI. The King of Great Britain cedes the islands of St. Pierre and Miquelon, in full right, to his most Christian Majesty, to serve as a shelter to the French fishermen: and his said most Christian Majesty engages not to fortify the said islands; to erect no building upon them, but merely for the convenience of the fishery; and to keep upon them a guard of fifty men only for the police.

VII. . . . It is agreed, that, for the future, the confines between the dominions of his Britannic Majesty, and those of his most Christian Majesty, in that part of the world, shall be fixed irrevocably by a line drawn along the middle of the river Mississippi, from its source to the river Iberville, and from thence, by a line drawn along the middle of this river, and the lakes Maurepas and Pontchartrain, to the sea; and for this purpose, the most Christian King cedes in full right, and guaranties to his Britannic Majesty, the river and port of the Mobile, and every thing which he possesses, or ought to possess, on the left side of the river Mississippi, except the town of New Orleans, and the island on which it is situated, which shall remain to France; provided that the navigation of the river Mississippi shall be equally free, as well to the subjects of Great Britain as to those of France, in its whole breadth and length, from its source to the sea, and expressly that part which is between the said island of New Orleans and the right bank of that river, as well as the passage both in and out of its mouth. It is further stipulated, that the vessels belonging to the subjects of either nation shall not be stopped, visited, or subjected to the payment of any duty whatsoever. The stipulations, inserted in the IVth article, in favour of the inhabitants of Canada, shall also take place with regard to the inhabitants of the countries ceded by this article.

VIII. The King of Great Britain shall restore to France the islands of Guadeloupe, of Marie Galante, of Desirade, of Martinico, and of Belleisle; and the fortresses of these islands shall be restored in the same condition they were in when they were conquered by the British arms. . . .

IX. The most Christian King cedes and guaranties to his Britannic Majesty, in full right, the islands of Grenada, and of the Grenadines, with the same stipulations in favour of the inhabitants of this colony, inserted in the IVth article for those of

Canada: and the partition of the islands, called Neutral, is agreed and fixed, so that those of St. Vincent, Dominica, and Tobago, shall remain in full right to Great Britain, and that of St. Lucia shall be delivered to France. . . .

CONCESSIONS TO SPAIN

XIX. The King of Great Britain shall restore to Spain all the territory, which he has conquered in the island of Cuba, with the fortress of the Havana, and this fortress, as well as all the other fortresses of the said island, shall be restored in the same condition they were in when conquered by his Britannic Majesty's arms. . . .

XX. In consequence of the restitution stipulated in the preceding article, his Catholic Majesty [the king of Spain] cedes and guaranties, in full right, to his Britannic Majesty, Florida, with Fort St. Augustin, and the Bay of Pensacola, as well as all that Spain possesses on the continent of North America, to the east, or to the south-east, of the river Mississippi; and, in general, every thing that depends on the said countries, and lands. . . . His Britannic Majesty agrees, on his side, to grant to the inhabitants of the countries, above ceded, the liberty of the Catholic religion: he will consequently give the most express and the most effectual orders, that his new Roman Catholic subjects may profess the worship of their religion, according to the rites of the Romish church, as far as the laws of Great Britain permit: [the Spanish inhabitants to be permitted to remove, or to sell their estates, under conditions as in Art. IV.] It is moreover stipulated, that his Catholic Majesty shall have power to cause all the effects, that may belong to him, to be brought away, whether it be artillery or other things.

THE WESTERN BOUNDARY OF THE ENGLISH COLONIES

DALE VAN EVERY

In 1763, shortly after the Treaty of Paris, George III of England issued a proclamation forbidding colonists from settling in lands west of the Appalachian Mountains. This was an attempt to establish peace following a Native American uprising known as Pontiac's War, and it showed that the British were sincere in their desire to see western lands reserved for the use of Native Americans. It is generally believed that the attempt by the British to restrict westward expansion was one of the unpopular policies (unpopular, that is, with American colonists) that eventually led to the American Revolution. In this selection Dale Van Every states that, although American settlers did eventually overrun the boundary, the Proclamation Line actually held as a stable boundary for about thirty years. It was not until after the revolutionary period that American settlers began their relentless westward push.

Dale Van Every has written a series of books on the American frontier experience. In addition to *Forth to the Wilderness*, this series includes *Ark of Empire: The American Frontier, 1784–1803* and *The Final Challenge: The American Frontier, 1804 to 1845*.

Not many of man's designs have absorbed more of his attention than his predilection for drawing lines upon the earth. A disposition to warn off trespassers has seemed

Dale Van Every, *Forth to the Wilderness: The First American Frontier, 1754–1774*, New York: William Morrow and Company, 1961. Copyright © 1961 by Dale Van Every. Reproduced by permission.

a human impulse almost as basic as that of the cell to reject foreign proteins. The most simple and primitive societies have been obsessed by it. Later and more elaborate examples have ranged from the frontier of Rome to the Great Wall of China to the Iron Curtain of our own time.

Experience has indicated that if such a man-made line is to endure for long, other than as a breeder of wars, certain attributes are invaluable. Most helpful of these assets are that the line should so conform to natural geographical features as to be readily recognizable, that it should separate areas and peoples sufficiently different for the separation to make at least some sense, and, unless the people on one side are so much more powerful than the other that there is no need for a line, that the peoples on either side should be reasonably reconciled to its existence.

THE PROCLAMATION LINE AS A PHYSICAL BOUNDARY

All three of these bolsters were possessed by the Proclamation Line of 1763 in overwhelming measure. No one could entertain a moment's doubt, real or pretended, as to its physical location. It loomed against the sky, since by official definition it coincided with the crestline of the Appalachian Mountain chain. From either side that vast forested height was visible from afar. Meeting the second test, it marked a natural dividing line between two regions and two peoples as dissimilar as this world could afford. On the one side was a civilized, politically and economically advanced community of industrious white men counseled by leaders of an intellectual capacity capable of identifying the lightning or composing a Declaration of Independence and on the other was a trackless, primordial wilderness infested by scattered tribes of irresponsibly belligerent savages. The contrast was between a time not so far from our own and the Stone Age. Finally, establishment of the line was opposed by nobody. It was welcomed and approved by every organized interest, racial, diplomatic, political, economic, whose aspirations were in any way involved.

The Proclamation Line was a mark drawn on a map by men who were none too certain about what they were accomplishing. What gave it some significance was that they were ministers of a nation just victorious in a world war. But what gave the mark much more significance was that it had represented something that had always been there. The mountain barrier with

which it coincided had so long as there had been a continent
been a rampart between the seaboard and the great interior valley. This had been a boundary so natural that even the buffalo
which had succeeded in spreading to the farthest reaches and
corners of the continent's middle had crossed it only in trickles.
The prehistoric mound-building Indians had left those monu-
mental demonstrations of their communal energy from end to
end of the Mississippi and along every one of the Mississippi's
eastern tributaries, but not one relic of their enterprise east of
the mountains. To the early English settler the line of cloud-
wreathed, blue heights looming against the western sky represented at once the edge of the unknown and the limit ordained
by nature to his own advance.

Formal history has tended to minimize the significance of the
Proclamation Line because it did not endure. As a matter of fact
it endured for the next thirty-one years. When the forces that
had originally sanctioned it were challenged by new forces it
continued to endure. The principle established by the Line was
to be bitterly contested through years of international negotiations at the highest level. It was a principle that died slowly and
very hard. Twenty of those thirty-one years were years of war
with armies in the field fighting to hold or breach the Line. But
we are not yet concerned with the circumstances accompanying the Line's ultimate overthrow. Let us first examine the circumstances accompanying its conception in 1763.

INTERNATIONAL POLITICAL OPINION

Among the great powers there was unanimity. The other two
with interests in the Mississippi Valley, France and Spain, could
only applaud England's declaration. They recognized the real
purpose behind the move and the foreseeable long-range effects
had for them the same appeal that they had for England's
imperial-minded Board of Trade. The significance of that same
real purpose began speedily to dawn on the least informed English minister who had so hastily concurred in the decision.
Avoiding the expense of recurrent Indian wars was only a stop-
gap purpose. No one could imagine that the wilderness was to
remain for all time a wilderness. Occupation and development
by white men, possibly accompanied by civilization of the Indians, sooner or later was bound to come. The advantage of taking care that that development be one over which England
could continue to exercise an appropriate imperial control was,

so soon as it was contemplated, self-evident. The real and not so hidden purpose of the Proclamation was thus to nip in the bud any incipient migration of turbulent American frontiersmen into the great central valley. With this purpose France and Spain could not have more heartily agreed.

France had under duress divested herself of her immense North American dominions. She had ceded the territory east of the Mississippi to England and that west of the river, plus New Orleans, to Spain. But she was in no way reconciled to the loss. She still retained the residual advantages of her immemorial influence over the Indians and of a French population on the St. Lawrence, at the mouth of the Mississippi, and in wilderness villages scattered through the interior. She was resolved upon the recovery of her empire at the first shadow of an opportunity. The more favorable fortunes of the next world war might open the way. The one event certain to close the way forever was an intrusion of American settlers into the central valley. This France was determined to resist and meanwhile to encourage the English, the Spanish, and the Indians to resist. At the peace table following the Revolution her resistance was to be all but successful.

Spain's American empire began at the Mississippi and extended south and west in an unbroken sweep across two continents to immeasurably distant Cape Horn. This was an unconscionable area to defend. She was peculiarly susceptible to any threat, however remote, to her central treasure house in Mexico. The appearance of a few Russian fur traders in the northwest Pacific was presently to cause her hastily to extend a line of missions and presidios hundreds of miles northward into previously ignored California. Any movement of American settlers across the Appalachian Mountains would represent a threat a thousand times more ominous. Spain could not have regarded the Proclamation Line more highly unless she were in a position to hold it herself. Sixteen years later she was to move fleets and armies in a vigorous attempt to do just that.

THE LINE IS SUPPORTED BY COLONISTS AND INDIANS

Along with the attitudes of the several great powers the attitude of Americans, in view of their proximity, was an international consideration. Americans were not yet independent but they were very independent minded. Their elected assemblies exercised a measure of self-government which had necessarily to be taken into account by the parent English government. Paris and Madrid were as much relieved as London to note that neither then nor for years to come was there appreciable American opposition to the Line. On a clear day the average American, even though he lived in the tidewater centers of population, could see the mountains. Their blue crests suggested the existence of a physical screen between him and the dangers of the wild region beyond them. So far the screen had not proved too substantial. During the French and Indian War his own home had for a time seemed as threatened as any settler's. Always the Indians had been able to cross the mountains at will. It had been passage the other way that had proved enormously difficult. In 1755 an English army had marched over them to destruction. In 1758 a second army three times as strong had succeeded only after months of agonizing effort. Another must presently make the supremely critical attempt. It followed that the average American was moved to trust and pray that this newly proclaimed Line might somehow be finally and firmly established as a permanent boundary. The possibility of future settlement west of the mountains appeared a prospect too distant to be seriously considered. Of much greater concern was the possibility of forestalling Indian wars in the present. Every colonial assembly, including notably the New York, Pennsylvania, Virginia, and South Carolina assemblies most involved in the Indian problem, gave the establishment of the Line their unreserved approval. This American political acceptance of the underlying principle persisted. Eighteen years later, toward the end of the Revolution, the Continental Congress by a vote of nine states to two was to instruct its peace commissioners to satisfy the demands of those great and good wartime allies, France and Spain, by accepting, if they continued to insist, the crest of the Appalachians as the permanent western boundary of the United States about to be.

Last among the international and political pressures at work, but the most effective for years to come, was that applied by the Indians. The Indian nations were as politically independent as communities can be. Much of their freedom of action from the earliest time of which they had memory had been directed to disputes with each other. In this respect they rivaled the ingrained contentiousness of the nations of Europe. Some of them on the other hand were gathered into more or less loosely knit regional confederations. But all were in constant touch with each other and all were united in their fierce opposition to any further advance of the white frontier. All realized that their very existence depended on the Line being held.

A line does not become a boundary merely by being drawn upon a map in a government office. More also is required than the affirmation, however ardent, of distant chancelleries or nearer legislatures and tribal councils. To invest a boundary with reality there must be the presence of physical force, or, at least, the imminent threat of force. Two such physical forces existed and they were equally committed to the maintenance of the Proclamation Line. The one organized military force in the area was the English regular army. Its garrisons were established at every more strategic point in the west. During the French War it had learned wilderness mobility the hard way. Under the direction of the English commander-in-chief in North America its primary duty was to enforce the formally announced will of the king. The other physical force in being and so situated as to make itself instantly effective was the Indian warrior class. Indian military power was handicapped by divided counsels and much innate heedlessness. Yet it remained a terrifying force, capable of a forever baffling swiftness of movement and peculiarly adapted to the unparalleled complexities of war in the forest. Even were the English army withdrawn a perpetual guardianship of the Line was vested in the long-continued Indian capacity to exact fearful penalties for every violation.

International, political, and military pressures were not, of course, the only influence bearing upon the stability of the Line. There was public opinion and in the colonies public opinion was becoming each year more violently articulate. But no important segment of that opinion regarded the King's Proclamation in any other light than as an eminently rational provision for public peace and safety. Little was to be lost and much was to be gained, it was generally agreed, if Indians and whites were to be kept to their own sides of the mountains. Church leaders earnestly advocated peace with the Indians, moved by the hope that this might lead to their eventual conversion. Commercial circles were eager to avoid the tax burden of new Indian wars. Most bankers, merchants, shippers, and shipbuilders were faced toward the sea and the trade with the West Indies and Europe. Large landowners deplored the westward drift of their tenants and indentured servants. An exceptionally vocal school of

American thought which was to persist for generations to come was opposed in principle to westward expansion. According to this strongly advocated theory the area east of the mountains provided ample room for a population of untold millions and the public welfare was to be far better served by a homogeneous development of this area than by a reckless westward dispersal of the community's energies. No American of 1763 foresaw a United States and still less a United States inheriting a relentless and unlimited westward extension of its dominion. Manifest destiny was a conception that followed events, not one that produced them.

Two towering economic interests, the fur trade and the great land companies, were specially concerned with the west. Both were endowed with enormous political and economic influence, in London as well as in the colonies. Both supported the establishment of the Line, the one actively and the other passively. The fur trade, which represented a substantial share of North America's total commerce, by the very nature of its operations was very nearly as opposed to the westward extension of white settlement as were the Indians themselves. The land companies had been formed in the decade preceding the French War and their activities had had much to do with precipitating it. Their common design was the acquisition of immense land grants beyond the mountains upon which they could ultimately profit by eventual sale to carefully shepherded colonies of actual settlers. After the rout of the French the prospects opening to them appeared more glittering than ever. Nevertheless they accepted the Line as a preliminary necessity. They much preferred to await an orderly and discreet negotiation with the crown than to see their prospective tracts prematurely overrun by an unmanageable rush of land-grabbing frontiersmen.

It was these land-grabbing frontiersmen whose individual inclination was to prove finally decisive. But that decision was not yet in sight. What was in sight was the mountains. They appeared an insurmountable barrier. The generations of their forebears who during the last century and a half had edged the frontier slowly westward from the seacoast had been confronted by no such obstacle. The landless man who ventured to carve a place for himself out of the forest had had only to go into it a little way. Even though living on the outer fringe of settlement he was not totally isolated. He could feel just behind him the support of his increasingly numerous neighbors. Next year there would be neighbors in front of him. Year by year, a cabin at a time and a mile at a time, the frontier had inched westward. Like water trickling through grass it was a process difficult to stem. The Indians had periodically eased the tension by withdrawing. They required wide hunting grounds which in turn required their keeping a distance from the frontier. Finally, most of the Shawnee and Delaware, the principal nations on the middle border, had moved to the freer hunting grounds on the Ohio on the other side of the mountains. Within another ten years, however, the slow and apparently inexorable advance of the frontier had come to a halt at the foot of the mountains. The former cabin-by-cabin and mile-by-mile advance was no longer possible. Ahead among the forested heights were only rocky and isolated creek bottoms in which a first settler would be defenselessly exposed. For the generation before 1763 the frontier instead of moving westward had skirted the mountains and pushed southward down the Valley of Virginia. But by now this slack had been taken up. There was no more wild free land to be had for the taking. There were only the mountains. And beyond them the vengefully waiting Indians. The fierce Indian inroads of the French War and now of Pontiac's War had demonstrated how fearful was this Indian danger. The frontiersman who might not hesitate to clear a corn patch and build a cabin a mile in advance of his neighbors had to think hard before deciding to subject his family to this two-hundred-mile jump into the fire. The King's Proclamation meant no more to him than had the many former attempts of provincial governments to set a limit to his land seeking. What gave him pause were the physical facts with which he had immediately and personally to deal. The mountains and the Indians and the distance were brutal facts.

The foregoing were among the forces, physical and psychological, that suggested in the fall of 1763 that the Line was a fixture likely to remain as long as any man living could foresee.

The Calm Before the Storm, 1763–1774

CHAPTER 3

ECONOMIC RIVALRY BETWEEN ENGLAND AND ITS COLONIES

LAWRENCE HENRY GIPSON

The period following the Seven Years' War was one of peace and prosperity for the English colonies in America. In fact, the colonies were *too* prosperous. If one single factor led to the American Revolution, it was the growing economic rivalry between the American colonies and the British motherland. The British, hoping to protect their own economic position, passed a number of laws restricting colonial trade and attempted to get a piece of the commercial action through various tariffs and taxes. The colonists naturally resented these laws and began to resist them.

Lawrence Henry Gipson (1880–1971) was a professor of history at numerous universities, from the University of Idaho in 1903 to Oxford University in 1951, and is the author of many books on American history. He is best known for his thirteen-volume series, the British Empire Before the American Revolution. In this selection he presents American population, commerce, and trade statistics that reveal just how rich and powerful the English colonies were becoming.

L et us consider the internal situation in the American colonies in 1763. While there are no accurate population figures for the thirteen colonies for that year, it would appear that they numbered at least 1,750,000 and perhaps as many

Lawrence Henry Gipson, *The Coming of the Revolution, 1763–1775*, New York: Harper & Brothers, 1954. Copyright © 1954 by Harper & Brothers. Reproduced by permission.

as 2,000,000, including blacks as well as whites. They were scattered along the Atlantic seaboard from upper Maine to the borders of Florida and had penetrated points far inland, following as a rule either the course of rivers or, in the case of such colonies as Pennsylvania and Massachusetts Bay, such artificial means of communication as Indian paths and roads. However, they were not evenly distributed. In some of the colonies, such as Connecticut, the population was fairly dense and had already settled the lands most suitable for cultivation, with the result that many families were restlessly seeking new homes beyond their bounds; in other colonies, as was true of New York, much of the good land was still held by great families either for speculative purposes or for tenantry, and these areas were therefore avoided by people seeking to acquire farms.

DIVERSITY IN THE ENGLISH COLONIES

While most colonials dwelt either in the open country, particularly in the South, or in small towns and villages, after the pattern of New England, there were also some seaports that indicated the presence of a real concentration of wealth and of people, such as Boston with a population of some 22,000 inhabitants, Newport with perhaps 10,000, New York City with about 18,000, Philadelphia surpassing Boston in size, and Charles Town (Charleston), the metropolis of the South, with some 10,000. As the result of huge demands for provisions at high prices paid by the British army contractors for supplying the armed forces, the late war had brought added prosperity to the colonies. Nowhere was there manifest the type of squalor that marked the low standard of living of people in many parts of the Old World. For, rude as were the conditions under which many, if not most, frontier families lived, these were accepted as an inevitable part of the task of subduing the wilderness and were lightened by the ever-present anticipation of future rewards for present hardships. Colonials in 1763 were, by and large, self-confident, resourceful, energetic, and positive, and they displayed a forthrightness born of these qualities. This forthrightness had its expression even in religious matters. The homogeneity that had distinguished, for example, both New England and Virginia in 1663 no longer existed a century later. Both the established Congregational Church of New England and the Anglican Church of Virginia had suffered heavy blows to their prestige from the Great Awakening and the resultant secessions from the local churches. In 1763 such heterodox groups as the Baptists were boldly challenging the older religious establishments, and outside of the organized churches there were other movements, such as deism, that appealed to the more intellectually inclined. Further, by 1763 the weekly press all along the Atlantic seaboard constituted a formidable threat to the position that clergymen had long enjoyed in America as oracles on social as well as religious and ethical issues, and exerted a powerful influence along secular lines.

To repeat, the great wilderness of North America was slowly helping to create a new kind of Briton—the American. But the American was not shaped from any one mold. Certainly the ranchers of the western Carolinas, who tended the great herds of cattle that roamed and fattened upon the marshy uplands about the sources of the Santee and other rivers, were by 1763 as distinct in pattern of living as were the cowboys of the western plains in the nineteenth century. Quite distinct were the western traders and trappers, who lived a life not unlike that of the Indians and one very different from other frontiersmen primarily interested in husbandry and homebuilding. In the more settled parts of the colonies, not only the wealthy tobacco and rice planters of the South but the merchant princes of the North had become as dissimilar from their prototypes in England as were American farmers, sailors, fishermen, small tradesmen, and mechanics. Moreover, the woodsmen, both of Maine and New Hampshire and of the pine barrens of the Carolinas, represented types that had no counterpart in the mother country. There were also extensive communities of German-speaking people in Pennsylvania, western Maryland, and western Virginia who preserved much of the culture of their ancestral homeland, as did the Ulster Scots—more familiarly known as Scotch-Irish—who remained a border people much like their ancestors in northern Ireland and earlier in the Lowlands of Scotland. Finally, there were the Negroes, probably numbering by 1763 almost 175,000. The impact of their mores, as well as their mere presence as slaves, upon the English civilization of the New World was clearly evident and as much as any other social institution distinguished it sharply from that of the mother country.

In short, many distinct groups were jostling one another in the British North America of 1763. Some were pacifistic like the Quakers, the Mennonites, and Dunkards in Pennsylvania, and others decidedly militant, like the Presbyterian Ulster Scots and the New England Congregationalists; many were devout communicants and others were apparently disassociated from any church or religion; most of them used the tongue of England, and yet thousands spoke some other language. Thus, there was a vital need of the spirit of tolerance in the colonies, were conditions of living not to be rendered unbearable. That this spirit of toleration was growing cannot be doubted; that it still fell far short of the present American ideal is not to be denied. In 1763, Roman Catholics as well as non-Christians, including Jews, were denied the franchise and other rights of citizenship even in Rhode Island, that colony of "soul freedom." Nor was religious freedom of Catholics protected in Massachusetts Bay under its charter, while in the province of Maryland a harsh code directed toward the complete suppression of their religion still remained on the statute books. In Connecticut men were being haled into court and fined or imprisoned for the crime of separatism; neither "unitarians" nor "deists" were capable of holding any office. In Virginia, Baptist and other dissenting preachers were liable to persecution for carrying on their activities, and so late as 1768 many of them were actually imprisoned as disturbers of the peace. Nevertheless, the spirit of the times was hostile to this intolerance, under whatever name it presented itself, and such popular leaders as Patrick Henry came powerfully to the defense of those who suffered for their nonconformity.

It is quite evident, in surveying their progress in the eighteenth century, that the American continental colonies had attained a large measure of maturity by 1763. Since this maturity had a very direct bearing upon their ultimate relationship to the rest of the British Empire and particularly to the mother country, it is important to indicate its characteristics with some clearness.

INDUSTRIAL DEVELOPMENT IN THE ENGLISH COLONIES

Economically, no colonial people had ever made such progress in the course of half a century. Although the American iron industry had its real beginnings only with the opening of the eighteenth century, it had by 1750 reached such proportions as bade fair to drive the iron manufactures of England from the markets of the Empire. In face of the danger of unemployment at home, an attempt was made in that year, with the passage by Parliament of the Iron Act, to curb colonial competition. The act placed restrictions on the manufacturing of American iron by positive prohibitions against the erection in the New World of additional slitting, plating, or steel mills, while at the same time it encouraged the increased production of American pig iron and bar iron in the vain hope that these products would be sent in large quantities to the mother country. Not only was no effective check placed upon colonial iron production and manufacturing by the act, but expansion of the industry in open violation of it continued. By the time of the outbreak of the American Revolution there were actually more furnaces and forges in operation in the continental colonies than in England and Wales, and the amount of both pig iron and bar iron flowing from them was larger than the total output of Great Britain. Moreover, the quality of American steel and iron manufactures was excellent.

The explanation of this phenomenon lies in the fact that sufficient capital had accumulated in the colonies to finance these costly undertakings; that managerial and technical skill of high order was available to conduct them successfully; and that the American iron industry was free of many handicaps facing English ironmasters. Virgin forests of hardwood provided at low cost an apparently inexhaustible supply of essential charcoal, an article that in England could be secured only in measured quantities upon the basis of the most careful planning well in advance of the need; iron ore of high quality was also abundant; and, finally, markets for all the iron and steel produced in America were close at hand, involving no such expensive carrying charges as those facing the British ironmaster who sought to compete in the markets of the New World. While this industry had its chief concentration in Pennsylvania, it was at the same time widely spread throughout the colonies and the prosperity that it enjoyed was therefore broadly distributed.

Not only was British North America by 1763 one of the world's leading centers for iron production; it had acquired too a leading position in shipbuilding. Although ships were built in most of the colonies, the largest and the best constructed in the New World came from the shipyards of New England and, particularly, Massachusetts Bay. The building of good sailing vessels demanded both a high degree of skill and proper facilities. Where else within the Empire were these so happily combined as in New England where shipways were scattered along the coasts at places favorable for launching? The beginning of this industry goes back to the seventeenth century: its foundation rested in the Navigation Act of 1660, which provided that ships flying the merchant flag of England and entitled to the privileges therein stated must not only have crews that were chiefly of English nationality, but must be of English or colonial construction. As a result, early in the eighteenth century as many as 140 ships were being launched each year by the Massachusetts Bay shipyards alone. By the year 1715 some forty or fifty of these were being sold annually to merchants in England, and by 1775 it was estimated that some 30 per cent of all the ships employed in the commerce of the mother country had been built in America. In this industry, as in iron production, the colonials had a tremendous advantage over their competitors in Great Britain. Not only was the oak of New England unsurpassed in quality, but the quantity—unlike the limited supply available in the mother country—could be measured only by the ability of loggers to float it down the rivers to the sawmills of the coastal towns. In that area was also the great white-pine belt, the trees of which were ideal for masts, bowsprits, and yardarms, which English shipwrights had to import at high cost. Moreover, naval stores, such as pitch for calking, tar and turpentine, anchors, chains, and other ship metal, sails and cordage, were all being produced in abundance in America by the year 1763. In fact, it was estimated that it cost about twice as much to build a merchant ship in England as in Massachusetts Bay—the difference being from £15.5 to £16.5 sterling per ton as against £8 per ton.

FISHING, TRADE, AND AGRICULTURE

Although many of these ships were sold in Great Britain, they were built principally for colonial needs. A large proportion of them were at all times employed in the fisheries. As early as the seventeenth century the men of Massachusetts Bay had appropriated the great cod and mackerel beds in the Gulf of Maine at the expense of the fishermen of western England, and in the next century they came to dominate the still more important cod fisheries to the south of the Strait of Canso in Nova Scotia, also in competition with the fishing fleets of the mother country. By 1750 some six hundred New England vessels were engaged in this activity and by 1771, including the whalers, they numbered over a thousand, and gave profitable employment to thousands of people during the open season. There was, indeed, deep apprehension in England even before the middle of the eighteenth century that English ships would be driven from the Banks of Newfoundland by this competition, just as they had earlier been driven from the Gulf of Maine and by 1750 from the Canso fisheries. There was good reason for this fear. The cod caught by New Englanders was cured under conditions much more favorable than was possible for the English "bankers" to enjoy, obliged as they were to dry their catch on the damp, foggy southeastern coast of Newfoundland. As a result the New England cod early commanded a much higher price in the Portuguese markets than did that carried there by the English sack ships from the port of St. John's.

Nor does this tell the whole story of the successful competition of American businessmen with those of the mother country. The carrying trade as well had an importance to Great Britain equal to, if not surpassing, the fisheries in providing sources of revenue and in the training of men to a seafaring life who would be available in times of emergency to man the great Royal Navy and thus protect England and her possessions. But the carrying trade that involved the continental colonies was in the course of the eighteenth century gradually taken over not only by colonial-made ships but by those with colonial registration. In 1753, of 496 vessels that legally cleared from Boston harbor, according to its port records, all but sixty-four were constructed within the province of Massachusetts Bay itself, only five carried a London registration, and only seven others that of an English or Scottish outport. By 1775, three quarters of all the commerce of the continental colonies, it has been estimated, was carried on in ships belonging to them. It is thus clear that the enterprise of American shipmasters and ship captains was gradually driving the ships of Great Britain from the waters of the New World outside of the West Indies.

In other fields the people of the colonies were indicating by 1763 that they were very well able to compete with those at home—for example, in the production of pottery and stoneware and even glassware. From American distilleries there came an immense volume of rum, the drink of the common people and an article of high esteem to those employed in the Indian trade, in the purchase of Negro slaves off the coast of Guinea, and in supplying the demands of the loggers and those engaged in the fisheries. As much as 2,000,000 gallons of this heady potation were being exported by the sixty-three distilleries of Massachusetts Bay alone in 1750, and in 1764 the merchants of Rhode Island asserted that not all of the molasses produced in the British West Indies was sufficient to meet the demands of their distilleries, which required at least 15,000 hogsheads each year. Other colonies, such as Pennsylvania and New York, were also heavily involved in this activity. In this connection, it is clear that the spirits produced in England, such as gin, could not compete in the New World with this beverage either in popularity or in price, nor could these compete easily even along the African coast where rum was brought in great quantity by Rhode Island slavers.

If American colonials were driving hard and successfully against their competitors in the British Isles in many fields of industry and in commerce, the same was true in agriculture, in milling, and in the meat-packing industry. This was especially the case of the men of the middle colonies and Virginia, who shipped great surpluses of wheat, flour, bread, beef, and pork as well as horses to the West Indies and elsewhere. In fact, it was asserted by Governor Morris of Pennsylvania in 1755 that that colony alone was able to export each year enough food to sustain a 100,000 people. By 1775 its people were annually sending abroad some 350,000 barrels of flour and other commodities in like proportions. It is clear that there was no difficulty in disposing of these food supplies profitably in the West Indian and other markets in competition with English flour and pork and Irish beef, and equally clear is it that in 1763 agriculture in these colonies was riding on a crest of prosperity. This was also true of the rice-producing colonies, especially South Carolina, which faced no competition from the British Isles where rice could not be raised. In competing with Mediterranean rice in the markets of Europe, the American product was so superior in quality as to obtain premium prices. In 1740 some 90,000 barrels of this commodity were exported from Charleston. In view of the abundance of other foods, such as vegetables and fruits, eggs, and poultry, that were consumed locally rather than exported, it is needless to point out that American colonials were not only a well-nourished people but were able to provide from their own fertile lands practically all the food that sustained them.

From the continental colonies also came enormous crops of tobacco, a great deal of indigo, and some silk; from the southern pine belt, abundant naval stores, such as pitch, resin, tar, and turpentine; and from the northern hardwood areas, large amounts of lumber, pearl ash, and potash—none of these articles in competition with the products of the mother country and all of them, in fact, enjoying special encouragement by Parliament in the way of either tariff protection or bounties. Indeed, not only did North American tobacco—the great staple of the Chesapeake Bay—enjoy a virtual monopoly of the markets of the British Isles through the early discrimination against foreign-grown tobacco by means of very high tariffs, but it was able in the century under consideration to dominate those of all northern Europe as well. This was owing to its high quality and reasonable price and to the fact that shipping was adequate to maintain a constant flow in quantity of the aromatic weed from British ports to those of the Continent. Upon its culture was largely based the impressive prosperity of both Virginia and Maryland, a prosperity that in the final analysis was, as a rule, only seriously affected by the careless business methods and extravagant tastes of the planters and the tendency at times to increase the area of tobacco culture within these and neighboring colonies more rapidly than the demand would warrant without a fall in price.

Finally, from the North American interior there moved to the coast in times of peace a great volume of furs and skins, secured in trade with the natives, which were thereupon exported to Great Britain, chiefly from the ports of New York, Philadelphia, and Charleston. From Charleston, for example, in 1748 deerskins to the value of £252,000 South Carolina currency were shipped and, between 1739 and 1759, an annual average of 200,000 pounds of buckskin.

These trade statistics attest the fact that the British colonials of North America in 1763 were among the most fortunate people in the world and also among the most enterprising.

Benjamin West and John Singleton Copley: America's First Notable Artists

David Bjelajac

The era between the Seven Years' War and the American Revolution saw the first flowering of American high culture, including the first notable artists, poets, and musicians. American painter Benjamin West sparked a new movement in art with his painting *The Death of General Wolfe*, which was shown in London in 1770. Up to that time the painting of events drawn from history had been restricted to events in "classical"—that is, Greek and Roman—history. Only such events were considered grand enough to be a suitable subject for a painting. By portraying the death of General James Wolfe at the Battle of Quebec, and doing so in the same epic style that had previously been reserved for paintings of classical history, West was making the statement that American history was just as grand and important as the history of the Roman empire. This statement was both shocking and irresistible. Soon, a number of talented young painters, including John Singleton Copley, were also creating paintings based on recent history.

David Bjelajac teaches art history at George Washington University and has written several books and articles on the subject. His special area of emphasis is American art of the eighteenth and nineteenth centuries. In this selection, he explains the political imagery in important paintings by West and Copley.

W orking within the English school of painting, Americans created a revolution in history painting: they chose modern subjects that portrayed the New World as a land of millennial promise, redemption, and brotherhood. Painters also elevated portraiture toward the moral seriousness of history painting, creating an American pantheon of virtuous patriots and notables.

BENJAMIN WEST AND THE REVOLUTION IN HISTORY PAINTING

Before the Revolution, Benjamin West became the founder of an American school of painting. But he did so only after he left his native Pennsylvania for Europe, never to return. Born to humble innkeepers, West received basic instruction from the Philadelphia painter William Williams. More importantly, West's early interest in history painting and the academic tradition brought him to the attention of the Anglican clergyman William Smith, provost of the College of Philadelphia and a Masonic chaplain of the Grand Lodge of Pennsylvania. Smith mentored West in ancient history, but he also taught the aspiring painter that America was a sacred space, a remote refuge for Liberty and pure religion.

Financed by Smith and other prominent Philadelphians, West traveled to Italy in 1760 to study the great masterpieces of antiquity and the Renaissance. Three years later, moving to London, he helped to establish the academic tradition of grand-manner history painting in Britain. His London studio became a magnet for aspiring American artists seeking instruction in drawing and painting. West's first American pupil, Matthew Pratt (1734–1805), represented him instructing four young men in *The American School*, a painting exhibited in London in 1766. Pratt portrays West standing at the left. He is wearing a green suit and tricorn hat, which signifies the Pennsylvanian's self-identification with the Quaker founders of that colony. Quaker reliance upon an inner voice or spiritual light appealed to an artist who wished to assert his independence from the material luxuries of European civilization.

Moralizing subjects such as *The Departure of Regulus from Rome* won West the patronage of George III, who was renowned for his religious piety. The painting's depiction of an ancient Roman hero solemnly departing for a certain death during the Punic Wars pleased the British monarch's desire for patriotic, self-sacrificing subjects; and soon afterward, he named West court history painter.

A year after *Regulus,* in 1770, West disturbed both his royal patron and the Royal Academy president with *The Death of General Wolfe,* a painting that radically paralleled Anglo-American agitation for political democratization. West's painting appealed to a far wider audience because he chose a celebrated modern subject, the victory over the French at the Battle of Quebec on September 13, 1759, and dared to clothe the figures in contemporary costume. [English portrait painter] Sir Joshua Reynolds regarded West's turn toward realism as a vulgarization of high art, a descent from the universal ideals of classicism.

West's aesthetic rebellion against Reynolds and European academic tradition served the cause of American nationalism. He argued that the pivotal battle of Quebec, which decided the Seven Years' War, occurred:

> in a region of the world unknown to the Greeks and the Romans, and at a period of time when no such nations, nor heroes in their costumes, any longer existed. The subject I have to represent is the conquest of a great province of America by the British troops. It is a topic that history will proudly record, and the same truth that guides the pen of the historian should govern the pencil of the artist. I consider myself as undertaking to tell this great event to the eye of the world; but if, instead of the facts of the transaction, I represent classical fictions, how shall I be understood by posterity!

West insisted upon representing both the geographical specificity and historical uniqueness of the New World. However, far from being non-fictional, his picture imaginatively manipulated facts. Beholders recognized the composition's religious associations with representations of Christ's disciples lamenting over his crucified body. As an immortalized type for Christ's sacrifice, Wolfe's martyred blood sanctified American soil. The battle, which West sketchily represented in the background, was fought outside Quebec's walls upon the "Plains of Abraham," evoking Old Testament associations for Anglo-Americans, who traditionally identified themselves as God's new chosen people. Over the conquered city, the dark storm clouds and battle smoke clear for the divine light of Providence to proclaim Britain's victory.

West created a strongly competing secondary focus at the far left of the composition to underscore the specifically American nature of the victory. A seminude Iroquois Indian, wearing body paint and red feathers, gazes contemplatively upon the dying general. Romantically associating Indians with a higher, secret knowledge of nature's vitalistic powers, West identified his art with the image of the noble Indian. The muscular warrior, in a dignified and melancholic pose, personifies the ancient ideal of a spartan lifestyle. A man of Nature, West's deferential Indian universalizes the selfless moral content of Wolfe's martyrdom, while his red flesh and exotic costume insistently specify the North American locale. Hovering over the Indian, wearing a green jacket, moccasins, and beaded breeches, stands a white man, whom West explicitly identifies as William Johnson. His name and a map with the geographical names "Mohawk Valley" and "Ontario" are inscribed upon the powder horn strapped to his body, equating Johnson's personal identity with property ceded to him by the Mohawk Indians. As a superintendent of Indian affairs, Johnson had learned Iroquois customs and language and married a Mohawk woman, more easily enabling him to convince some Native Americans to ally with Britain against France.

West's explicit inclusion of this colonial New Yorker belied the fact that Johnson, the hero of earlier battles at Lake George and Fort Niagara, was not actually present at the Battle of Quebec. Ignoring literal details of the battle, West was politically motivated to foreground the heroic American role in the Seven Years' War lest that fact be forgotten by imperial policymakers and the British public. A painted snake that decorates the Indian's back recalls Benjamin Franklin's widely published print *Join or Die,* which equates a segmented snake with the politically divided American colonies. Only by uniting into a sinuous whole could America defend itself against French and Indian threats.

Although an English aristocrat purchased *The Death of General Wolfe* and George III later ordered a copy, West began the original painting without a commission or certain patron. Through public exhibition and engraved prints of the composition, he reached out for a wider, international audience that included the growing middle class. The central portion of the painting even decorated English ceramic mugs and earthenware for the domestic and export market.

JOHN SINGLETON COPLEY

West's success intensified John Singleton Copley's desire to escape the heated environment of Boston for a career abroad. The Boston Massacre of 1770 had dramatically intensified the conflict, as British troops shot and killed five Boston laborers protesting the army occupation. The polarizing event made life more difficult for a painter heavily dependent upon the patronage of the colonial political establishment. Copley's half brother Henry Pelham designed an engraving of *The Bloody Massacre* that was rapidly plagiarized by Paul Revere. Unlike Pelham and Copley, Revere enthusiastically supported the colonial rebels and added the sign "Butcher's Hall" over the heads of the British troops.

The massacre divided Boston along class, ethnic, and racial lines. Even critics of imperial rule feared mob violence and supported the British version of events that soldiers had fired in self-defense at a rowdy mob. The number of poor adult males in Boston, many of them African Americans and Irish Catholics, had doubled since 1687 to almost one-third of the adult male population. John Adams probably spoke for most of the Boston elite when he denigrated the massacre victims as "a motley rabble of saucy boys, negroes and mulattoes, Irish teagues and outlandish jack tarrs." Defending the British troops in court, he sarcastically singled out an escaped African-American slave, Crispus Attucks, who "appears to have undertaken to be the hero of the night; and to lead this army with banners . . . and march them up to *King street* with their clubs."

Three years later, during the Boston Tea Party, Revere and other Sons of Liberty threw into Boston harbor a shipment of tea belonging to Copley's father-in-law, Richard Clarke, a merchant for London's East India Company. Copley left America for Europe. First studying art in Italy, he then settled in London, and like West, never returned to his native land.

Copley's first major history painting in London demonstrated his commitment to modern American subject matter and contemporary costume, emulating West's *The Death of General Wolfe*. During the Revolution, Copley enigmatically elevated a black man to the top of a visual pyramid in his history painting *Watson and the Shark*. A political and religious allegory, the picture's symbolism of white-black or light-dark expresses the tension between imperial order and revolutionary chaos. Painted for Brook Watson, a wealthy London merchant and Tory critic of the Revolution, Copley's composition tells the story of how Watson, as a young cabin boy, had lost his right leg to a shark while swimming near his ship anchored in the harbor at Havana, Cuba.

As described by London notices of the 1778 Royal Academy exhibition, Copley's painting represents the dramatic moment when a group of sailors in a rowboat finally rescued Watson "at the very instant he was about to be seized the third time," and "the shark was struck with the boat hook, and driven from his prey." London newspapers emphasized the success of the third rescue attempt, implicitly comparing Watson's plight with Christ's Resurrection on the third day. Further borrowing from Christian iconography, Copley heroicized the lowly sailors, one of whom is about to spear the shark like St. George or St. Michael slaying the dragon. Above the dark waters, the dawn's golden light promises salvation. The cross-shaped masts of ships on the horizon join the crosses of Havana's cathedral and convent towers. They suggest that Watson's rescue symbolized his spiritual rebirth during the Christian voyage of life.

IMAGES OF REVOLUTION AND INDEPENDENCE

On a political level, Brook Watson's dismembered body symbolized the damaged body politic of the British Empire, which was founded upon the shipping and commercial wealth of Watson and other London merchants. Watson's lost leg evoked associations with numerous revolutionary-era prints of a dismembered Britannia such as Benjamin Franklin's *Magna Britannia*. By 1778, when *Watson and the Shark* was exhibited, France had allied with America, and British troops had lost the previous year's pivotal Battle of Saratoga. Furthermore, the French threatened British control of the West Indies, including Caribbean ports such as Havana, the setting for Copley's painting.

Watson and the Shark encouraged contemporary beholders to identify with Watson's fate, knowing that this cabin boy more than survived despite the loss of a leg. The British Empire also would renew itself through revolutionary trial by fire. Similarly, after the initial 1775 battles at Lexington and Concord, Copley had prophesied from his safe haven in London that America "will finally emerge from her present Callamity and become a Mighty Empire. And it is a pleasing reflection that I shall stand amongst the first of the Artists that shall have led the country to the knowledge and cultivation of the fine Arts."

Copley's optimistic faith in divine providence led him to believe that both America and Britain would prosper once the revolutionary floodwaters had subsided. He interpreted the American Revolution as a divinely ordained natural disaster akin to the biblical Flood or to the drowning of a youth in shark-infested waters.

Copley's fatalistic view of the Revolution as an unavoidable act of God or Nature may explain why a black man stands at the compositional apex of the picture. London reviewers criticized the relative passivity of his black sailor: "It would not be unnatural to place a woman in the attitude of the *black*; but he, instead of being terrified, ought, in our opinion, to be busy. He has thrown a rope over to the boy. It is held, unsailorlike . . . and he makes no use of it." For London critics, Copley's "idle Black" was like a child or a woman, too frozen by fear to take action. While not blatantly caricatured, the black sailor's passivity made him appear less a man than an abstract personification of the emotional horror associated with the shark. Both the shark and the black sailor symbolized the darkness of the underworld. Critics also referred to the African's fellow sailors as "tars," short for tarpaulin sails. But the word also punned with the visual image of the black to suggest sticky, oily tar, a dangerously combustible, yet healing black substance that was used to caulk leaking ships and cauterize amputation wounds. Copley had heard John Adams employ the term "tar" to characterize the politically volatile racial mixture that triggered the Boston massacre. Indeed, Watson's helpless nude body is strikingly similar to the figure of the dying man in the left foreground of Revere's *The Bloody Massacre*, originally composed by Copley's half brother.

Headed by the African who holds a serpentine towline, the sailors form part of an elemental circle connecting them with the monstrous shark that surrounds the boat. While the shark's open jaws approach the youth, his tail in middle ground points upward toward the harpoonist and African at the top of the compositional circuit. Beholders may have associated this violent circle of fiery tars versus watery serpentine monster with the emblematic *uroboros* or circular serpent. Biting its own tail to form a perfect circle, the serpent regenerated itself, eating its old skin to signify nature's seasonal cycle or daily revolution from night to day. The circular serpent often decorated Masonic lodge certificates and furniture, expressing Freemasons' faith that nature's cyclical laws were divinely ordained. During the Revolution, the *uroboros* appeared on the mastheads of city newspapers and government treasury notes. This image reassured citizens that a millennial dawn was emerging from the darkness of revolutionary violence.

In addition to the original version sold to Watson, Copley hung a replica of *Watson and the Shark* in his studio and sold engraved prints of the composition. Thanks to the success of "the Shark painting," Copley became a favorite with London merchants, painting their portraits and histories of their martyred heroes. At the same time, Copley portrayed statesmen and citizens of the new republic. Four years after *Watson and the Shark*, he painted the portrait of an entirely different Watson, a young American merchant, who wished to commemorate the dawn of a new empire. Elkanah Watson later recalled the circumstances of the portrait in his journal:

> The painting was finished in most admirable style, except the background, which Copley and I designed to represent a ship, bearing to America the intelligence of the acknowledgement of independence, with a sun just rising upon the stripes of the Union, streaming from her gaff. All was complete save the flag, which Copley did not deem prudent to hoist under present circumstances, as his gallery is a constant resort of the royal family and the nobility. I dined with the artist, on the glorious 5th of December, 1782, after listening with him to the speech of the King, formally recognizing the United States of America as in the rank of nations. . . . He invited me into his studio; and there with a bold hand, a master's touch, and I believe an American heart, attached to the ship the Stars and Stripes. This was, I imagine, the first American flag hoisted in Old England.

Elkanah Watson implicitly contrasts Copley's "bold hand" and "master's touch" with the artist's political timidity and unwillingness to jeopardize lucrative commissions from the British aristocracy. Copley's reputation in the United States soon suffered precisely because more radical nationalists questioned the sincerity of the artist's "American heart." Though the painting elevated his career beyond portraiture, *Watson and the Shark* became fodder for Copley's American critics, who condemned its heroic commemoration of a British Tory. William Dunlap (1766–1839), the first historian of American art, perpetuated the myth that "Copley was, when removed to England no longer an American painter in feeling." Yet Copley, like West, could never shed his American identity while living in London even if he wanted to, since English critics often referred to his American origins.

AGAINST THE STAMP ACT

WILLIAM PITT

Pressured by English businessmen, the British Parliament passed laws designed to regulate trade with the colonies to England's advantage. One of the most disliked laws in the colonies was the Stamp Act of 1765, which taxed printed materials, including business and legal documents, newspapers, and pamphlets.

American lawyers argued that there was no precedent for the British government to impose taxes without also allowing representation in Parliament. William Pitt, an elder statesman in the British Parliament, agreed with the colonists on this point and argued their case forcefully. This speech was delivered in 1766 as a reply to a previous speech by Prime Minister George Grenville, Pitt's brother-in-law, who had sponsored the Stamp Act and frequently spoke in its defense. In this speech Pitt goes so far as to call the taxation of the colonies a kind of slavery. As a result of his tireless advocacy of colonial interests, William Pitt became a hero to the Americans. The newly founded town of Pittsburgh was named after him.

I have been charged with giving birth to sedition in America. They have spoken their sentiments with freedom against this unhappy act, and that freedom has become their crime. Sorry I am to hear the liberty of speech in this house, imputed as a crime. But the imputation shall not discourage me. It is a liberty I mean to exercise. No gentleman ought to be afraid to exercise it. It is a liberty by which the gentleman who calumniates it might have profited, by which he ought to have profited.

William Pitt, "Speech on the Stamp Act , January 14, 1766," *Great Issues in American History: From the Revolution to the Civil War, 1765–1865*, edited by Richard Hofstadter, New York: Vintage Books, 1958.

He ought to have desisted from his project. The gentleman [Prime Minister George Grenville] tells us, America is obstinate; America is almost in open rebellion. I rejoice that America has resisted. Three millions of people so dead to all feelings of liberty, as voluntarily to submit to be slaves, would have been fit instruments to make slaves of the rest. I come not here armed at all points, with law cases and acts of parliament, with the statute book doubled down in dogs'-ears, to defend the cause of liberty: if I had, I myself would have cited the two cases of Chester and Durham [cities in northern England]. I would have cited them, to have shown that even under former arbitrary reigns, parliaments were ashamed of taxing a people without their consent, and allowed them representatives. Why did the gentleman confine himself to Chester and Durham? He might have taken a higher example in Wales; Wales, that never was taxed by parliament till it was incorporated. I would not debate a particular point of law with the gentleman. I know his abilities. I have been obliged to his diligent researches: but, for the defence of liberty, upon a general principle, upon a constitutional principle, it is a ground upon which I stand firm; on which I dare meet any man. The gentleman tells us of many who are taxed, and are not represented. The India Company, merchants, stock-holders, manufacturers. Surely many of these are represented in other capacities, as owners of land, or as freemen of boroughs. It is a misfortune that more are not equally represented: but they are all inhabitants, and as such, are they not virtually represented? . . . they have connections with those that elect, and they have influence over them. The gentleman mentioned the stock-holders: I hope he does not reckon the debts of the nation as a part of the national estate. Since the accession of King William, many ministers, some of great, others of more moderate abilities, have taken the lead of government. ([Grenville] then went through the list of them, bringing it down till he came to himself, giving a short sketch of the characters of each of them.)

None of these thought, or ever dreamed, of robbing the colonies of their constitutional rights. That was reserved to mark the era of the late administration: not that there were wanting some, when I had the honour to serve his Majesty, to propose to me to burn my fingers with an American stamp-act. With the enemy at their back, with our bayonets at their breasts, in the day of their distress, perhaps the Americans would have submitted to the imposition; but it would have been taking an ungenerous and unjust advantage. The gentleman boasts of his bounties to America. Are not those bounties intended finally for the benefit of this kingdom? If they are not, he has misapplied the national treasures. I am no courtier of America; I stand up for this kingdom. I maintain, that the parliament has a right to bind, to restrain America. Our legislative power over the colonies is sovereign and supreme. When it ceases to be sovereign and supreme, I would advise every gentleman to sell his lands, if he can, and embark for that country. When two countries are connected together, like England and her colonies, without being incorporated, the one must necessarily govern; the greater must rule the less; but so rule it, as not to contradict the fundamental principles that are common to both. If the gentleman does not understand the difference between external and internal taxes, I cannot help it; but there is a plain distinction between taxes levied for the purposes of raising a revenue, and duties imposed for the regulation of trade, for the accommodation of the subject; although, in the consequences, some revenue might incidentally arise from the latter.

The gentleman asks, when were the colonies emancipated? But I desire to know, when were they made slaves. But I dwell not upon words. When I had the honour of serving his Majesty, I availed myself of the means of information which I derived from my office: I speak, therefore, from knowledge. My materials were good; I was at pains to collect, to digest, to consider them; and I will be bold to affirm, that the profits to Great Britain from the trade of the colonies, through all its branches, is two millions a year. This is the fund that carried you triumphantly through the last war. . . . You owe this to America: this is the price that America pays you for her protection. And shall a miserable financier come with a boast, that he can bring a pepper-corn into the exchequer, to the loss of millions to the nation? I dare not say, how much higher these profits may be augmented. Omitting the immense increase of people by natural population, in the northern colonies, and the emigration from every part of Europe, I am convinced the whole commercial system of America may be altered to advantage. You have prohibited where you ought to have encouraged, encouraged where you ought to have prohibited. Improper restraints have been laid on the continent, in favour of the islands. You have but two nations to trade with in America. Would you had twenty! Let acts of parliament in consequence of treaties remain, but let not an English minister become a custom-house officer for Spain, or for any foreign power. Much is wrong; much may be amended for the general good of the whole. . . .

The gentleman must not wonder he was not contradicted, when, as the minister, he asserted the right of parliament to tax America. I know not how it is, but there is a modesty in this House, which does not choose to contradict a minister. I wish gentlemen would get the better of this modesty. Even that chair, Sir, sometimes looks towards St. James's. If they do not, perhaps the collective body may begin to abate of its respect for the representative. . . .

THE STRENGTH OF AMERICA

A great deal has been said without doors of the power, of the strength of America. It is a topic that ought to be cautiously meddled with. In a good cause, on a sound bottom, the force of this country can crush America to atoms. I know the valour of your troops. I know the skill of your officers. There is not a company of foot that has served in America out of which you may not pick a man of sufficient knowledge and experience to make a governor of a colony there. But on this ground, on the Stamp Act, when so many here will think a crying injustice, I am one who will lift up my hands against it.

In such a cause, your success would be hazardous. America, if she fell, would fall like the strong man. She would embrace the pillars of the state, and pull down the constitution along with her. Is this your boasted peace? Not to sheathe the sword in its scabbard, but to sheathe it in the bowels of your countrymen? Will you quarrel with yourselves, now the whole House of Bourbon is united against you? . . .

The Americans have not acted in all things with prudence and temper. They have been wronged. They have been driven to madness by injustice. Will you punish them for the madness you have occasioned? Rather let prudence and temper come first from this side. I will undertake for America, that she will follow the example. There are two lines in a ballad . . . of a man's behaviour to his wife, so applicable to you and your colonies, that I cannot help repeating them:

"Be to her faults a little blind;
Be to her virtues very kind."

Upon the whole, I will beg leave to tell the House what is really my opinion. It is, that the Stamp-Act be repealed absolutely, totally, and immediately; that the reason for the repeal should be assigned, because it was founded on an erroneous principle. At the same time, let the sovereign authority of this country over the colonies be asserted in as strong terms as can be devised, and be made to extend to every point of legislation whatsoever: that we may bind their trade, confine their manufactures, and exercise every power whatsoever—except that of taking money out of their pockets without their consent.

PHILLIS WHEATLEY: AMERICA'S FIRST NOTABLE POET

JOHN C. SHIELDS

Several Americans published books of poems during the revolutionary period. However, it is interesting that the first American poet to achieve anything like an international reputation, and the only poet from the period who is still remembered today, was a young African American woman who was, in fact, a first-generation slave. No doubt her youth had something to do with her success, and perhaps her gender and race did as well. She was only fourteen years old when her first poem was published and only seventeen when her elegy to the beloved Methodist minister George Whitefield brought her to the attention of London society in 1770. At that time, fourteen-year-old Wolfgang Amadeus Mozart was giving concerts in Europe, having established his reputation as a child prodigy. English society, like European society, was fascinated by child prodigies and was eager to discover more of them. A young slave who could write poetry as well as most of her contemporaries, although she had not even learned to speak English until she arrived from Africa in Boston at the age of seven or eight, certainly qualified.

In this selection John C. Shields, who teaches English at Illinois State University and is the editor of *The Collected Works of Phillis Wheatley*, summarizes Phillis Wheatley's life and career.

John C. Shields, *Encyclopedia of African-American Culture and History*, vol. 5, edited by Jack Salzman, David Lionel Smith, and Cornel West, New York: Macmillan, 1996. Copyright © 1996 by Simon & Schuster and The Trustees of Columbia University in the City of New York. Reproduced by permission.

Phillis Wheatley was born, according to her own testimony, in Gambia, West Africa, along the fertile lowlands of the Gambia River. She was abducted as a small child of seven or eight, and sold in Boston to John and Susanna Wheatley on July 11, 1761. The horrors of the middle passage very likely contributed to the persistent asthma that plagued her throughout her short life. The Wheatleys apparently named the girl, who had nothing but a piece of dirty carpet to conceal her nakedness, after the slaver, the *Phillis*, that transported her. Nonetheless, unlike most slave owners of the time, the Wheatleys permitted Phillis to learn to read, and her poetic talent soon began to emerge.

AN EARLY TALENT FOR POETRY

Her earliest known piece of writing was an undated letter from 1765 (no known copy now exists) to Samson Occom, the Native American Mohegan minister and one of Dartmouth College's first graduates. The budding poet first appeared in print on December 21, 1767, in the *Newport Mercury* newspaper, when the author was about fourteen. The poem, "On Messrs. Hussey and Coffin," relates how the two gentlemen of the title narrowly escaped being drowned off Cape Cod in Massachusetts. Much of her subsequent poetry deals, as well, with events occurring close to her Boston circle. Of her fifty-five extant poems, for example, nineteen are elegies; all but the last of these are devoted to commemorating someone known by the poet. Her last elegy is written about herself and her career.

In early October 1770, Wheatley published an elegy that was pivotal to her career. The subject of the elegy was George Whitefield, an evangelical Methodist minister and privy chaplain to Selina Hastings, countess of Huntingdon. Whitefield made seven journeys to the American colonies, where he was known as "the Voice of the Great Awakening" and "the Great Awakener." Only a week before his death in Newburyport, Mass., on September 30, 1770, Whitefield preached in Boston, where Wheatley very likely heard him. As Susanna Wheatley regularly corresponded with the countess, she and the Wheatley household may well have entertained the Great Awakener. Wheatley's vivid, ostensibly firsthand account in the elegy, replete with quotations, may have been based on an actual acquaintance with Whitefield. In any case, Wheatley's deft elegy became an overnight sensation and was often reprinted.

It is almost certain that the ship that carried news of Whitefield's death to the countess also carried a copy of Wheatley's elegy, which brought Wheatley to the sympathetic attention of the countess. Such an acquaintance ensured that Wheatley's elegy was also reprinted many times in London, giving the young poet the distinction of an international reputation. When Wheatley's *Poems* was denied publication in Boston for racist reasons, the countess of Huntingdon generously financed its publication in London by Archibald Bell.

Wheatley's support by Selina Hastings and her rejection by male-dominated Boston signal her nourishment as a literary artist by a community of women. All these women—the countess, who encouraged and financed the publication of her *Poems* in 1773; Mary and Susanna Wheatley, who taught her the rudiments of reading and writing; and Obour Tanner, who could empathize probably better than anyone with her condition as a slave—were much older than Wheatley and obviously nurtured her creative development.

A Celebrity in London

During the summer of 1772, Wheatley actually journeyed to England, where she assisted in the preparation of her volume for the press. While in London she enjoyed considerable recognition by such dignitaries as Lord Dartmouth, Lord Lincoln, [philanthropist and scholar] Granville Sharp (who escorted Wheatley on several tours about London), Benjamin Franklin, and Brook Watson, a wealthy merchant who presented Wheatley with a folio edition of John Milton's *Paradise Lost* and who would later become lord mayor of London. Wheatley was to have been presented at court when Susanna Wheatley became ill. Wheatley was summoned to return to Boston in early August 1773. Sometime before October 18,

Phillis Wheatley

1773, she was granted her freedom, according to her own testimony, "at the desire of my friends in England." It seems likely, then, that if Selina Hastings had not agreed to finance Wheatley's *Poems* and if the poet had not journeyed to London, she would never have been manumitted [freed from slavery].

As the American Revolution erupted, Wheatley's patriotic feelings began to separate her even more from the Wheatleys, who were loyalists. Her patriotism is clearly underscored in her two most famous Revolutionary War poems. "To His Excellency General Washington" (1775) closes with this justly famous encomium: "A crown, a mansion, and a throne that shine, / With gold unfading WASHINGTON! be thine." "Liberty and Peace" (1784), written to celebrate the Treaty of Paris (September 1783), declares: "And new-born Rome [i.e., America] shall give *Britannia* Law."

Phillis Wheatley's attitude toward slavery has also been misunderstood. Because some of her antislavery statements have been recovered only in the 1970s and '80s, she has often been criticized for ignoring the issue. But her position was clear: In February 1774, for example, Wheatley wrote to Samson Occom that "in every human breast, God has implanted a Principle, which we call Love of Freedom; it is impatient of Oppression, and pants for Deliverance." This letter was reprinted a dozen times in American newspapers over the course of the next twelve months. Certainly Americans of Wheatley's time never questioned her attitude toward slavery after the publication of this letter.

In 1778 Wheatley married John Peters, a free African American who was a jack-of-all-trades, serving in various capacities from storekeeper to advocate for African Americans before the courts. But given the turbulent conditions of a nation caught up in the Revolution, Wheatley's fortunes began to decline steadily. In 1779 she published a set of *Proposals* for a new volume of poems. While the *Proposals* failed to attract subscribers, these *Proposals* attest that the poet had been diligent with her pen since the 1773 *Poems* and that she had indeed produced some 300 pages of new poetry. This volume never appeared, however, and most of its poems are now lost.

Phillis Wheatley Peters and her newborn child died in a shack on the edge of Boston on December 5, 1784. Preceded in death by two other young children, Wheatley's tragic end resembles her beginning in America. Yet Wheatley has left to her largely unappreciative country a legacy of firsts: She was the first African American to publish a book, the first woman writer whose publication was urged and nurtured by a community of women, and the first American woman author who tried to earn a living by means of her writing.

REPORT ON THE BOSTON MASSACRE

JAMES BOWDOIN

Emotions were running high in the city of Boston due to the quartering of British soldiers in private homes. The resentment led to a violent confrontation between a group of British soldiers and a mob of citizens. The soldiers, in panic, fired on the unarmed mob, killing several people. This further enraged the public, and the British decided to withdraw their soldiers to their barracks on Castle Island.

As the head of an investigative committee, James Bowdoin collected accounts of the incident and reported the committee's findings to the Boston town council. At the time, Bowdoin was a prominent Boston businessman. He was later appointed to represent Massachusetts at the Continental Congress, but poor health prevented him from attending. He helped write the constitution for the Commonwealth of Massachusetts, and he served as its second governor. He was also an amateur scientist and served as the first president of the American Academy of Sciences.

A t a Meeting of the Freeholders and other Inhabitants of the Town of Boston assembled at Faneuil Hall, on Monday the 12th day of March, Anno Domini, 1770. The following Report, containing a narrative of the late Massacre, is submitted to the Town. In the name of the Committee, James Bowdoin. By the foregoing depositions it appears very clearly, there was a general combination among the soldiers of the 29th regiment at least, to commit some extraordinary act of violence

James Bowdoin, "A Short Narrative of the Horrid Massacre in Boston," *The American Revolution: A Short History*, edited by Richard B. Morris, New York: D. Van Nostrand, 1955.

upon the town; that if the inhabitants attempted to repel it by firing even one gun upon those soldiers, the 14th regiment were ordered to be in readiness to assist them; and that on the late butchery in King Street they actually were ready for that purpose, had a single gun been fired on the perpetrators of it.

It appears by a variety of depositions, that on the same evening between the hours of six and half after nine (at which time the firing began), many persons, without the least provocation, were in various parts of the town insulted and abused by parties of armed soldiers patrolling the streets; particularly: Samuel Drowne declares that, about nine o'clock of the evening of the fifth of March current, standing at his own door in Cornhill, he saw about fourteen or fifteen soldiers of the 29th regiment, who came from Murray's barracks, armed with naked cutlasses, swords, etc., and came upon the inhabitants of the town, then standing or walking in Cornhill, and abused some, and violently assaulted others as they met them; most of whom were without so much as a stick in their hand to defend themselves, as he very clearly could discern, it being moonlight, and himself being one of the assaulted persons. All or most of the said soldiers he saw go into King Street (some of them through Royal Exchange Lane), and there followed them, and soon discovered them to be quarrelling and fighting with the people whom they saw there, which he thinks were not more than a dozen, when the soldiers came first, armed as aforesaid.

These assailants after attacking and wounding divers persons in Cornhill, proceeded (most of them) up the Royal Exchange Lane into King Street; where, making a short stop, and after assaulting and driving away the few they met there, they brandished their arms and cried out:

"Where are the boogers! Where are the cowards!"

ATTACKED BY SNOWBALLS

The outrageous behavior and the threats of the said party occasioned the ringing of the meeting-house bell near the head of King Street, which bell ringing quick, as for fire, it presently brought out a number of the inhabitants, who being soon sensible of the occasion of it, were naturally led to King Street, where the said party had made a stop but a little while before, and where the stopping had drawn together a number of boys, round the sentry at the Custom house. Whether the boys mistook the sentry for one of the said party, and thence took occasion to differ with him, or whether he first affronted them, which is affirmed in several depositions; however that may be, there was much foul language between them, and some of them, in consequence of his pushing at them with his bayonet, threw snowballs at him, which occasioned him to knock hastily at the door of the Custom house. The officer on guard was Capt. Preston, who with seven or eight soldiers, with firearms and charged bayonets, issued from the guard house, and in great haste posted himself and his soldiers in front of the Custom house. In passing to this station the soldiers pushed several per-

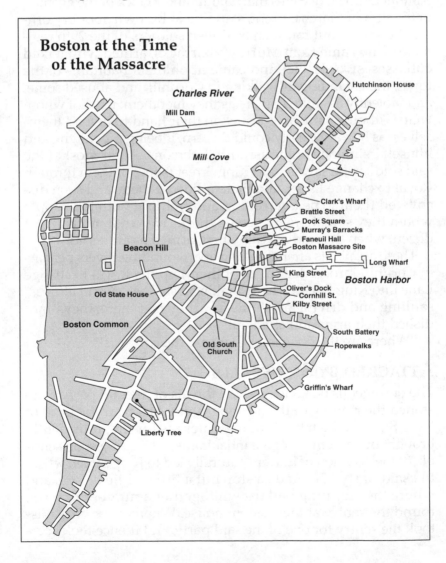

Boston at the Time of the Massacre

sons with their bayonets, driving through the people in so rough a manner that it appeared they intended to create a disturbance. This occasioned some snowballs to be thrown at them, which seems to have been the only provocation that was given.

Mr. Knox (between whom and Capt. Preston there was some conversation on the spot) declares, that while he was talking with Capt. Preston, the soldiers of his detachment had attacked the people with their bayonets; and that there was not the least provocation given to Capt. Preston or his party; the backs of the people being toward them when the people were attacked. He also declares that Capt. Preston seemed to be in great haste and much agitated, and that, according to his opinion, there were not then present in King Street above seventy or eighty persons at the extent.

The said party was formed into a half circle; and within a short time after they had been posted at the Custom house, began to fire upon the people. Capt. Preston is said to have ordered them to fire, and to have repeated that order. One gun was fired first, then others in succession, and with deliberation, till ten or a dozen guns were fired; or till that number of discharges were made from the guns that were fired. By which means eleven persons were killed and wounded. These facts, with divers circumstances attending them, are supported by the depositions of a considerable number of persons.

Soon after the firing, a party from the main guard went with a drum to Murray's and the other barracks, beating an alarm as they went, which, with the firing, had the effect of a signal for action. Whereupon all the soldiers of the 29th regiment, or the main body of them, appeared in King Street under arms, and seemed bent on a further massacre of the inhabitants, which was with great difficulty prevented. They were drawn up between the State house and main guard, their lines extending across the street and facing down King Street, where the townspeople were assembled. The first line kneeled, and the whole of the first platoon presented their guns ready to fire, as soon as the word should be given. They continued in that posture a considerable time; but by the good providence of God they were restrained from firing.

FRANCIS HOPKINSON AND WILLIAM BILLINGS: AMERICA'S FIRST NOTABLE COMPOSERS

RONALD L. DAVIS

The revolutionary period coincides with the classical period in Western music. Music composition in Europe was dominated by court composers writing for the social elite under the patronage of kings and princes. Joseph Haydn and Wolfgang Amadeus Mozart were among the important and typical composers of the period. Of course, Americans had little use for court music and few opportunities to hear it in any case. America's first composers were more interested in writing music for people to sing in church and in their homes.

Ronald L. Davis teaches history at Southern Methodist University and specializes in the history of American music. His other books include *A History of Opera in the American West*. In this selection he describes the sharp contrast between America's first two notable composers, Francis Hopkinson and William Billings.

W hile the musical tradition of Anglo-America doubtlessly goes back to the founding of Jamestown, the earliest composition in the English colonies did not

Ronald L. Davis, *A History of Music in American Life*, vol. I, Malabar, FL: Robert Krieger, 1982. Copyright © 1982 by Robert E. Krieger Publishing Co., Inc. Reproduced by permission.

appear until the latter half of the eighteenth century, virtually on the eve of the Revolution. Before music could be written in the New World, an urban base of leisure and cultural sophistication had to be achieved. Just who the first American composer was is difficult to establish, although Francis Hopkinson is generally awarded the distinction. Whether this genesis is justified or not is ultimately of less significance than Hopkinson's approach to music, which was that of the aristocratic amateur steeped in the genteel English tradition. Hopkinson's songs, so cherished by the pre-Revolutionary elite, assume an artificial, stilted quality that reflects the self-conscious atmosphere in which the composer dwelt.

His contemporary William Billings, on the other hand, wrote music that is now considered more important—music that is crude, if not downright gauche, but nevertheless vibrant and alive, bearing little resemblance to what the colonial gentry coddled and admired. A man of modest circumstances, Billings was a product of the Puritan heritage, yet demonstrated himself an individualist of the highest order. His music was written with virtually no formal knowledge, and he broke rules he had never heard of or with which he was only casually acquainted. His compositions, however, are as genuine and original as Hopkinson's are pallid and imitative. The contrast between them well illustrates the parallel trends already developing in American music—the one spontaneous and distinctive, the other contrived and mannered.

A RENAISSANCE GENTLEMAN

Francis Hopkinson was only incidentally a musician, for he dabbled in practically everything. Like his friend Benjamin Franklin, Hopkinson was an American Renaissance man, versatile in his interests and abilities. Although his enthusiasm for the arts ran deep, he approached art with a social rather than a professional attitude, always remaining the adept gentleman. Born on September 21, 1737, Hopkinson lived his entire life in and around Philadelphia. He was enrolled by his father, the lawyer Thomas Hopkinson, in the College of Philadelphia (later the University of Pennsylvania) supposedly as the school's first student. During his last year as an undergraduate a group of classmates staged *The Masque of Alfred the Great*, which the English composer Thomas Arne had set to music. Young Hopkinson is thought to have been the harpsichordist for the production. Certainly his interest in music and writing verse became evident during his college days, although after receiving the bachelor's degree in 1757 he studied law under Benjamin Chew, the attorney-general of Pennsylvania. Shortly after completing his legal training, Hopkinson began a long career of public service, first acting as secretary to an Indian commission.

Already Hopkinson had developed something of a local reputation as a man of letters, for he was frequently asked to compose verses for recitation on public occasions or to commemorate a birth, marriage, or death in one of Philadelphia's important families. He became a regular contributor to the *American Magazine*, although most of the poems found there are of more interest to the historian than to the literary critic. In May, 1766, he left for a year abroad, where he continued writing, mostly trivial verses complimenting ladies and flattering benefactors. While in London he spent some time improving his musical skills and is thought to have studied painting with Benjamin West, the noted American artist who had become the darling of the British court.

Soon after his return to Philadelphia, Hopkinson set up a shop as a retail merchant and married Ann Borden. Something of a dawdler before marriage, he now became more serious about economic matters and more ambitious. Either late in 1773 or early in 1774 Hopkinson moved across the Delaware River to nearby Bordentown, New Jersey, probably because he felt the chances for political advancement were better there. His friend William Franklin was governor of that colony, and his father-in-law, Joseph Borden, was a leader in provincial affairs there. In New Jersey Hopkinson began a law practice, was appointed collector of customs and provincial councilor, and quickly emerged as a prosperous man of affairs. His literary interests continued, although his writing became less directed toward poetry and more toward essays—for which he showed greater talent—modeled after the writings of Joseph Addison. After 1775 he contributed regularly to the *Pennsylvania Magazine* or *American Monthly Museum*, a new but highly influential Philadelphia periodical.

As the Revolution approached, Hopkinson became increasingly alarmed over what he considered British abuses. He protested loudly in 1774 against the punishment of Boston and two years later came out boldly in favor of separation from England. As a member of the Second Continental Congress he was one of the signers of the Declaration of Independence. During the war he served as chairman of the Navy Board, successfully administering naval affairs during an extremely difficult period. He was also treasurer of loans, a job involving infinite detail and demanding painstaking accuracy, and was appointed Judge of the Admiralty from Pennsylvania. Most historians now agree that Hopkinson rather than Betsy Ross designed the first American flag, a design which the seamstress merely executed. He was later active in the convention of 1787 that framed the Constitution of the United States.

Despite his official duties Hopkinson found time during the Revolution to complete a sizeable amount of writing. He wrote articles, poems, and pamphlets ridiculing the British and encouraging the patriots. He penned a series of incendiary ballads aimed at destroying the legend of British invincibility, the most famous of which is "The Battle of the Kegs." Set to music, possibly by Hopkinson himself, and republished as a broadside, "The Battle of the Kegs" became one of the most popular songs among the armies at the front. Hopkinson apparently was fairly pleased with the ballad, for he sent Benjamin Franklin a copy of it in his own handwriting.

After the war Hopkinson continued an active life in public affairs, remaining a civic leader of Philadelphia, and serving as a federal judge until his death in 1791. At the same time he enjoyed sufficient leisure to write on subjects ranging from political "squibs" to learned articles on education. He developed a fascination for science, became active in the American Philosophical Society, and found time to work out a number of inventions, most of them more interesting than practical. He experimented with the principles of aviation and designed a dirigible. He developed a spring block to aid in sailing, devised an instrument for measuring distances on the high seas, found an improved way to grease the wheels of carriages, invented an improved form of candlestick, and even discovered a method for coloring artificial pearls.

A MUSICIAN IN THE GENTEEL TRADITION

But Hopkinson's major personal interests lay in the arts. In addition to his prolific writing, he tried his hand at painting and even before his trip to Europe had established a reputation in Pennsylvania as an authority on music. Having grown up in a family that was fond of the arts, Hopkinson began to study the harpsichord at age seventeen. He became quite proficient on the instrument and shortly wrote an "Ode to Music." His first song, "My Days Have Been So Wondrous Free," was composed in 1759, just two years after his graduation from college. Before leaving on his European tour Hopkinson made a metrical version of the Psalms for the Dutch Reformed Church in New York, using the payment to help finance his trip. He later studied the organ with Joseph Bremmer, an English musician who had arrived in Philadelphia in 1763, and with Bremmer's departure from the city Hopkinson succeeded him as organist of Christ Church.

Recognized as a musical light of Philadelphia before the Revolution, he became a member of a group of amateur and professional musicians who met in one another's homes to play the popular chamber works of their day. By Hopkinson's day subscription concerts had made their appearance in the seaboard cities of colonial America, and the composer became an active force in organizing Philadelphia's early concert life. London music teachers who had settled in the colonies around the middle of the century had introduced wealthier townspeople to arias by [George] Handel and compositions by [Alessandro] Scarlatti, [Antonio] Vivaldi, [Giovanni] Pergolesi, and [Arcangelo] Corelli, preparing the way for public concerts. Hopkinson's familiarity with the works of these European masters is evident from his extensive music library, most of which has been preserved by his heirs and much of it transcribed in the musician's own hand. . . .

His most ambitious undertaking as a composer was the oratorio *The Temple of Minerva,* for which Hopkinson wrote both the libretto and music. Performed privately in Philadelphia on December 11, 1781, before a fashionable gathering that included General and Mrs. George Washington, General and Mrs. Nathanael Greene, and the minister from France, so far as it is known the work never received a public hearing. The complete libretto was published in the *Freeman's Journal* a week after its presentation in Philadelphia, but the music has not survived. Blatant in its postwar patriotism, the piece consists of two scenes in which the goddess Minerva and her high priest join with the Genius of America and the Genius of France to laud General Washington and the French-American alliance. Referred to on occasions as the first American opera, *The Temple of Minerva* was more dramatic cantata than opera, since it lacked a plot and consisted merely of a series of musical declamations on a political theme. . . .

The originality which later generations found lacking in Hopkinson's music bothered his contemporaries scarcely at all. Since music was looked upon by eighteenth-century connoisseurs of culture as a bond with the past, innovation would have been more suspect than admired. Hopkinson wrote his songs using the European masters as his model, and while posterity would find him no genius of expression, he reflected well the dreams and ideals of the society in which he lived. If his songs lack vigor, it was not vigor he sought. Strength and vitality for him had their place in economic matters and in securing the foundations of a new country, but the arts were the reserve of delicacy and refinement. Music to Hopkinson was a polite luxury, a symbol of good breeding. To have injected the utilitarian impulses of the workaday American experience into his songs would have been to debase his concept of art and strip music of its gentlemanly qualities. Hopkinson's musical world, observes Oscar Sonneck, his first biographer, "was an untrue Arcadia, populated with over-sentimental shepherds and shepherdesses, or with jolly tars, veritable models of sobriety and good behavior, even when filling huge bumpers for drinking-bouts."

The composer represented the social and intellectual establishment of America, and his contact with the common man, both in the city and on the frontier, was limited. Before his death on May 9, 1791, his patrician notions had received public criticism from more democratically inclined spokesmen. By working to create a cultured climate in Philadelphia, Hopkinson certainly played a significant role in establishing drama and concert life in colonial America. Yet as a composer, he exerted virtually no influence on later American music. His songs began no trend, laid no foundation on which future composers could build, but merely perpetuated a dilettante tradition rooted in the past. When the democratic impulses of the new nation swelled in the next century, Hopkinson's way of life would vanish. As it passed, his music remained a fragile reminder of a colonial aristocracy that time and an industrializing social system had left behind.

A TANNER TURNED SINGING TEACHER

The essentially comfortable world enjoyed by Francis Hopkinson bore little resemblance to that of the more inventive colonial composer William Billings. Born in Boston on October 7,

1746, Billings was the son of a middle-aged, yeoman shop-keeper. His rudimentary common school education was cut short at age fourteen when his father died, leaving young Billings to be apprenticed to a tanner. The foul smells and dirt of the leather business held but slight fascination for the youth, while his interest in music, curiously enough, seems to have appeared quite early. During his adolescence Billings may have received brief musical instruction from John Barry, for a time choral director at New South Church, and who is thought to have acquired a copy of Tans'ur's *Musical Grammar*. So inflamed did Billings' passion for music become that tradition has it that he whiled away spare moments at the tannery by chalking tunes on sides of leather and over the walls of the shop.

The extent of Billings' formal training in music is uncertain, although he is considered to have been primarily self-taught. He doubtlessly participated in some of the early Boston singing schools, usually church-sponsored classes designed to teach young singers the fundamentals of reading music, and he apparently became associated with leaders in the movement toward regular singing, or singing by note. That Billings was active in the community's budding concert life or was intimately acquainted with the compositions of the European masters is doubtful. His interest in music largely emerged out of a religious atmosphere, and he remained basically a product of a folk heritage descended from Puritanism. He saw music in terms of the psalms, hymns, and anthems he had grown up with, while music as conscious art rarely entered his mind.

Little is known about the details of Billings' life. In 1774 he married Lucy Swan, a member of his singing class at Stoughton, and the couple had six surviving children—five girls and a boy. Sometime before 1770 Billings opened a music shop near the Boston post office, although he continued to practice the tanner's trade throughout most of his life. The plight of the professional musician in eighteenth-century America was at best financially precarious, and Billings especially seems to have been viewed by fellow Bostonians with mingled respect and curiosity. Surely he was vulnerable to more than his share of bantering, for a social dandy in appearance he was not. Blind in one eye, with one leg shorter than the other and a considerably withered arm, he possessed a raspy voice that became less offensive when he sang. To add to nature's afflictions, he was uncommonly slovenly in his dress and had a propensity for taking incredible quantities of snuff, which he carried around in his coat pocket. Every few minutes he would pull out a handful of snuff, and instead of taking it in the usual manner, daintily with thumb and finger, he would snuff it from his clenched fist. At the same time he manifested an infectious personality, appeared unlimited in vitality and enthusiasm, and displayed an aggressive drive approximating the Yankee Peddler stereotype.

All of this made Billings the frequent brunt of pranksters' jokes. The musician, for instance, was startled one evening by a loud screeching outside his door. Upon checking he discovered two cats, their hind legs tied together, unceremoniously thrown across the sign of his shop reading "Billings' Music." On another occasion the ungainly music master was asked by a wag whether he considered snoring vocal or instrumental music!

At his music shop Billings sold instruments and tunebooks, but his major interest was in organizing and teaching singing schools in and around Boston. Billings' aim was to teach musical notation without robbing his students of the joy of singing, and he represents the peak of the singing school tradition. Unlike his Puritan ancestors, who prized solemnity above everything else in sacred music, Billings assumed a downright playful attitude. He looked upon hymns and anthems as an amusement, rather than a sober duty to God. Singing schools lasted something like three months, with two or three meetings a week. Students were mostly teenagers and young adults, and Billings viewed these occasions as social as well as instructional. As his fame spread, his classes became so large that rehearsal rooms could not hold all those wanting to attend. Some had to content themselves with crowding outside the door to listen. Locally printed tunebooks were published for singing school use, and by the Revolution a growing proportion of the music included originated in America.

Billings himself would publish six tunebooks, the first of which was the *New England Psalm Singer.* Issued in 1770, the collection contained 120 hymns and several anthems, all composed by Billings. It was the first tunebook produced of entirely American music. Barely twenty-four years old at the time the compilation was published, Billings sought to invigorate the old psalm-settings, add variety to hymns like Watts', and create religious music that would be interesting and fun for his singing school participants. He wrote his compositions "as plain and simple as possible," and yet wanted his music to be "most majestic" and "so exceedingly grand" that the floors would tremble when choirs sang it. The composer later claimed that the pieces contained in the *New England Psalm Singer* were "more than twenty times as powerful as the old slow tunes." Possessing little more than a rudimentary knowledge of music, he professed breezy disregard for accepted rules. "I think it best," he declared with youthful brashness, "for every *Composer* to be his own *Carver.*" He insisted, *"Nature is the Best Dictator,* for all the hard dry studied Rules . . . will not enable any Person to form an Air . . . without Genius. It must be Nature, Nature must lay the Foundation, Nature must inspire Thought."

And yet in practice Billings does not seem to have stood in open rebellion against the musical canons of his time, for certainly his works were influenced by the British models he knew. Within pre-existing forms, however, he was able to add variety and find a highly personal tone. Nor was his originality confined to music. He possessed a sensitivity to words, enjoyed wordplay for its own sake, and was not reluctant to alter even Biblical texts to suit his purpose. The composer held up publication on the *New England Psalm Singer* until he could have it printed on American paper, while its frontispiece was engraved by Paul Revere. The tune titles—several of them named after local places or referring to recent events—help give the collection a native flavor. Billings had a penchant for combining politically inspired texts with sacred music that was unprecedented. But above all it is the composer's energy that shines through, animating the words and invigorating their meaning.

His second collection, *The Singing Master's Assistant,* issued eight years later, showed the musician's talent and imagination to have advanced considerably. Often referred to as "Billings' Best," *The Singing Master's Assistant* reflects the composer's growing self-confidence, firmly established his reputation, and went through four editions. Published about the time the British were beginning to feel the determination and strength of the colonial armies, *The Singing Master's Assistant* was far more nationalistic than any American tunebook to date, containing several texts dealing with the war. The composer reworked "Chester," his most famous tune, adding four stanzas in which the references to British tyranny were made more specific. This revision captured the defiant spirit of the moment and was sung around campfires and played by fifers all along the Atlantic coast, becoming almost a battle cry for the Continental Army. . . .

A COMPOSER FOR THE PEOPLE

As was customary with compilers of singing books, Billings, undaunted by lack of formal education, undertook to explain the rules of music in the introductions to his various collections and expound his views on a variety of musical subjects. His prose proved as eccentric, homespun, and personal as his music. He later recounted his excitement while the *New England Psalm Singer* was at press: "Oh! how did my foolish heart throb and beat with tumultuous joy." He could scarcely wait, he said, for the sheets to be stitched together and the cover put on. When the book emerged at last, he cried, "Go forth, my little book, go forth and immortalize the name of your Author; may your sale be rapid and may you be a welcome guest in all companies, and what will add tenfold to thy dignity, may you find your way into the Libraries of the Learned."

A man of Billings' spirit and self-confidence was not about to be hemmed in by established musical laws any more than he was to be intimidated by precedent or authority. Gentility was so far removed from his spectrum that cultivating the airs of refinement seldom entered his head. He wrote songs that grew out of his experience, music that to him was exciting. Billings wanted not only to supply the New England singing schools with American tunes, he also wanted to delight them with music that was fresh and alive, inviting a greater degree of involvement than the old psalm books permitted. The psalters and hymnals that had been used in New England for the past century and a half Billings considered monotonous and dull.

His major vehicle for enlivening vocal music was the fuging-tune, which he neither invented nor introduced to America, although he did become New England's most successful exponent of the fuging style. The fuging-tunes composed by Billings had almost nothing in common with the formal fugues of [German composer Johann Sebastian] Bach and the European masters. Instead they were a form of hymnody in which, after an introduction, the usual homophonous technique of harmony is forsaken in favor of polyphony, the voices entering one after the other in round-like fashion, but at the close returning to the more conventional homophony. "The parts come after each other, with the same notes," Billings himself said of the fuging-tune. Then with a characteristic burst of color and enthusiasm he explained:

Each part striving for mastery and victory. The audience entertained and delighted, their minds surprisingly agitated and extremely fluctuated, sometimes declaring for one part and sometimes for another. Now the solemn bass demands their attention; next the manly tenor; now the lofty counter; now the volatile treble. Now here, now there, now here again! O ecstatic! Rush on, you sons of harmony!

The fuging-tunes that Billings became so identified with had definite antecedents in England. They were actually survivals of the polyphonic motets sung in British cathedrals during the Elizabethan period. For a brief time in the eighteenth-century English fuging-tunes appeared as a temporary union between metrical psalmody and the contrapuntal technique, achieving considerable popularity in the rural sections of Great Britain but very little in the cities. By the 1760s the fuging-tune was out of favor in England, although emigrants in America undoubtedly brought some knowledge of it to the New World. By the time Billings arrived on the scene the fuging method had been incorporated into an amalgamating folk tradition, and the Boston tanner merely injected his ideas into a musical vernacular that provided him the flexibility he desired.

Three of Billings' fuging-tunes appeared in his *New England Psalm Singer*, and they evoked protests from the beginning. Samuel Holyoke argued early in the 1790s that the fuging style produced "a mere jargon of words." A generation later the method had come to symbolize for sophisticates all that was crude in the Yankee singing tradition. Billings had no notion that he was writing an American version of a Bach fugue, and those who have viewed his fuging-tunes as raw attempts to imitate the Baroque masters have missed the point. Billings' concern was with devising effective hymns for his friends and neighbors; he made no pretense at anything more aesthetic. As with much of colonial culture, the fuging-tune in America represented not so much an innovation as an adaptation of an English folkway. Billings was not unique in his method of composition, but in writing music that he felt would be meaningful to common people he was sensitive to the pulse of the New England environment and aware of changing currents in the American folk experience. Unlike Hopkinson, Billings was not patterning his songs after a rigid British concept of art nor striving to enhance his gentlemanly image by creating mirages of elegance. Whereas Hopkinson's approach to music was static, imitating as it did a formal English archetype, Billings' tunes were based on a less crystalized tradition that permitted the freedom for growth. . . .

By the time of Billings' death the new nation had turned away from the singing schools toward the more sophisticated choruses of Handel, the anthems of [Thomas] Arne and [Henry] Purcell, and eventually the compositions of Mozart and Haydn. In the urban East the old tunebooks were replaced by the more "correct" hymns of [Isaac] Watts and later [Samuel] Wesley and [Lowell] Mason, although in the rural sections of the country folk hymnody continued throughout the nineteenth century. In the southern shape-note collections Billings' music was well represented long after the northern advocates of taste had denounced the fuging-tunes as "a sort of musical horse-race."

Then beginning in the 1930s Billings' significance as a composer was restored, and he is now considered the foremost American musician of the eighteenth century. Once released from a European standard, Billings was recognized as an unconventional genius, often unconcerned with and hence unhampered by propriety. It is perhaps a fitting symbol of a democratic society that a Boston tanner was America's first great musical talent. Surely it was a mark of his century that Billings was able to do the variety of things he did. But he was a practical musician, whose tunes touched his countrymen in a personal way, revealing to them a musical energy they had almost forgotten they possessed. This was Billings' real triumph. His songs are as individualistic as the frontier spirit, consistent with the life he knew, an instinctive expression of the American experience.

THE BOSTON TEA PARTY

GEORGE HEWES

Nowadays tea is associated with the English and coffee is considered a more typically American drink. In 1773 the reverse was true. Coffee was popular in England, and American colonists drank enormous quantities of tea, which was imported to America from the East Indies. Tea was one of the products that the British attempted to regulate through the imposition of tariffs. In order to establish the principle that the British government was entitled to impose tariffs, the British artificially lowered the cost of legally imported tea to the point that it was actually cheaper than tea smuggled in illegally. Afraid that the cheap tea would in fact lead people to accept the tariffs, some Bostonians decided to prevent the tea from being brought ashore and sold. Disguised as Indians, they boarded the three ships carrying the tea and dumped the cargo into Boston Harbor.

In this selection, one of the participants, George Hewes, offers a firsthand account of the events of that night. Hewes was a Boston shoemaker who supported the patriot cause. During the Revolution he served as a common sailor on American privateering ships and as a soldier with the militias. After the war he moved to New York and returned to his trade as a shoemaker.

T he tea destroyed was contained in three ships, lying near each other, at what was called at that time Griffin's wharf, and were surrounded by armed ships of war; the commanders of which had publicly declared, that if the rebels, as

George Hewes, "Mohawks Spill Tea in Boston Harbor," *The Heritage of America: Readings in American History for High Schools*, edited by Henry Steele Commager and Allan Nevins, Boston: Little, Brown and Company, 1941.

they were pleased to style the Bostonians, should not withdraw their opposition to the landing of the tea before a certain day, the 17th day of December, 1773, they should on that day force it on shore, under the cover of their cannon's mouth. On the day preceding the seventeenth, there was a meeting of the citizens of the county of Suffolk, convened at one of the churches in Boston, for the purpose of consulting on what measures might be considered expedient to prevent the landing of the tea, or secure the people from the collection of the duty. At that meeting a committee was appointed to wait on Governor Hutchinson, and request him to inform them whether he would take any measures to satisfy the people on the object of the meeting. To the first application of this committee, the Governor told them he would give them a definite answer by five o'clock in the afternoon. At the hour appointed, the committee again repaired to the Governor's house, and on inquiry found he had gone to his country seat at Milton, a distance of about six miles. When the committee returned and informed the meeting of the absence of the Governor, there was a confused murmur among the members, and the meeting was immediately dissolved, many of them crying out, "Let every man do his duty, and be true to his country"; and there was a general huzza for Griffin's wharf.

"INDIANS" DESTROY THE TEA

It was now evening, and I immediately dressed myself in the costume of an Indian, equipped with a small hatchet, which I and my associates denominated the tomahawk, with which, and a club, after having painted my face and hands with coal dust in the shop of a blacksmith, I repaired to Griffin's wharf, where the ships lay that contained the tea. When I first appeared in the street, after being thus disguised, I fell in with many who were dressed, equipped, and painted as I was, and who fell in with me, and marched in order to the place of our destination. When we arrived at the wharf, there were three of our number who assumed an authority to direct our operations, to which we readily submitted. They divided us into three parties, for the purpose of boarding the three ships which contained the tea at the same time. The name of him who commanded the division to which I was assigned was Leonard Pitt. The names of the other commanders I never knew. We were immediately ordered by the respective commanders to board all the ships at the same time, which we promptly obeyed. The commander of the division to which I belonged, as soon as we were on board the ship, appointed me boatswain, and ordered me to go to the captain and demand of him the keys to the hatches and a dozen candles. I made the demand accordingly, and the captain promptly replied, and delivered the articles; but requested me at the same time to do no damage to the ship or rigging. We then were ordered by our commander to open the hatches, and take out all the chests of tea and throw them overboard, and we immediately proceeded to execute his orders; first cutting and splitting the chests with our tomahawks, so as thoroughly to expose them to the effects of the water. In about three hours from the time we went on board, we had thus broken and thrown overboard every tea chest to be found in the ship, while those in the other ships were disposing of the tea in the same way, at the same time. We were surrounded by British armed ships, but no attempt was made to resist us. We then quietly retired to our several places of residence, without having any conversation with each other, or taking any measures to discover who were our associates; nor do I recollect of our having had the knowledge of the name of a single individual concerned in that affair, except that of Leonard Pitt, the commander of my division, whom I have mentioned. There appeared to be an understanding that each individual should volunteer his

In December 1773, Boston residents disguised as Native Americans boarded ships carrying tea, dumping all of the cargo into Boston Harbor.

services, keep his own secret, and risk the consequences for himself. No disorder took place during that transaction, and it was observed at that time, that the stillest night ensued that Boston had enjoyed for many months.

ATTEMPTS TO SAVE SOME OF THE TEA

During the time we were throwing the tea overboard, there were several attempts made by some of the citizens of Boston and its vicinity to carry off small quantities of it for their family use. To effect that object, they would watch their opportunity to snatch up a handful from the deck, where it became plentifully scattered, and put it into their pockets. One Captain O'Connor, whom I well knew, came on board for that purpose, and when he supposed he was not noticed, filled his pockets, and also the lining of his coat. But I had detected him, and gave information to the captain of what he was doing. We were ordered to take him into custody, and just as he was stepping from the vessel, I seized him by the skirt of his coat, and in attempting to pull him back, I tore it off; but springing forward, by a rapid effort, he made his escape. He had, however, to run a gauntlet through the crowd upon the wharf; each one, as he passed, giving him a kick or a stroke.

Another attempt was made to save a little tea from the ruins of the cargo by a tall, aged man who wore a large cocked hat and white wig, which was fashionable at that time. He had sleightly slipped a little into his pocket, but being detected, they seized him, and taking his hat and wig from his head, threw them, together with the tea, of which they had emptied his pockets, into the water. In consideration of his advanced age, he was permitted to escape, with now and then a slight kick.

The next morning, after we had cleared the ships of the tea, it was discovered that very considerable quantities of it were floating upon the surface of the water; and to prevent the possibility of any of its being saved for use, a number of small boats were manned by sailors and citizens, who rowed them into those parts of the harbor wherever the tea was visible, and by beating it with oars and paddles, so thoroughly drenched it, as to render its entire destruction inevitable.

Declaring Independence, 1775–1776

CHAPTER 4

THE FIRST BATTLE OF THE AMERICAN REVOLUTION

ERIC W. BARNES

By 1775 colonists had begun preparing for armed resistance to British authority. This involved organizing troops of volunteers who could be called to arms at short notice, much like a fire brigade. These local militias were known as minutemen. Of course, the minutemen needed weapons, so they began buying guns, ammunition, and gunpowder and stockpiling them at strategic locations. The British were aware, through loyalist informants, that such stockpiles were being created. Obviously, to prevent violence and put down the rebellion, the British needed to seize the stockpiled weapons. Their attempts to do this created the first confrontations of the Revolutionary War. The most famous such confrontation took place at Lexington and Concord, but there was an earlier, similar confrontation at Salem.

Eric W. Barnes (1907–1962) taught English at the Loomis School in Connecticut after serving as director of the Institute for American Studies at the Free University of Berlin. In this selection he recounts the events of the Salem confrontation, at which no shots were fired but blood was spilled.

Lexington and Concord may argue for another hundred years about where the shot heard round the world was actually fired, but to the town of Salem, over on the Massachusetts coast, the question will remain largely academic. The

point of the discussion, after all, is where the War of Independence began, and Salem has her own claims to the honor. It was
at Salem's North River Bridge, two months before the clashes
at Lexington and Concord, that British troops first met armed
American resistance—and retreated. Although no shots were
fired at the North Bridge (not to be confused with the Concord
landmark of the same name), at least one bayonet was brought
into play, and the first American blood was shed.

A Cache of Weapons in Salem

All during the winter of 1774–75 rumors of patriot activity at
Salem had been drifting through British headquarters in Boston.
The military governor of Massachusetts, Lieutenant General the
Honorable Thomas Gage, had kept a suspicious eye on the
town ever since autumn when the colony's General Court,
meeting in Salem against his express orders, had set itself up as
the Provincial Congress, thus bringing rebellion more or less
into the open. Then, in February, 1775, Gage learned from a
well-placed informer that the Congress was creating an ord-
nance depot at Salem and had assembled there a sizable number of cannon. Gage decided to act. If he did not seize the
weapons at once, his troops would soon be facing them on the
battlefield. By taking the Americans by surprise, he might still
avoid an armed collision.

But secrecy was of the utmost importance. Since Gage was
aware that all British troop movements in the city of Boston
were closely watched by the patriot information service, he assigned the Salem mission to the 64th Infantry Regiment, stationed at Castle William on an island in Boston Harbor. The regiment was commanded by Colonel Alexander Leslie, son of a
Scottish earl and an experienced soldier. On February 24, Gage
ordered Leslie to have his men ready to embark for Marblehead, the small port next to Salem, the following night.

The regiment sailed on schedule at midnight Saturday, February 25, without being noticed by the ever-vigilant patriot
spies. Only one near-slip occurred. In the early morning after
the departure of the troops, Castle William's milk supplier arrived in his wherry to find the fort deserted except for a skele-
ton guard. To keep this information from reaching the patriots
in Boston, the milkman was held until the regiment returned.

Shortly after noon on Sunday, the ship dropped anchor in
Marblehead Bay; to all appearances she was merely a British

vessel on patrol. Only members of the crew were visible on her decks; Leslie's orders were to keep his men under hatches until two o'clock when the townspeople would have returned to church after the noontime intermission in the all-day service. Gage was no stranger to New England. He knew her inhabitants well and had timed the expedition accordingly.

A RIDER CARRIES A WARNING

Gage was right about New England piety; but he had overlooked New England common sense. While the majority of Marblehead's citizens were at church, a careful watch was kept on the British ship, and the troops were counted as they landed at Homan's Cove. As soon as the column had marched out of earshot on the road to Salem, drums began to beat at all the church doors, and the call to arms was sounded throughout the town. Long before Marblehead's eight companies of militia had formed, a horseman was galloping to overtake the redcoats and warn Salem.

The messenger had been well chosen. Not only was Major John Pedrick an expert rider, but his presence on the road would not be likely to arouse the suspicion of the British. He was well known to Colonel Leslie, who had been a guest at his house, and he was generally regarded as loyal to the Crown. Leslie could not know that Major Pedrick had just recently gone over to the other side, following the lead of his attractive young daughter. It seemed that Miss Pedrick had found the attentions of a certain British officer so wearing that when she finally got rid of him, she switched her allegiance to the patriot cause.

When he caught up with the British column Pedrick slowed his horse to a canter. The soldiers, noting his fine broadcloth cloak and the silver mountings of his saddle, probably assumed that this was some neighborhood squire taking advantage of the unusually mild February weather for a ride in the country. Colonel Leslie, however, recognized his acquaintance at once and greeted him cordially, ordering his men to file right and left so that the gentleman might pass. Pedrick thanked Leslie for his courtesy, expressed the hope that they might soon meet again, and jogged down between the files. He kept on at an easy pace until he came to a bend in the road where a low growth of scrub hid him from sight. Then he dug in his spurs and galloped toward Salem.

Half an hour later he was clattering through the empty streets of the town, headed toward the North River. At the North Meet-inghouse, just below the bridge, he pulled up sharply and sprang from his horse.

Afternoon service was in progress. The Reverend Thomas Barnard, famed throughout the countryside for his fine voice and commanding logic, had scarcely reached the mid-point of his sermon when the door crashed open and the congregation was brought to its feet by John Pedrick's loud call to arms and his announcement that the British were headed for Salem. Five minutes later the Reverend Mr. Barnard—himself a staunch loy-alist—was gazing at empty pews.

Among the first to leave the church was Benjamin Daland, Salem's leading liveryman. He rushed for his stable and, sad-dling his fastest horse, headed for nearby Danvers to alert the militia there. While the alarm coursed through Salem and mili-tia members scattered to their homes for equipment, Colonel Timothy Pickering, recently elected commander of the Essex County Militia Regiment, dispatched forty minutemen to Cap-tain Robert Foster's forge, close by the North River Bridge. Here nineteen cannon were being fitted with carriages, and it was im-perative to hide them before the British troops arrived.

At the time, the North River Bridge was approached by a causeway extending to the ship channel, where there was a draw that could be lifted to let vessels pass. The draw was op-erated from the north side, and when the leaf was up, access to the forge was cut off from the Salem side of the river, from which direction the British were approaching. As soon as the draw had been raised and secured, the minutemen began to haul the guns out of the forge. Some of them were buried un-der the thick bed of leaves in a nearby oak grove (there was no snow on the ground); others were carted off to a safer and more distant hiding place at Orne's Point.

The men worked furiously under the anxious eye of Captain David Mason, Engineer to the Committee of Public Safety. Ma-son, who had collected the cannon and was supervising their conversion for field use, was a man of varied talents. In regular life he was a carriage gilder and finisher—a japanner—and on occasion, a portrait painter. He was also highly regarded as a man of science and had made rather a good thing of his lectures on "the new electrical fire" (admission: one pistareen). Benjamin Franklin was an old acquaintance, and Mason's experiments with electricity had been commended by the great man. Mason had also given time to the study of explosives. This knowledge, as well as his ingenuity in constructing all sorts of mechanical devices, had won him the appointment with the committee.

Present at the forge with Mason and its owner, Captain Foster, was another important Salemite, the Honorable Richard Derby. A member of the Provincial Congress, Derby was Salem's richest shipowner; in fact he had already laid the foundations of America's first really great fortune. But it was not Derby's wealth alone that commanded general respect; he had a reputation for courage. During the Seven Years' War, when French privateers began to harass American shipping, Derby had defiantly mounted cannon on all his vessels, even small schooners, and literally fought his way from market to market in the West Indies. Thus it seemed perfectly natural that he should command the defense of the forge—all the more so since eight of the nineteen cannon had been removed from his own ships and loaned to the Provincial Congress.

CONFRONTATION AT THE BRIDGE

As the last gun was hauled to safety, word came that the British had arrived. There had been a short delay at the South Mills Bridge to replace a few planks that the patriots had torn up. A small detachment of troops had then marched off to the east, down Fish Street to the Long Wharf, presumably to create a diversion. But the main column headed straight for Town House Square, where it halted while someone went to find Mr. John Sargent, half brother of Salem's most eminent Tory, Colonel William Browne. Sargent appeared at once, having obviously expected the summons, and spoke a few words in Leslie's ear. Then he took his place beside the redcoat commander, and the column started off in the direction of the North River Bridge.

As the troops were getting under way, a gentleman rushed up to Leslie to ask what the presence of soldiers on the Sabbath meant. Since Leslie was on the King's business, he merely looked at the stranger with cold annoyance and told him to mind his own business. But the gentleman—another Salem shipowner, named Captain John Felt—was not to be put off; he foresaw trouble and wanted to prevent it. As the column moved up the street with the informer Sargent on one side of Colonel Leslie, Felt marched along on the other.

By now the churches were emptied and people were crowding along the way, edging up toward the North Bridge in the wake of the redcoats. Though few knew about the hidden cannon, no one doubted that something eventful was about to happen. There was a grim alertness as well as curiosity on the faces that followed the marching troops.

The troops headed straight out upon the causeway leading to the drawbridge; they had almost reached the open gap before Leslie realized that the leaf was up. He looked at the icy current streaming in fast with the tide, then across to the line of men on the wharf jutting out beside the draw. His color changed. He stamped his foot and swore (the witnesses all agree on the vigor of the Colonel's oaths throughout the affair), asking what these people meant by obstructing the King's highway, and ordering them to lower the bridge at once.

In 1775 British forces stormed towns trying to find and confiscate weapons stockpiles.

A little knot of townsmen had collected at the end of the causeway. One of the group, Joseph Barr, calmly informed Leslie that this was not the King's highway; the road and the bridge were private. They belonged to the owners of the property on the other side of the draw, who could do with them as they saw fit. After all, they had their rights.

Rights! This was the monotonous theme of everything these

troublemakers said and did. Leslie had heard enough. He called out loudly that if the draw was not lowered at once, his men would fire.

The shipowner John Felt, who had refused to leave the Colonel's side, now exploded with the kind of remark that goes down in history (thanks to the prompt recording of the Salem *Gazette*, in this case). "Fire and be damned!" he shouted. "You've no right to fire without further orders. If you fire you'll all be dead men."

To give emphasis to Felt's words, Captain Mason spoke up from the other side. Colonel Leslie had indeed better look to the safety of his men; the whole countryside had been alerted, and militiamen would soon be pouring into Salem. Mason was hardly bluffing for the liveryman Daland had done his work well. In addition to the eight companies awaiting orders at Marblehead, other patriots were on the march from as far away as Amesbury. Before the afternoon was over, some three thousand men (one exaggerated account placed the number at ten thousand) would be on the roads leading to Salem.

Leslie saw his position clearly. The pale February sun was sinking fast, and the thought of his small force trying to reach Marblehead after dark was not comforting. Yet he had his mission; he could not let a mob of peasants and shopkeepers stand in his way. Angrily he glanced back at the crowd of Salemites. His eye moved up the riverbank, and suddenly he saw the solution to his problem.

Captain Felt had seen it too, a moment sooner. Two scows ("gundalows," according to the records) were drawn up on the bank near the end of the causeway. Just as Leslie's eye fixed on them, Felt spoke quickly to a fellow citizen standing nearby. The man started running down the causeway, joined by half a dozen volunteers with axes and crowbars that seemed to have appeared from nowhere. Before a detachment of redcoats could reach the scow, which was the property of John Felt himself, her bottom was stove in.

Blood Is Spilled

Farther down the bank was the second boat, owned by Joseph Sprague, a deacon of the North Meetinghouse and proprietor of a distillery situated near the bridge. Sprague was in the crowd, and when he saw what was happening, he started for his scow, calling to one of his workmen, Joseph Whicher, to follow. At his master's summons, Whicher gave a whoop and, seizing a mattock, rushed for the deacon's boat, followed by eager assistants.

The redcoats, having arrived too late to save the first scow, lowered their bayonets and ran toward the second, shouting to the wreckers to desist (a detail over which the *Gazette* grew particularly indignant: by what law was a man forbidden to put a hole in his own gondola if he was so minded?). They were too late. Joseph Whicher, conscious of his role in a drama on which all attention was fastened, gave a mighty blow that sent his mattock crunching through the bottom of the boat. A great cheer went up from the American audience. At this, Whicher leaped to the bow of the scow and, tearing open his shirt, defied the nearest redcoat to touch him. The invitation was irresistible. The soldier gave a smart jab with his bayonet, and Whicher fell back wide-eyed into the arms of his companions. The wound was slight, but blood spurted over the hero's chest; the crowd groaned with sympathy and admiration. This was patriots' blood, and in Salem's mind it would color the incident for all time. Whicher himself made certain that his gallant effort was not forgotten as long as he lived. With slight urging, the distiller's assistant would bare his chest and display the mark of "the first wound received in the War of Independence."

Frustrated in his attempt to use the scows, Leslie turned furiously to Captain Felt and swore that he would cross the river if it took till autumn. He pointed to a dilapidated warehouse on the wharf alongside the causeway: if necessary he would barrack his men right there. Felt pulled his collar higher against the bitter wind sweeping in from the ocean and said he guessed nobody would mind.

Then another bystander asked the Colonel why he wanted to cross the bridge in the first place. By its very impertinence, the question threw Leslie into such a rage that he momentarily forgot discretion. He blurted out that he had come for the cannon he knew to be stored on the other side of the river. The words reached old Richard Derby standing among the defenders by the draw. According to eyewitness accounts, he bellowed across the gap: "Find the cannon if you can! Take them if you can! They will never be surrendered."

With this challenge, Leslie's patience came to an end. He nodded to the officer beside him. "Turn this company about," he commanded, "and have the men fire." Twelve steps and eight separate orders were involved in the long process of priming, loading, presenting, and firing the "Brown Bess" musket of the English infantryman. The soldiers had scarcely begun this elaborate operation when a figure in a long black gown came rushing through the crowd toward Leslie, and a voice, obviously accustomed to making itself heard, implored him to halt.

The newcomer was none other than the Reverend Mr. Barnard. Until now he had remained discreetly in the background with Major Pedrick, who for reasons of delicacy did not wish to disclose his presence to Colonel Leslie. But with a climax rapidly approaching over the bridge, both men felt that something must be done to avert bloodshed. At Pedrick's urging, Barnard agreed to try to dissuade Leslie from his course.

The minister's words must have impressed Leslie—or perhaps he never intended to shoot in the first place. At any rate, he rescinded the order to fire. But the situation was still unresolved. Since Leslie had declared within the hearing of everybody present that he would cross the bridge whatever the consequences, his personal honor was now at stake.

HONORABLE WITHDRAWAL

Barnard recognized this, and, thinking quickly, ventured a suggestion. Leslie's purpose now was simply to cross the bridge. The Colonel knew that he could not hope to find the cannon before dark, and to delay would only invite disaster, hopelessly outnumbered as he was. What if the bridge were lowered? asked Mr. Barnard. Would Colonel Leslie be satisfied to march his men across to some specified point, say thirty rods distant, then turn and march them back again without further action?

The sun was brushing the treetops now. Leslie may have caught sight of Colonel Pickering, the militia commander, moving among his men, and decided that the Americans would not remain passive forever. He did not know, of course, that Colonel Pickering was also in a quandary, that he had been practically immobilized all afternoon on a fine point of ethics. It was only ten days since Pickering had taken command of the Essex Regiment, still a part of the colony's legally constituted defense force, and his oath to the King was worrisomely fresh in his mind. He would act only in the last extremity.

After a brief consultation with his officers, Leslie told Barnard that he accepted the proposal. The minister promptly stepped to the edge of the bridge and asked the defenders to lower the draw, explaining the agreement with Colonel Leslie.

The proposal was greeted with a chilling silence. After a long moment someone called over: "We don't know you in this business." Here was a blow to Barnard's good intentions, as well as his pride. He had not considered that though he may have been the logical man to approach Leslie, his loyalist sympathies could hardly inspire confidence in the defenders of the forge.

Obviously somebody closer to the patriot cause would have to speak. Leslie looked at Captain Felt, whom he had treated with a good deal of disdain up to now, and asked if he had any authority with the unruly crowd. Felt said that he did not know about authority, but he might have a little influence. This was a modest assumption, since Felt was not only a leader among the patriots but one of the owners of the bridge. It needed only his assurance that Colonel Leslie had indeed given his word, and the draw came rattling down.

The fifes struck up "Yankee Doodle," which had not yet become the exclusive property of the Americans, and five minutes later the redcoats were tramping up the north bank of the river. As they neared the turning place, the window of a house was thrown open and a sharp-voiced dame, one Sarah Tarrant, cried: "Go home! Go home!"

Of all the afternoon's humiliations none seemed to strike Colonel Leslie so deeply as these inhospitable words. His face purpled, but he kept his eyes ahead and strode grimly to the place where forty minutemen stood solidly across the road. There he gave the order to halt, face about, and march again. Once more as the troops passed her window Mrs. Tarrant leaned out of it and was reported to have shouted: "Go home and tell your master he has sent you on a fool's errand, and broke the peace of our Sabbath. What? Do you think we were born in the woods to be frightened by owls? Fire at me if you have the courage, but I doubt it." As she spoke, [she] waved a turkey-wing duster for emphasis.

The redcoats did not stop again until they reached Marblehead. Once more Major Pedrick galloped ahead of them; he had started back as soon as the column recrossed the bridge. It had occurred to him that after the fatigues and frustrations of the day, Colonel Leslie might seek the hospitality of his house, and he must set out the Madeira.

But Leslie did not dally for refreshment at Marblehead. He sailed at once for Boston. His report confirmed General Gage's bleak surmise: the Americans were not only arming, they were on the march. The war that men in England still talked of preventing had begun. Even London realized this when the *Gentleman's Magazine* for April, 1775, published the first dispatches on the North Bridge affair with the comment, "The Americans have hoisted their standard of liberty at Salem," and the conclusion that "there is no doubt that the next news will be an account of a bloody engagement between the two armies." The last dispatch was received just before the magazine went to press, on April 29. By that time, of course, the fuse lit at Salem had exploded the powder at Lexington and Concord.

THE BATTLE FOR BUNKER HILL

RICHARD M. KETCHUM

In the first skirmishes of the Revolution, British forces faced only independent local militias made up mostly of untrained volunteers. Many patriot leaders believed that such local militias, fighting for their own homes, would be sufficient to prevail against the British, and the success of the militias in early battles encouraged this belief. However, other leaders, including George Washington, realized that the colonies would have to put a professional army into the field. Two months after the skirmishes at Lexington and Concord this army was ready to challenge British control of Boston.

Richard M. Ketchum has written eleven books on the Revolutionary War, including *Saratoga: Turning Point of America's Revolutionary War* and *The Winter Soldiers: The Battles for Trenton and Princeton*. He works as an editor for American Heritage Publishing Company. In this selection he describes the Battle of Bunker Hill as a major milestone in the Revolution. There was, in fact, nothing decisive about the battle itself since neither side achieved a clear victory. Nevertheless, prior to the battle the British believed they were dealing with a handful of dissatisfied rebels who would be easily put down; after the battle the British knew they were at war.

F or a battle that proved to be so decisive it was a curious one, in that neither side at first claimed to have won a victory. It was not a particularly large engagement; there were, after all, only about twelve hundred Americans arrayed

Richard M. Ketchum, *Decisive Day: The Battle for Bunker Hill*, New York: Anchor Books, 1974. Copyright © 1974 by Richard M. Ketchum. Reproduced by permission.

against twice that many British. Ironically, people could not even agree on a name for it at the time. Battles are usually called after the place where they occur, but there was such widespread uncertainty about the location of the action that some referred to it as the battle of Charlestown, some as Bunker Hill, still others as Breed's Hill.

THE PAGEANTRY OF BATTLE

For those who like to imagine the ultimate drama of war in picture-book terms, this was one of the few genuine setpieces of the Revolutionary War—a pitched battle in which the pride of the British army, after being rowed across a body of water in full view of the mesmerized citizenry of Boston, lined up as if on parade and marched in precise order up a hill to storm a fort by direct, frontal assault. It was a scene difficult for novelist or filmmaker to surpass in terms of sheer pageantry.

War demands a final reckoning in human terms, however, and the casualties at the Battle for Bunker Hill were altogether staggering. Nearly half of the scarlet-coated regulars who stormed the redoubt fell in the attack, more than a third of the American defenders were killed, wounded, or captured, and in these grim statistics lies the true significance of the matter.

Under cover of darkness on June 16, 1775, the rebels had constructed an earthen fort directly opposite British-held Boston, and when General Thomas Gage saw it the next morning he recognized it for what it was—a challenge that could not possibly be ignored. The engagement that ensued was, quite literally, a fight to the death, signifying once and for all that both sides meant business—meant, in fact, to settle their differences through bloodshed instead of further talk. What occurred on the slopes of Breed's Hill differed substantially from the events of April 19, 1775, when British troops marched out into the countryside and were compelled to fall back in confusion from Lexington and Concord, pursued by bands of men who harried them, guerrilla-fashion, from the cover of trees and stone walls.

Two months separated Lexington and Concord from Bunker Hill, and during that period the rebellious Americans cobbled together an army of sorts—not a very well-organized or efficient one, to be sure, but an army nevertheless, and when several units marched from Cambridge to Charlestown peninsula on the night of June 16 they were the first of a long line of American expeditionary forces setting out to meet the foe in some sort of planned movement.

THIS MEANS WAR

The Battle for Bunker Hill had a powerful effect on George III's government in London. Although further efforts would be made from time to time to reach a negotiated settlement with the Americans, those efforts were undertaken not in a spirit of conciliation, but as one enemy toward another. Bunker Hill, in other words, forced Great Britain to commit itself to war, and after the battle relationships between mother country and colonies were never the same again.

If the events of June 17 forced Britain's hand, they had a profound effect on America as well. Here were thirteen ill-assorted colonies, each tied more closely to London than to each other, and because two small armies met head to head in mortal combat they found themselves at war with the nation to which they owed allegiance. Suddenly there was an imperative need for the untried Continental Congress to act, to take charge of events—to behave, in fact, like a real governing body, supplying a fragile unity and direction where little or none had existed before. Equally suddenly, individual Americans discovered that they had to take a stand, to choose between one side and the other for better or for worse.

Bunker Hill became a ray of hope to Congress and the various colonies, not because they thought the New Englanders had won, but because they had survived. Taken together with Lexington and Concord, the engagement demonstrated that the British army was not invincible after all and that an aroused citizenry was capable of resisting trained professional soldiers in red coats.

The lesson of Bunker Hill was not lost on Britain's military leaders. It is difficult to prove that a single battle affected the subsequent conduct of an army and its commanders, but the fact is that the British never again revealed quite the same aggressiveness after Bunker Hill. The recollection of the awful slaughter, where more British officers were killed than in any battle in memory, remained with General William Howe as long as he served in America. Not again did he risk a full-scale frontal assault on an entrenched rebel position.

None of these aftereffects was apparent to the men joined in battle in the fierce heat of June 17, 1775. Someone had ordered

them to fight and most of them—British and American alike—
did so with unsurpassed ferocity and courage despite the mis-
calculations of their commanders. The story of that decisive day,
as the historian Allen French realized, was "a tale of great blunders heroically redeemed. Each side committed an unexplain-
able, inexcusable error in strategy; and each side paid in blood
according to the magnitude of its mistake."

THE DECLARATION OF THE CAUSES AND NECESSITY OF TAKING UP ARMS

JOHN DICKINSON AND THOMAS JEFFERSON

To coordinate the actions of the colonies, colonial leaders decided to create the Continental Congress to debate issues and make joint decisions. The First Continental Congress was an assembly of delegates from twelve colonies (Georgia did not send a delegation). It met briefly in 1774 to organize a boycott of British goods following the enactment of onerous new laws, including the Quartering Act, which allowed the British to house soldiers in private homes. Following the confrontation at Lexington and Concord, a second Continental Congress was convened in Philadelphia. This time all thirteen colonies sent delegations. The Second Continental Congress became the central government of the thirteen colonies, issuing money, directing the war, and maintaining international relations.

This declaration, passed on July 6, 1775, almost exactly a year prior to the Declaration of Independence, authorized the use of force against England. A first draft of the declaration was written by Thomas Jefferson, but it was considered too inflammatory. A second draft, written primarily by John Dickinson, which retained only the final four and a half paragraphs of Jefferson's draft, was adopted instead. Dickinson, a representative from Pennsylvania, was opposed to independence. He later voted against the Declaration of Independence and briefly resigned

John Dickinson and Thomas Jefferson, "Declaration of the Causes and Necessity of Taking Up Arms," *Documentary Source Book of American History, 1606–1926,* edited by William MacDonald, New York: The Macmillan Company, 1926.

from the Continental Congress in protest following its passage. However, he then rejoined the Continental Congress to become one of the chief architects of the Articles of Confederation.

I f it was possible for men, who exercise their reason to believe, that the divine Author of our existence intended a part of the human race to hold an absolute property in, and an unbounded power over others, marked out by his infinite goodness and wisdom, as the objects of a legal domination never rightfully resistible, however severe and oppressive, the inhabitants of these colonies might at least require from the parliament of Great-Britain some evidence, that this dreadful authority over them, has been granted to that body. But a reverence for our great Creator, principles of humanity, and the dictates of common sense, must convince all those who reflect upon the subject, that government was instituted to promote the welfare of mankind, and ought to be administered for the attainment of that end. The legislature of Great-Britain, however, stimulated by an inordinate passion for a power not only unjustifiable, but which they know to be peculiarly reprobated by the very constitution of that kingdom, and desperate of success in any mode of contest, where regard should be had to truth, law, or right, have at length, deserting those, attempted to effect their cruel and impolitic purpose of enslaving these colonies by violence, and have thereby rendered it necessary for us to close with their last appeal from reason to arms.—Yet, however blinded that assembly may be, by their intemperate rage for unlimited domination, so to slight justice and the opinion of mankind, we esteem ourselves bound by obligations of respect to the rest of the world, to make known the justice of our cause.

HISTORY OF THE BRITISH COLONIES

Our forefathers, inhabitants of the island of Great-Britain, left their native land, to seek on these shores a residence for civil and religious freedom. At the expense of their blood, at the hazard of their fortunes, without the least charge to the country from which they removed, by unceasing labour, and an unconquerable spirit, they effected settlements in the distant and inhospitable wilds of America, then filled with numerous and warlike nations of barbarians.—Societies or governments, vested with perfect legislatures, were formed under charters

from the crown, and an harmonious intercourse was established
between the colonies and the kingdom from which they derived
their origin. The mutual benefits of this union became in a short
time so extraordinary, as to excite astonishment. It is universally
confessed, that the amazing increase of the wealth, strength, and
navigation of the realm, arose from this source; and the minister, who so wisely and successfully directed the measures of
Great-Britain in the late war, publicly declared, that these
colonies enabled her to triumph over her enemies.—Towards
the conclusion of that war, it pleased our sovereign to make a
change in his counsels.—From that fatal moment, the affairs of
the British empire began to fall into confusion, and gradually
sliding from the summit of glorious prosperity, to which they
had been advanced by the virtues and abilities of one man, are
at length distracted by the convulsions, that now shake it to its
deepest foundations.—The new ministry finding the brave foes
of Britain, though frequently defeated, yet still contending, took
up the unfortunate idea of granting them a hasty peace, and of
then subduing her faithful friends.

These devoted colonies were judged to be in such a state, as
to present victories without bloodshed, and all the easy emolu-
ments of statuteable plunder.—The uninterrupted tenor of their
peaceable and respectful behaviour from the beginning of col-
onization, their dutiful, zealous, and useful services during the
war, though so recently and amply acknowledged in the most
honourable manner by his majesty, by the late king, and by parliament, could not save them from the meditated innovations.—
Parliament was influenced to adopt the pernicious project, and
assuming a new power over them, have in the course of eleven
years, given such decisive specimens of the spirit and consequences attending this power, as to leave no doubt concerning
the effects of acquiescence under it. They have undertaken to
give and grant our money without our consent, though we have
ever exercised an exclusive right to dispose of our own property; statutes have been passed for extending the jurisdiction of
courts of admiralty and vice-admiralty beyond their ancient
limits; for depriving us of the accustomed and inestimable privilege of trial by jury, in cases affecting both life and property; for
suspending the legislature of one of the colonies; for interdict-
ing all commerce to the capital of another; and for altering fundamentally the form of government established by charter, and
secured by acts of its own legislature solemnly confirmed by the

crown; for exempting the "murderers" of colonists from legal trial, and in effect, from punishment; for erecting in a neighbouring province, acquired by the joint arms of Great-Britain and America, a despotism dangerous to our very existence; and for quartering soldiers upon the colonists in time of profound peace. It has also been resolved in parliament, that colonists charged with committing certain offences, shall be transported to England to be tried.

But why should we enumerate our injuries in detail? By one statute it is declared, that parliament can "of right make laws to bind us in all cases whatsoever." What is to defend us against so enormous, so unlimited a power? Not a single man of those who assume it, is chosen by us; or is subject to our controul or influence; but, on the contrary, they are all of them exempt from the operation of such laws, and an American revenue, if not diverted from the ostensible purposes for which it is raised, would actually lighten their own burdens in proportion, as they increase ours. We saw the misery to which such despotism would reduce us. We for ten years incessantly and ineffectually besieged the throne as supplicants; we reasoned, we remonstrated with parliament, in the most mild and decent language.

Administration sensible that we should regard these oppressive measures as freemen ought to do, sent over fleets and armies to enforce them. The indignation of the Americans was roused, it is true; but it was the indignation of a virtuous, loyal, and affectionate people. A Congress of delegates from the United Colonies was assembled at Philadelphia, on the fifth day of last September. We resolved again to offer an humble and dutiful petition to the king, and also addressed our fellow-subjects of Great-Britain. We have pursued every temperate, every respectful measure: we have even proceeded to break off our commercial intercourse with our fellow-subjects, as the last peaceable admonition, that our attachment to no nation upon earth should supplant our attachment to liberty.—This, we flattered ourselves, was the ultimate step of the controversy: but subsequent events have shewn, how vain was this hope of finding moderation in our enemies.

THE PRESENT TYRANNY

Several threatening expressions against the colonies were inserted in his majesty's speech; our petition, tho we were told it was a decent one, and that his majesty had been pleased to receive it graciously, and to promise laying it before his parliament, was huddled into both houses among a bundle of American papers, and there neglected. The lords and commons in their address, in the month of February, said, that "a rebellion at that time actually existed within the province of Massachusetts-Bay; and that those concerned in it, had been countenanced and encouraged by unlawful combinations and engagements, entered into by his majesty's subjects in several of the other colonies; and therefore they besought his majesty, that he would take the most effectual measures to inforce due obedience to the laws and authority of the supreme legislature."—Soon after, the commercial intercourse of whole colonies, with foreign countries, and with each other, was cut off by an act of parliament; by another several of them were intirely [sic] prohibited from the fisheries in the seas near their [coasts], on which they always depended for their sustenance; and large reinforcements of ships and troops were immediately sent over to general [Thomas] Gage.

Fruitless were all the entreaties, arguments, and eloquence of an illustrious band of the most distinguished peers, and commoners, who nobly and [strenuously] asserted the justice of our cause, to stay, or even to mitigate the heedless fury with which these accumulated and unexampled outrages were hurried on.—Equally fruitless was the interference of the city of London, of Bristol, and many other respectable towns in our favour. Parliament adopted an insidious manoeuvre calculated to divide us, to establish a perpetual auction of taxations where colony should bid against colony, all of them uninformed what ransom would redeem their lives; and thus to extort from us, at the point of the bayonet, the unknown sums that should be sufficient to gratify, if possible to gratify, ministerial rapacity, with the miserable indulgence left to us of raising, in our own mode, the prescribed tribute. What terms more rigid and humiliating could have been dictated by remorseless victors to conquered enemies? in our circumstances to accept them, would be to deserve them.

Soon after the intelligence of these proceedings arrived on this continent, general Gage, who in the course of the last year had taken possession of the town of Boston, in the province of Massachusetts-Bay, and still occupied it is [as] a garrison, on the 19th day of April, sent out from that place a large detachment of his army, who made an unprovoked assault on the inhabitants of the said province, at the town of Lexington, as appears by the affidavits of a great number of persons, some of whom were officers and soldiers of that detachment, murdered eight of the inhabitants, and wounded many others. From thence the troops proceeded in warlike array to the town of Concord, where they set upon another party of the inhabitants of the same province, killing several and wounding more, until compelled to retreat by the country people suddenly assembled to repel this cruel aggression. Hostilities, thus commenced by the British troops, have been since prosecuted by them without regard to faith or reputation.—The inhabitants of Boston being confined within that town by the general their governor, and having, in order to procure their dismission, entered into a treaty with him, it was stipulated that the said inhabitants having deposited their arms with their own magistrates, should have liberty to depart, taking with them their other effects. They accordingly delivered up their arms, but in open violation of honour, in defiance of the obligation of treaties, which even savage nations esteemed sacred, the governor ordered the arms deposited as aforesaid, that they might be preserved for their owners, to be seized by a body of soldiers; detained the greatest part of the inhabitants in the town, and compelled the few who were permitted to retire, to leave their most valuable effects behind.

By this perfidy wives are separated from their husbands, children from their parents, the aged and the sick from their relations and friends, who wish to attend and comfort them; and those who have been used to live in plenty and even elegance, are reduced to deplorable distress.

The general, further emulating his ministerial masters, by a proclamation bearing date on the 12th day of June, after venting the grossest falsehoods and calumnies against the good people of these colonies, proceeds to "declare them all, either by name or description, to be rebels and traitors, to supersede the course of the common law, and instead thereof to publish and order the use and exercise of the law martial."—His troops have butchered our countrymen, have wantonly burnt Charlestown, besides a considerable number of houses in other places; our ships and vessels are seized; the necessary supplies of provisions are intercepted, and he is exerting his utmost power to spread destruction and devastation around him.

We have received certain intelligence, that general Carelton [Sir Guy Carleton], the governor of Canada, is instigating the people of that province and the Indians to fall upon us; and we have but too much reason to apprehend, that schemes have been formed to excite domestic enemies against us. In brief, a part of these colonies now feel, and all of them are sure of feeling, as far as the vengeance of administration can inflict them, the complicated calamities of fire, sword, and famine. We are reduced to the alternative of chusing an unconditional submission to the tyranny of irritated ministers, or resistance by force.—The latter is our choice.—We have counted the cost of this contest, and find nothing so dreadful as voluntary slavery.—Honour, justice, and humanity, forbid us tamely to surrender that freedom which we received from our gallant ancestors, and which our innocent posterity have a right to receive from us. We cannot endure the infamy and guilt of resigning succeeding generations to that wretchedness which inevitably awaits them, if we basely entail hereditary bondage upon them.

A Declaration of Intent to Take Up Arms

Our cause is just. Our union is perfect. Our internal resources are great, and, if necessary, foreign assistance is undoubtedly attainable.—We gratefully acknowledge, as signal instances of the Divine favour towards us, that his Providence would not permit us to be called into this severe controversy, until we were grown up to our present strength, had been previously exercised in warlike operation, and possessed of the means of defending ourselves. With hearts fortified with these animating reflections, we most solemnly, before God and the world, *declare*, that, exerting the utmost energy of those powers, which our beneficent Creator hath graciously bestowed upon us, the arms we have been compelled by our enemies to assume, we will, in defiance of every hazard, with unabating firmness and perseverance, employ for the preservation of our liberties; being with one mind resolved to die freemen rather than to live slaves.

Lest this declaration should disquiet the minds of our friends and fellow-subjects in any part of the empire, we assure them that we mean not to dissolve that union which has so long and so happily subsisted between us, and which we sincerely wish to see restored.—Necessity has not yet driven us into that desperate measure, or induced us to excite any other nation to war against them.—We have not raised armies with ambitious designs of separating from Great-Britain, and establishing independent states. We fight not for glory or for conquest. We exhibit to mankind the remarkable spectacle of a people attacked by unprovoked enemies, without any imputation or even suspicion of offence. They boast of their privileges and civilization, and yet proffer no milder conditions than servitude or death.

In our own native land, in defence of the freedom that is our birth-right, and which we ever enjoyed till the late violation of it—for the protection of our property, acquired solely by the honest industry of our fore-fathers and ourselves, against violence actually offered, we have taken up arms. We shall lay them down when hostilities shall cease on the part of the aggressors, and all danger of their being renewed shall be removed, and not before.

With an humble confidence in the mercies of the supreme and impartial Judge and Ruler of the Universe, we most devoutly implore his divine goodness to protect us happily through this great conflict, to dispose our adversaries to reconciliation on reasonable terms, and thereby to relieve the empire from the calamities of civil war.

THE LOYALIST CASE

PETER VAN SCHAACK

The debate over independence was, in one sense, a debate over the legitimate basis of government. Traditionally monarchs claimed that their right to govern had been granted to them "by God." If this claim were true, no rebellion against a king could be considered legitimate since such a rebellion would also be a rebellion against God. However, by the eighteenth century most people believed in the philosophy articulated by John Locke, that a government owed its legitimacy to the consent of the governed—that is, a government could be legitimate only if the people agreed to be governed by it. Naturally, under this theory a rebellion could be justified provided two further questions could be answered: (1) under what conditions may the governed withdraw their consent; and (2) have those conditions been met in the present case?

Peter Van Schaack was a loyalist from New York. In 1778 he went into exile in England, but he returned after the war when the New York legislature restored his citizenship in 1784. In this passage from his journal, Van Schaack agrees with views expressed by Thomas Jefferson in the Declaration of Independence concerning the legitimate basis of government and the conditions under which a governed people may withdraw their consent to be governed. He disagrees, however, that British treatment of its colonies has been harsh enough to meet these conditions.

T
he only foundation of all legitimate governments is certainly a compact between the rulers and the people, containing mutual conditions, and equally obligatory on both the contracting parties. No question can therefore exist, at this enlightened day, about the lawfulness of resistance, in cases of

Peter Van Schaack, "Life of Peter Van Schaack," *The Spirit of 'Seventy-Six: The Story of the American Revolution as Told by Participants*, vol. I, edited by Henry Steele Commager and Richard B. Morris, New York: Bobbs-Merrill, 1958.

gross and palpable infractions on the part of the governing power. It is impossible, however, clearly to ascertain every case which shall effect a dissolution of this contract; for these, though always tacitly implied, are never expressly declared, in any form of government.

As a man is bound by the sacred ties of conscience to yield obedience to every act of the legislature so long as the government exists, so, on the other hand, he owes it to the cause of liberty to resist the invasion of those rights which, being inherent and unalienable, could not be surrendered at the institution of the civil society of which he is a member. In times of civil commotions, therefore, an investigation of those rights which will necessarily infer an inquiry into the nature of government, becomes the indispensable duty of every man.

VALID GROUNDS FOR REBELLION

There are perhaps few questions relating to government of more difficulty than that at present subsisting between Great Britain and the Colonies. It originated about the *degree* of subordination we owe to the British Parliament, but by a rapid progress it seems now to be whether we are members of the empire or not. In this view, the principles of Mr. Locke and other advocates for the rights of mankind are little to the purpose. His treatise throughout presupposes rulers and subjects of the *same state,* and upon a supposition that we are members of the empire, his reasonings, if not inapplicable, will be found rather to militate against our claims; for he holds the necessity of a *supreme power,* and the necessary existence of *one legislature* only in every society, in the strongest terms.

Here arises the doubt: if we are parts of the same state, we cannot complain of a *usurpation,* unless in a qualified sense, but we must found our resistance upon an *undue and oppressive* exercise of a power we recognize. In short, our reasonings must resolve into one or the other of the following three grounds, and our right of resistance must be founded upon either the first or third of them; for either, first, we owe no obedience to any acts of Parliament; or, secondly, we are bound by all acts to which British subjects in Great Britain would, if passed with respect to them, owe obedience; or, thirdly, we are subordinate in a certain degree, or, in other words, certain acts may be valid in Britain which are not so here.

Upon the first point I am exceedingly clear in my mind, for I consider the Colonies as members of the British empire, and subordinate to the Parliament. But, with regard to the second and third, I am not so clear. The necessity of a supreme power in every state strikes me very forcibly; at the same time, I foresee the destructive consequences of a right in Parliament to bind us in all cases whatsoever. To obviate the ill effects of either extreme, some middle way should be found out, by which the benefits to the empire should be secured arising from the doctrine of a supreme power, while the abuses of that power to the prejudice of the colonists should be guarded against; and this, I hope, will be the happy effect of the present struggle.

The basis of such a compact must be the securing to the Americans the essential rights of Britons, but so modified as shall best consist with the general benefit of the *whole*. If upon such a compact we cannot possess the specific privileges of the inhabitants of Great Britain (as for instance a representation in Parliament we cannot), this must not be an obstacle; for there is certainly a point in which the general good of the whole, with the least possible disadvantage to every part, does centre, though it may be difficult to discern it, and every *individual* part must give way to the *general good*. . . .

GROUNDS FOR REBELLION ARE NOT PRESENT IN THIS CASE

It may be said that these principles terminate in passive obedience: far from it. I perceive that several of the acts exceed those bounds which, of right, ought to circumscribe the Parliament. But my difficulty arises from this, that, taking the whole of the acts complained of together, they do not, I think, manifest a system of slavery, but may fairly be imputed to human frailty and the difficulty of the subject. Most of them seem to have sprung out of particular occasions, and are unconnected with each other, and some of them are precisely of the nature of other acts made before the commencement of his present Majesty's reign, which is the era when the supposed design of subjugating the colonies began. If these acts have exceeded what is and ought to be declared to be the line of right, and thus we have been sufferers in *some respects* by the undefined state of the subject, it will also, I think, appear from such a union, when established, if past transactions are to be measured by the standard hereafter to be fixed, that *we* have hitherto been deficient in other respects, and derived *benefit* from the same unsettled state.

In short, I think those acts may have been passed without a preconcerted plan of enslaving us, and it appears to me that the more favorable construction ought ever to be put on the conduct of our rulers. I cannot therefore think the government *dissolved*; and as long as the society lasts, the power that every individual gave the society when he entered into it can never revert to the individuals again, but will always remain in the community.

If it be asked how we come to be subject to the authority of the British Parliament, I answer, by the same compact which entitles us to the benefits of the British constitution and its laws; and that we derive advantage even from some kind of subordination, whatever the degree of it should be, is evident, because, without such a controlling common umpire, the colonies must become independent states, which would be introductive of anarchy and confusion among ourselves.

Some kind of dependence being then, in my idea, necessary for our own happiness, I would choose to see a claim made of a constitution which shall concede this point, as, before that is done by us and rejected by the mother country, I cannot see any principle of regard for my country which will authorize me in taking up arms, as absolute *dependence* and *independence* are two extremes which I would avoid; for, should we succeed in the latter, we shall still be in a sea of uncertainty and have to fight among ourselves for that constitution we aim at.

There are many very weighty reasons besides the above to restrain a man from taking up arms, but some of them are of too delicate a nature to be put upon paper; however, it may be proper to mention what does *not* restrain *me*. It is not from apprehension of the consequences should America be subdued, or the hopes of any favor from government, both which I disclaim; nor is it from any disparagement of the cause my countrymen are engaged in, or a desire of obstructing the present measures.

I am fully convinced that men of the greatest abilities and the soundest integrity have taken parts in this war with America, and their measures should have a fair trial. But this is too serious a matter, implicitly to yield to the authority of any characters, however respectable. Every man must exercise his own reason and judge for himself; "for he that appeals to Heaven must be sure that he has right on his side," according to Mr. Locke. It is a question of morality and religion, in which a man cannot conscientiously take an active part without being convinced in his own mind of the justice of the cause; for obedience while government exists being clear on the one hand, the dissolution of the government must be equally so, to justify an appeal to arms; and whatever disagreeable consequences may follow from dissenting from the general voice, yet I cannot but remember that I am to render an account of my conduct before a more awful tribunal, where no man can be justified who stands accused by his own conscience of taking part in measures which, through the distress and bloodshed of his fellow-creatures, may precipitate his country into ruin.

THE DECLARATION OF INDEPENDENCE

THOMAS JEFFERSON

The motion to declare independence from Britain was introduced to the second Continental Congress on June 7, 1776, more than a year after the beginning of the war, by Richard Henry Lee, a delegate from Virginia. Of course, not everyone believed that the open hostilities with England would—or should—result in independence from England, and the question sparked a heated debate. A committee, composed of John Adams, Benjamin Franklin, Thomas Jefferson, Robert Livingston, and Roger Sherman, was appointed to create a draft resolution making the case for independence. Jefferson's draft, with only minor changes proposed by Adams and Franklin, was offered to the Congress, which then proceeded to make additional changes. The most important change was to drop a section complaining that Britain had encouraged the slave trade. The final version of the Declaration of Independence was approved on July 4, 1776.

Thomas Jefferson, the chief author, was a delegate from Virginia. Following the passage of the Declaration of Independence, he returned to Virginia to serve in the Virginia legislature and as governor of Virginia from 1779 to 1781. He succeeded Benjamin Franklin as ambassador to France, helped write the U.S. Constitution, and served two terms as the third president of the United States.

W hen in the Course of human events, it becomes necessary for one people to dissolve the political bands, which have connected them with another, and to as-

Thomas Jefferson, "The Declaration of Independence," *Great Issues in American History: From the Revolution to the Civil War, 1765–1865*, edited by Richard Hofstadter, New York: Vintage Books, 1958.

sume among the powers of the earth, the separate and equal station to which the Laws of Nature and of Nature's God entitle them, a decent respect to the opinions of mankind requires that they should declare the causes which impel them to the separation.—We hold these truths to be self-evident, that all men are created equal, that they are endowed by their Creator with certain unalienable Rights, that among these are Life, Liberty and the pursuit of Happiness.—That to secure these rights, Governments are instituted among Men, deriving their just powers from the consent of the governed,—That whenever any Form of Government becomes destructive of these ends, it is the Right of the People to alter or to abolish it, and to institute new Government, laying its foundation on such principles and organizing its powers in such form, as to them shall seem most likely to effect their Safety and Happiness. Prudence, indeed, will dictate that Governments long established should not be changed for light and transient causes; and accordingly all experience hath shewn, that mankind are more disposed to suffer, while evils are sufferable, than to right themselves by abolishing the forms to which they are accustomed. But when a long train of abuses and usurpations, pursuing invariably the same Object evinces a design to reduce them under absolute Despotism, it is their right, it is their duty, to throw off such Government, and to provide new Guards for their future security.— Such has been the patient sufferance of these Colonies; and such is now the necessity which constrains them to alter their former Systems of Government.

COMPLAINTS AGAINST THE KING

The history of the present King of Great Britain is a history of repeated injuries and usurpations, all having in direct object the establishment of an absolute Tyranny over these States. To prove this, let Facts be submitted to a candid world.—He has refused his Assent to Laws, the most wholesome and necessary for the public good.—He has forbidden his Governors to pass Laws of immediate and pressing importance, unless suspended in their operation till his Assent should be obtained; and when so suspended, he has utterly neglected to attend to them.—He has refused to pass other Laws for the accommodation of large districts of people, unless those people would relinquish the right of Representation in the Legislature, a right inestimable to them and formidable to tyrants only.—He has called together legislative bodies at places unusual, uncomfortable, and distant from the depository of their public Records, for the sole purpose of fatiguing them into compliance with his measures.—He has dissolved Representative Houses repeatedly, for opposing with manly firmness his invasions on the rights of the people.—He has refused for a long time, after such dissolutions, to cause others to be elected; whereby the Legislative powers, incapable of Annihilation, have returned to the People at large for their exercise; the State remaining in the meantime exposed to all the dangers of invasion from without, and convulsions within.— He has endeavoured to prevent the population of these States; for that purpose obstructing the Laws for Naturalization of Foreigners; refusing to pass others to encourage their migrations hither, and raising the conditions of new Appropriations of Lands.—He has obstructed the Administration of Justice, by refusing his Assent to Laws for establishing Judiciary powers.— He has made Judges dependent on his Will alone, for the tenure of their offices, and the amount and payment of their salaries.— He has erected a multitude of New Offices, and sent hither swarms of Officers to harrass our people, and eat out their substance.—He has kept among us, in times of peace, Standing Armies without the Consent of our legislatures.—He has affected to render the Military independent of and superior to the Civil power.—He has combined with others to subject us to a jurisdiction foreign to our constitution, and unacknowledged by our laws; giving his Assent to their Acts of pretended Legislation.—For quartering large bodies of armed troops among us:—For protecting them, by a mock Trial, from punishment for any Murders which they should commit on the Inhabitants of these States:—For cutting off our Trade with all parts of the world:—For imposing Taxes on us without our Consent:—For depriving us in many cases, of the benefits of Trial by Jury:— For transporting us beyond Seas to be tried for pretended offenses:—For abolishing the free System of English Laws in a neighboring Province, establishing therein an Arbitrary government, and enlarging its Boundaries so as to render it at once an example and fit instrument for introducing the same absolute rule into these Colonies:—For taking away our Charters, abolishing our most valuable Laws, and altering fundamentally the Forms of our Governments:—For suspending our own Legislatures, and declaring themselves invested with power to legislate for us in all cases whatsoever.—He has abdicated Government here, by declaring us out of his Protection and waging War against us.—He has plundered our seas, ravaged our Coasts, burnt our towns, and destroyed the lives of our people.—He is at this time transporting large Armies of foreign Mercenaries to compleat the works of death, desolation and tyranny, already begun with circumstances of Cruelty & perfidy scarcely paralleled in the most barbarous ages, and totally unworthy the Head of a civilized nation.—He has constrained our fellow Citizens taken Captive on the high Seas to bear Arms against their Country, to become the executioners of their friends and Brethren, or to fall themselves by their Hands.—He has excited domestic insurrections amongst us, and has endeavoured to bring on the inhabitants of our frontiers, the merciless Indian Savages, whose known rule of warfare, is an undistinguished destruction of all ages, sexes and conditions. In every stage of these Oppressions We have Petitioned for Redress in the most humble terms: Our repeated Petitions have been answered only by repeated injury. A Prince whose character is thus marked by every act which may define a Tyrant, is unfit to be the ruler of a free people. Nor have We been wanting in attentions to our Brittish brethren. We have warned them from time to time of attempts by their legislature to extend an unwarrantable jurisdiction over us. We have reminded them of the circumstances of our emigration and settlement here. We have appealed to their native justice and magnanimity, and we have conjured them by the ties of our common kindred to disavow these usurpations, which would inevitably interrupt our connections and correspondence. They too have been deaf to the voice of justice and of consanguinity. We must, therefore, acquiesce in the necessity, which denounces our Separation, and hold them, as we hold the rest of mankind, Enemies in War, in Peace Friends.—

FREE AND INDEPENDENT STATES

We, therefore, the Representatives of the united States of America, in General Congress, Assembled, appealing to the Supreme Judge of the world for the rectitude of our intentions do, in the Name, and by Authority of the good People of these Colonies, solemnly publish and declare, That these United Colonies are, and of Right ought to be Free and Independent States; that they are Absolved from all Allegiance to the British Crown, and that all political connection between them and the State of Great

Britain, is and ought to be totally dissolved; and that as Free and Independent States, they have full Power to levy War, conclude Peace, contract Alliances, establish Commerce, and to do all other Acts and Things which Independent States may of right do.—And for the support of this Declaration, with a firm reliance on the protection of divine Providence, we mutually pledge to each other our Lives, our Fortunes and our sacred Honor.

Losing Battles and Winning the War, 1776–1781

CHAPTER 5

MILITARY INTELLIGENCE DURING THE AMERICAN REVOLUTION

THOMAS FLEMING

George Washington gained his military experience fighting against the French and Native Americans during the Seven Years' War. In fact, the very first battles in the war were fought (and lost) under Washington's command. At the time he was a twenty-one-year-old inexperienced officer. With the outbreak of the Revolution he was elected to represent Virginia as a delegate to the Continental Congress. He was the only delegate with extensive military experience. Hence, on June 15, 1775, shortly after authorizing the use of force against Britain, Congress voted to put him in charge of the Continental army as its commander in chief. After losing a pitched battle to take New York City, Washington formulated a strategy of avoiding direct confrontations and choosing his battles wisely. Washington's careful strategy is generally credited with winning the war for the patriots. Following the Revolution Washington helped write the U.S. Constitution and served two terms as the first president of the United States.

Historian and novelist Thomas Fleming has written many books on the American Revolution. His nonfiction works include biographies of George Washington, Benjamin Franklin, and Thomas Jefferson, as well as histories of specific battles. His fiction works include *The Officers' Wives* and *Dreams of Glory*. In

Thomas Fleming, "George Washington, Spymaster," *American Heritage*, vol. 51, February/March, 2000. Copyright © 2000 by Forbes. Reproduced by permission.

this selection he describes Washington's masterful use of military intelligence to stay one step ahead of the British.

I t is commonly understood that without the Commander in Chief's quick mind and cool judgment the American Revolution would have almost certainly expired in 1776. It is less well known that his brilliance extended to overseeing, directly and indirectly, extensive and very sophisticated intelligence activities against the British.

A CHANGE IN STRATEGY

Washington had wanted to be a soldier almost from the cradle and seems to have acquired the ability to think in military terms virtually by instinct. In the chaos of mid-1776, with half his army deserting and the other half in a funk and all his generals rattled, he kept his head and reversed his strategy. The Americans had started with the idea that a general action, as an all-out battle was called, could end the conflict overnight, trusting that their superior numbers would overwhelm the presumably small army the British could afford to send to our shores. But the British sent a very big, well-trained army, which routed the Americans in the first several battles in New York. Washington sat down in his tent on Harlem Heights and informed the Continental Congress that he was going to fight an entirely different war. From now on, he wrote, he would "avoid a general action." Instead would "protract the war."

In his 1975 study of Washington's generalship, *The Way of the Fox*, Lt. Col. Dave Richard Palmer has called this reversal "a masterpiece of strategic thought, a brilliant blueprint permitting a weak force to combat a powerful opponent." It soon became apparent that for the blueprint to be followed, Washington would have to know what the British were planning to do, and he would have to be able to prevent them from finding out what he was doing. In short, espionage was built into the system.

Washington had been acquainted with British colonial officials and generals and colonels since his early youth, and he knew how intricately espionage was woven into the entire British military and political enterprise. Any Englishman's mail could be opened and read if a secretary of state requested it. Throughout Europe every British embassy had its intelligence network.

Thus Washington was not entirely surprised to discover,

shortly after he took command of the American army in 1775, that his surgeon general, Dr. Benjamin Church, was telling the British everything that went on in the American camp at Cambridge, Massachusetts. He was surprised to find out, not long after he had transferred his operations to New York in the spring of 1776, that one of his Life Guard, a soldier named Thomas Hickey, was rumored to be involved in a plot to kill him.

By that time Washington had pulled off his own opening gambit in a form of intelligence at which he soon displayed something close to genius: disinformation. Shortly after he took command in Cambridge, he asked someone how much powder the embryo American army had in reserve. Everyone thought it had three hundred barrels, but a check of the Cambridge magazine revealed most of that had been fired away at Bunker Hill. There were only thirty-six barrels—fewer than nine rounds per man. For half an hour, according to one witness, Washington was too stunned to speak. But he recovered and sent people into British-held Boston to spread the story that he had eighteen hundred barrels, and he spread the same rumor throughout the American camp.

THE BURNING OF NEW YORK

In chaotic New York, grappling with a large and aggressive British army, deserting militia, and an inapplicable strategy, Washington temporarily lost control of the intelligence situation. That explains the dolorous failure of Capt. Nathan Hale's mission in September 1776. Hale, sent to gather information behind British lines, was doomed almost from the moment he volunteered. He had little or no contact with the American high command, no training as a spy, no disguise worthy of the name, and an amorphous mission: to find out whatever he could wherever he went.

There is little evidence that Washington was even aware of Hale's existence. He was involved in something far more serious: figuring out how to burn down New York City in order to deprive the British of their winter quarters, despite orders from the Continental Congress strictly forbidding him to harm the place. He looked the other way while members of Hale's regiment slipped into the city; they were experts at starting conflagrations thanks to a tour of duty on fire ships—vessels carrying explosives to burn enemy craft on the Hudson.

On September 21 a third of New York went up in flames. The

timing was disastrous for Hale, who was captured the very same day. Anyone with a Connecticut accent became highly suspect, and the British caught several incendiaries and hanged them on the spot. They gave Hale the same treatment: no trial, just a swift, humiliating death. Hale's friends were so mortified by his fate, which they considered shameful, that no one mentioned his now-famous farewell speech ["I only regret that I have but one life to lose for my country"] for another fifty years. Then an old man told his daughter about it, and Yale College, seeking Revolutionary War heroes among its graduates, quickly immortalized him.

Washington never said a word about Hale. His only Intelligence comment at the time concerned New York. The fire had destroyed Trinity Church and about six hundred houses, causing no little discomfort for the British and the thousands of Loyalist refugees who had crowded into the city. In a letter, Washington remarked that "Providence, or some good honest fellow, has done more for us than we were disposed to do for ourselves."

One of Hale's best friends, Maj. Benjamin Tallmadge, never got over his death. He probably talked about it to Washington, who assured him that once they got the protracted war under control, all espionage would be handled from Army headquarters, and no spy's life would be wasted the way Hale's had been.

Surviving long enough to fight an extended conflict was no small matter. In the weeks after Hale's death, disaster after disaster befell the American army. Washington was forced to abandon first New York and then New Jersey. On the other side of the Delaware, with only the shadow of an army left to him, he issued orders in December 1776 to all his generals to find "some person who can be engaged to cross the river as a spy" and added that "expense must not be spared" in securing a volunteer.

He also rushed a letter to Robert Morris, the financier of the Revolution, asking for hard money to "pay a certain set of people who are of particular use to us." He meant spies, and he had no illusion that any spy would risk hanging for the paper money the Continental Congress was printing. Morris sent from Philadelphia two canvas bags filled with what hard cash he could scrape together on an hour's notice—410 Spanish dollars, 2 English crowns, 10 shillings, and 2 sixpence.

The search soon turned up a former British soldier named John Honeyman, who was living in nearby Griggstown, New Jersey. On Washington's orders Honeyman rediscovered his loyalty to the king and began selling cattle to several British garrisons along the Delaware. He had no trouble gaining the confidence of Col. Johann Rall, who was in command of three German regiments in Trenton. Honeyman listened admiringly as Rall described his heroic role in the fighting around New York and agreed with him that the Americans were hopeless soldiers.

On December 22, 1776, having spent about a week in Trenton, Honeyman wandered into the countryside, supposedly in search of cattle, and got himself captured by an American patrol and hustled to Washington's headquarters. There he was publicly denounced by the Commander in Chief as a "notorious" turncoat. Washington insisted on interrogating him personally and said he would give the traitor a chance to save his skin if he recanted his loyalty to the Crown.

A half-hour later the general ordered his aides to throw Honeyman into the guardhouse. Tomorrow morning, he stated, the Tory would be hanged. That night Honeyman escaped from the guardhouse with a key supplied by Washington and dashed past American sentries, who fired on him. Sometime on December 24 he turned up in Trenton and told Colonel Rall the story of his narrow escape.

The German naturally wanted to know what Honeyman had seen in Washington's camp, and the spy assured him that the Americans were falling apart. They were half-naked and freezing, and they lacked the food and basic equipment, such as shoes, to make a winter march. Colonel Rall, delighted, prepared to celebrate Christmas with no military worries to interrupt the feasting and drinking that were traditional in his country. He never dreamed that Honeyman had given Washington a professional soldier's detailed description of the routine of the Trenton garrison, the location of the picket guards, and everything else an assaulting force would need to know.

At dawn on December 26 Washington's ragged Continentals charged through swirling snow and sleet to kill the besotted Colonel Rall and capture most of his troops. New Jersey had been on the brink of surrender; now local patriots began shooting up British patrols, and the rest of the country, in the words of a Briton in Virginia, "went liberty mad again."

CIPHERS, INVISIBLE INK, AND CODE NAMES

Washington set up a winter camp in Morristown and went to work organizing American intelligence. He made Tallmadge his second-in-command, though he was ostensibly still a major in the 2d Continental Dragoons. That regiment was stationed in outposts all around the perimeter of British-held New York, and Tallmadge visited these units regularly, supposedly to make sure that all was in order but actually working as a patient spider setting up spy networks inside the British lines. His methods, thanks to Washington's tutelage, could not have been more sophisticated. He equipped his spies with cipher codes, invisible ink, and aliases that concealed their real identities. The invisible ink, which the Americans called "the stain," had been invented by Dr. James Jay, a brother of the prominent patriot John Jay, living in England. It was always in short supply.

Two of the most important American agents operating inside British-held New York were Robert Townsend, a Quaker merchant, and Abraham Woodhull, a Setauket, Long Island, farmer. Their code names were Culper Jr. and Culper Sr. As a cover, Townsend wrote violently Loyalist articles for the *New York Royal Gazette;* this enabled him to pick up information from British officers and their mistresses, and he sent it on to Woodhull via a courier named Austin Roe.

Woodhull would then have a coded signal hung on a Setauket clothesline that was visible through a spyglass to Americans on the Connecticut shore. A crew of oarsmen would row across Long Island Sound by night, collect Townsend's letters, and carry them to Tallmadge's dragoons, who would hurry them to Washington. The general applied a "sympathetic fluid" to reveal the secret messages written in Dr. Jay's "stain."

When the British occupied Philadelphia, in 1777, Washington salted the city with spies. His chief assistant there was Maj. John Clark, a cavalryman who became expert at passing false information about American strength at Valley Forge to a spy for the British commander General Howe. Washington laboriously wrote out muster reports of the Continental Army, making it four or five times its actual size; the British, recognizing the handwriting, accepted the information as fact and gave the spy who had obtained it a bonus. Washington must have enjoyed this disinformation game; at one point, describing a particularly successful deception, Clark wrote, "This will give you a laugh."

The most effective American spy in Philadelphia was Lydia Darragh, an Irish-born Quaker midwife and undertaker. The British requisitioned a room in her house to serve as a "council chamber" and discussed their war plans there. By lying with her ear to a crack in the floor in the room above, Mrs. Darragh could hear much of what they said. Her husband wrote the information in minute shorthand on scraps of paper that she hid in large cloth-covered buttons. Wearing these, her fourteen-year-old son would walk into the countryside to meet his brother, a lieutenant in the American army. He snipped off the buttons, and the intelligence was soon in Washington's hands.

Mrs. Darragh's biggest coup was getting word to Washington that the British were about to make a surprise attack on his ragged army as it marched to Valley Forge in early December 1777. When the attack came, the Continentals were waiting with loaded muskets and cannon, and the king's forces withdrew.

The British returned to Philadelphia determined to find whoever had leaked their plan. Staff officers went to Mrs. Darragh's house and demanded to know exactly when everyone had gone to bed the previous night—except one person. "I won't ask you, Mrs. Darragh, because I know you retire each night exactly at nine," the chief interrogator said. Lydia Darragh smiled and said nothing. After the war she remarked that she was pleased that as a spy she had never had to tell a lie.

BRITISH SPIES

The British, of course, had a small army of spies working for them as well, and they constantly struggled to penetrate Washington's operations. Toward the end of 1779, one of their Philadelphia spies wrote to Maj. John Andre, the charming, witty, artistically talented director of British intelligence: "Do you wish to have a useful hand in their army and to pay what you find his services worth? The exchange is 44 to £" The numbers refer to the vertiginous depreciation of the Continental dollar; British spies, too, wanted to be paid in hard money.

The Americans did their best to make trouble for Andre by spreading around Philadelphia and New York the rumor that he was given to molesting boys. It is not clear whether Washington was involved in these particular smears, and they hardly chime with Andre's reputation for charming women, notably a Philadelphia belle named Peggy Shippen, who eventually married Gen. Benedict Arnold.

In any event, Andre was very successful at keeping tabs on the Americans. Surviving letters from his spies show him obtaining good estimates of American army strength in 1779. At one point Gen. Philip Schuyler made a motion in the Continental Congress that it leave Philadelphia because "they could do no business that was not instantly communicated" to the British.

Andre's most successful agent was a woman named Ann Bates, a former schoolteacher who married a British soldier while the army was in Philadelphia. Disguised as a peddler, she wandered through the American camp, counted the cannon there, overheard conversations at Washington's headquarters, and accurately predicted the American attack on the British base in Newport, Rhode Island, in 1778.

The intelligence war reached a climax, or something very close to one, between 1779 and 1781. American morale was sinking with the Continental currency, and trusting anyone became harder and harder. Washington could never be sure when a spy had been "turned" by British hard money, and the British tried to accelerate the decline of the paper dollar by printing and circulating millions of counterfeit bills.

Soon an astonished American was writing, "An ordinary horse is worth twenty thousand dollars." In despair Congress stopped producing money; this brought the army's commissary department to a halt. The Continental desertion rate rose, with veterans and sergeants among the chief fugitives.

Washington struggled to keep the British at bay with more disinformation about his dwindling strength. His spies had achieved such professionalism that he had to appeal to Gov. William Livingston of New Jersey to spare three men arrested in Elizabethtown for carrying on an illegal correspondence with the enemy. That was exactly what they had been doing—as double agents feeding the British disinformation.

The three spies stood heroically silent. Washington told Livingston they were willing to "bear the suspicion of being thought inimical." But realism could not be carried too far; the Continental Army could not hang its own agents. Would the governor please do something? Livingston allowed the spies to escape, and intelligence documents show that three years later they were still at work.

By June 1780 agents had given the British high command accurate reports of the American army's weakness in its Morristown camp. The main force had diminished to four thousand men; because of a shortage of fodder, there were no horses, which meant the artillery was immobilized. The British had just captured Charleston, South Carolina, and its garrison of five thousand, demoralizing the South. They decided a strike at

Washington's force could end the war, and they marshaled six thousand troops on Staten Island to deliver the blow.

A few hours before the attack, a furtive figure slipped ashore into New Jersey from Staten Island to warn the Continentals of the enemy buildup. He reached the officer in command in Elizabethtown, Col. Elias Dayton, and Dayton sent a rider off to Morristown with the news. Dayton and other members of the New Jersey Continental line, backed by local militia, were able to slow the British advance for the better part of a day, enabling Washington to get his army in motion and seize the high ground in the Short Hills, aborting the British plan.

It was a very close call. Without the warning from that spy, the British army would certainly have come over the Short Hills, overwhelmed Washington's four thousand men in Morristown, and captured their artillery. This probably would have ended the war.

After the royal army retreated to New York, word reached them that a French expeditionary force was landing in Newport, Rhode Island, to reinforce the struggling Americans. The British commander, Sir Henry Clinton, decided to attack before the French had a chance to recover from the rigors of the voyage and fortify.

This was the Culper network's greatest moment. Robert Townsend, alias Culper Jr., discovered the plan shortly after Clinton put six thousand men aboard transports and sailed them to Huntington Bay on the north shore of Long Island. They waited there while British frigates scouted Newport Harbor to assess the size of the French squadron.

Townsend's warning sent Washington's disinformation machine into overdrive. Within twenty-four hours a double agent was in New York, handing the British top-secret papers, supposedly dropped by a careless courier, detailing a Washington plan to attack the city with every Continental soldier and militiaman in the middle states.

The British sent horsemen racing off to urge Sir Henry Clinton in Huntington Bay to return to New York with his six thousand men. Clinton, already discouraged by the British admiral's lack of enthusiasm for his plan to take Newport, glumly agreed and sailed his soldiers back to their fortifications. There they waited for weeks for an assault that never materialized.

While Clinton was in Huntington Bay, he and two aides were made violently ill by tainted wine they drank with dinner aboard the flagship. He ordered the bottle seized and asked the physician general of the British army to examine the dregs in the glasses. The doctor said the wine was "strongly impregnated with arsenic." During the night the bottle mysteriously disappeared, and Clinton was never able to confirm the assassination attempt or find the perpetrator. This may have been Washington's way of getting even for the Hickey plot.

BENEDICT ARNOLD

The main event in the later years of the intelligence war was the treason of Benedict Arnold in 1780. However, the American discovery of Arnold's plot to sell the fortress at West Point to the British for six thousand pounds—about half a million dollars in modern money—was mostly luck. There was little that Benjamin Tallmadge or his agents could claim to their credit except having passed along a hint of a plot involving an American general a few weeks before.

There is no doubt that West Point would have been handed over and Benedict Arnold and John Andre given knighthoods if three wandering militiamen in Westchester County had not stopped Andre on his return to New York with the incriminating plans in his boot. The motive of these soldiers was not patriotism but robbery; Westchester was known as "the neutral ground," and Loyalists and rebels alike wandered there in search of plunder.

Hanging John Andre was one of the most difficult things Washington had to do in the intelligence war. The major was the object of universal affection, and Alexander Hamilton and others on Washington's staff urged him to find a way to commute the sentence. Washington grimly replied that he would do so only if the British handed over Arnold. That of course did not happen, and Andre died on the gallows. In the next twelve months, Washington made repeated attempts to capture Arnold. He ordered an American sergeant named Champe to desert and volunteer to join an American legion that Arnold was trying to create. To give Champe a convincing sendoff, Washington ordered a half a dozen cavalrymen to pursue him, without telling them he was a fake deserter. Champe arrived in the British lines with bullets chasing him.

Washington would seem to have liked these little touches of realism. Unusually fearless himself, he had once said as a young man that whistling bullets had "a charming sound." One won-ders if spies such as Honeyman and Champe agreed.

Soon Champe was a member of Arnold's staff, living in the former general's house on the Hudson River in New York. Through cooperating agents, Champe communicated a plan to knock Arnold unconscious when he went into his riverside garden to relieve himself one moonless night. A boatload of Americans would be waiting to carry him back to New Jersey and harsh justice.

On the appointed night the boat was there, and Arnold went to the garden as usual, but Champe was on a troopship in New York Harbor. Clinton had ordered two thousand men, including Arnold's American legion, south to raid Virginia. Champe had to watch for an opportunity and deserted back to the American side.

Arnold's defection badly upset American intelligence operations for months. He told the British what he knew of Washington's spies in New York, and they made several arrests. Townsend quit spying for six months, to the great distress of Washington and Tallmadge.

THE BATTLE OF YORKTOWN

The intelligence war continued during the year remaining until Yorktown. Washington's reluctant decision to march south with the French army to try to trap a British army in that small Virginia tobacco port was accompanied by strenuous disinformation efforts intended to tie the British army to New York for as long as possible. In the line of march as the allied force moved south through New Jersey were some thirty large flatboats. British spies reported that the Americans were constructing large cooking ovens at several points near New York. Both seemed evidence of a plan to attack the city.

Benedict Arnold, now a British brigadier, begged Sir Henry Clinton to ignore this deception and give him six thousand men to attack the long, vulnerable American line of march. Clinton said no. He wanted to husband every available man in New York. By the time the British commander's Philadelphia spies told him where Washington was actually going, it was too late. The royal army under Charles Lord Cornwallis surrendered after three weeks of pounding by heavy guns, the blow that finally ended the protracted war.

Even after the fighting wound down, intelligence activity went on. In the fall of 1782, a year after Yorktown, a French officer stationed in Morristown wrote, "Not a day has passed since we have drawn near the enemy that we have not had some news of them from our spies in New York." For a final irony, the last British commander in America, Sir Guy Carleton, sent Washington a report from a British agent warning about a rebel plot to plunder New York and abuse Loyalists as the British army withdrew, and Washington sent in Major Tallmadge and a column of troops—not only to keep order but also to protect their agents, many of whom had earned enmity for appearing to be loyal to George III.

Among the American spies in New York was a huge Irish American tailor named Hercules Mulligan who had sent Washington invaluable information. His greatest coup was a warning that the British planned to try to kidnap the American commander in 1780. Mulligan reported directly to Washington's aide Col. Alexander Hamilton.

Another of the deepest agents was James Rivington, editor of the unctuously loyal *New York Royal Gazette.* He is believed to have stolen the top-secret signals of the British fleet, which the Americans passed on to the French in 1781. The knowledge may have helped the latter win the crucial naval battle off the Virginia capes that September, sealing Cornwallis's fate at Yorktown.

The day after the British evacuated New York, Washington had breakfast with Hercules Mulligan—a way of announcing that he had been a patriot. He also paid a visit to James Rivington and apparently gave him a bag of gold coins. When he was composing his final expense account for submission to the Continental Congress with his resignation as Commander in Chief, Washington included from memory the contents of the bag of coins Robert Morris had rushed to him in late December 1776: 410 Spanish dollars, 2 English crowns, 10 shillings, and 2 sixpence. The circumstances under which he received it, Washington remarked, made it impossible for him ever to forget the exact amount of that crucial transfusion of hard money. It is another piece of evidence, barely needed at this point, that intelligence was a centerpiece of the strategy of protracted war—and that George Washington was a master of the game.

FOREIGN RELATIONS DURING THE AMERICAN REVOLUTION

SAMUEL FLAGG BEMIS

It is unlikely that the American colonies could have won their independence from Britain without the aid of foreign allies. The French and the Spanish, who had lost territory to the British during the Seven Years' War and still felt humiliated by the defeat, were eager to help. At the beginning of the Revolution this took the form of money and arms funneled secretly to the Americans. By the end of the war the French were contributing troops and naval support as well.

For the French monarchy, assisting the Americans turned out to be a fatal mistake, for two reasons. First, since the American Revolution was understood to be a rebellion against a monarchy, the rhetoric justifying the revolution promoted such concepts as liberty, equality, and the rights of man. French soldiers fighting beside the Americans returned to France inspired by democratic ideals and by a conviction that such ideals could actually be put into practice. Second, the financial burden of a renewed conflict with Britain brought the king's financial dealings to the attention of the Estates General (the French parliament), which was among the important events leading to the French Revolution in 1789. The French king might have done better to save his money and keep his troops at home.

Samuel Flagg Bemis (1891–1973) was the Stirling Professor of

Samuel Flagg Bemis, *The Diplomacy of the American Revolution*, Bloomington: Indiana University Press, 1957.

Diplomatic and Inter-American Relations at Yale from 1935 to 1960. He received two Pulitzer Prizes for his work on American diplomatic history. In this selection he looks at the American Revolution from the French perspective.

———

That [French minister of foreign affairs Étienne-François de] Choiseul and his successors at Versailles were determined to undo the prostration of their country in 1763 by getting revenge on Great Britain as soon as the proper opportunity should present itself is the basic explanation of French foreign policy from 1763 to 1783. The American Revolution presented that opportunity.

FRANCE TRIES TO REGAIN ITS POSITION

Though France immediately after the Peace of Paris reconciled herself to a renunciation of colonial interests on the continent of North America, she never accepted, except by *force majeure*, the status of a cipher in European international politics—and France was as near a cipher after 1763 as such a power can be. No sooner had the Peace of Paris been settled than Choiseul turned his attention and energy to that necessary rebuilding of military and naval power and of the finances, so indispensable if the monarchy were to retrieve its position as a great power, and to a study of ways and means to bolster the diplomatic position of France *vis-à-vis* England. There is no evidence that he had purposely ceded Canada to Great Britain, as some historians once guessed, in order to remove the need of the English colonies in America for protection against the French on their northern frontier. But it is certain that he realized the political significance of the cession of Canada in the development of an independent spirit in America and that he began to study the American situation most attentively, with the definite hope that Britain's troubles with the colonies might be France's opportunity.

Choiseul sent secret observers to the English Colonies in America in 1764 and thereafter to report on the military resources of Great Britain and the political temper of the colonists. England herself was overrun by his spies. These persons found much more preference in their employer's favor when they reported what he wanted to believe—that an American rebellion was close at hand—than they did when they reported (as did the cool-headed [soldier Johann Kalb], who visited the Colonies

after the Stamp Act had been repealed) that there was little immediate likelihood that discontented Americans would seek
French assistance to settle grievances with England. Choiseul
fell from power in 1770, convinced that insurrection in America
and consequent independence were sure in the future, though
not in his generation. Before he quitted office he had already diverted his attention to a study of the chance of combating Great
Britain in the field of strictly European diplomacy, but he left
the French Foreign Office full of reports and memoranda on the
colonial difficulties of Great Britain and France's prime interest
therein. This material served for useful reference when, four
years later, [Charles Gravier] de Vergennes became Minister of
Foreign Affairs under the new king Louis XVI, in the year 1774,
on the eve of the American Revolution.

Vergennes was a methodical thinker with the habit—so illu-
minating for the historian—of crystallizing his ideas on paper.
When he assumed office in 1774 he mapped out the principles
on which French diplomacy was to operate: maintenance of the
Family Compact with Spain as the essential mainstay of
France's military and naval support against England; holding
to the Austrian alliance of 1756 in a purely defensive sense
only—it might prevent England from setting Prussia against the
Rhine again, in case of Anglo-French troubles; eventual war
with England only when France could envisage such a contin-
gency with a sure chance of success; in short, the policy of
Choiseul in the hands of a more circumspect and prudent man.
To Vergennes was to come France's opportunity, for which
Choiseul had waited in vain.

TROUBLE IN THE ENGLISH COLONIES

Vergennes's first reaction to the news of the American troubles
of Great Britain was one of perspicacious but cautious interest.
The alert French chargé at London . . . pointed out the international significance of Britain's predicament. He reported, as
early as December 19, 1774, that friends of the insurgents had
approached him with suggestions of an alliance, or at least the
secret assistance of France. They had mentioned the precedent
afforded by the British in supplying munitions to the Corsicans,
in their insurrection against France a few years before. To
French observers in 1774, however, the American insurrection
appeared at first merely as the reflection of issues in English
party politics, which might cease at any time with the fall of the

actual ministry. In that way the earlier troubles over the colonial Stamp Tax had abruptly ended. In such an overturn Vergennes and every Frenchman feared a possible return of Lord Chatham [William Pitt] to leadership of the British Government. The correspondence of the French Foreign Office for 1774 and the first half of 1775 was full of alarm as to this contingency.

It was well known that the former prime minister had considered the Peace of Paris too lenient. In Paris they really feared that if Chatham came back to power he might heal the breach with the Colonies and then, uniting American and assembled British forces, descend on the French West India Islands and the colonial possessions of Spain. This possibility undoubtedly speeded French and Spanish military and naval preparation, but it lost its real horror when the British prohibitory acts and proclamations were announced to the world and made it apparent that the American Revolution would become a long and bitter contest. After that Vergennes reverted to this danger when it suited his purpose to argue to the King of France or of Spain for a policy of intervention in American affairs. The predicament of England became so involved after 1775 that it is impossible to believe that he was really afraid of any immediate danger from a British attack in American waters. Had the French and Spanish powers cared to remain passive spectators of the American Revolution, they could have had adequate assurances and guaranties from England for the security of their American possessions. They were in no real danger. It is significant that Vergennes carefully avoided any opportunity for an understanding with the British as to the safety of French and Spanish possessions and rejected British offers for mutual limitation of armaments on the ground that any such arrangement would leave the British forces superior to those of the French and Spanish. What Vergennes wanted was not the continuance of peace with Great Britain but a chance to meet that power, on better than even terms, in a war for the recovery of French power and prestige.

Realization that the opportunity for reversing the balance of British power was imminent began to dawn on Vergennes in the summer of 1775 after promptings from the adventurous courtier and dramatist [Pierre-Augustin] Caron de Beaumarchais. It was in these very summer months that the young author of *The Barber of Seville*, now a French political agent in London who had developed abundant contacts with English and American radicals in that city, began to send in to Vergennes ob-

servations on the course of contemporary English politics, particularly on the American question. We do not know what the
text of these earliest reports was, and because of this we cannot
trace precisely the initiative behind them or the exact measure
of their influence on French policy; at any rate Beaumarchais
crossed to France in September, 1775, and had long conferences
with Vergennes and Sartine, the Minister of Marine, on the matter of establishing some sort of understanding with the American insurrectionists. It was on this occasion that he drew up for
the King's perusal his first memorial on the American crisis. He
pictured it as likely to produce great political turbulence in England, even a civil war, if the [Lord Frederick] North Ministry
should be overthrown. "It is indispensable to have a superior
and vigilant man in London at present," he said, reflecting on
the ineptitude of the regular ambassador there. Equipped with
a supply of secret service money, and understanding that he
was in no way to compromise anybody, he went back to London, as he wrote Vergennes, "well informed of the King's intentions and your own." These intentions are not revealed, but
Beaumarchais alludes, in another letter, to "the necessity of undertaking, the facility of doing, the certainty of succeeding, and
the immense harvest of glory and repose which this little sow-
ing of seed will yield to his reign."

Coincident with Beaumarchais's urgings Vergennes in September, 1775 sent to the English Colonies a secret observer, who
had previously traveled in America and therefore knew something of the country and language. This officer, Achard de Bonvouloir, had verbal instructions to assure colonial leaders that
France did not want to get back Canada and was far from being unfriendly to the independence of the old English Colonies.
On the contrary, she admired the greatness and nobleness of
their efforts. "Without any interest to harm them we would be
pleased to see fortunate circumstances enable them to frequent
our ports; the facilities which they would find there for their
commerce would soon prove the esteem which we hold for
them." Bonvouloir was not to make any official representations.
He must not commit the French Ministry to anything.

PERSUADING THE FRENCH KING

Thereafter Beaumarchais, again in Paris, addressed another letter, December 7, 1775, to the King, the purpose of which was to
overcome royal personal scruples which revolted at "the pro-

posed expedient." "The objection, then," wrote Beaumarchais, "has no bearing on the immense utility of the project, nor on the danger of carrying it out, but solely on the delicate conscientiousness of your Majesty. . . . But, Sire, the policy of governments is not the moral law of their citizens. . . . It is the English, Sire, which it concerns you to humiliate and to weaken, if you do not wish to be humiliated and weakened yourself on every occasion."

The project alluded to was that of assisting the American insurrectionists by supplying them with munitions, and even money, in so secret a way as not to compromise the French authorities.

While Vergennes was watching the situation and standing ready to present his American policy to the King for approval, Bonvouloir's report from Philadelphia arrived, February 27, 1776, assuring the French Government that the revolted Colonies were rapidly preparing to assert their independence and to fight for it, and telling of the hopes he had given—without committing the French Ministry—to expect shelter for their trade in French harbors, perhaps even more material assistance. It was immediately following reception in Paris of Bonvouloir's communication that Beaumarchais sent his famous "Peace or War" memoir "to the King alone," which first went to Vergennes unsealed. Perhaps Beaumarchais had read Bonvouloir's report, but most likely his new memoir was based rather on representations made to him by an American in London, Arthur Lee, the correspondent of the Secret Committee of Correspondence of the Continental Congress. These he reported to be to the effect that if the American insurrectionists should become too discouraged at the futility of their efforts to obtain from the French Ministry aid in the shape of powder and munitions, they might in exasperation join forces to those of England and fall on the French sugar islands. After analyzing the British colonial situation, Beaumarchais put the question to the King:

> What shall we do in this extremity to win peace and save our islands?
>
> Sire, the only means is to give help to the Americans, so as to make their forces equal to those of England. . . . Believe me, Sire, the saving of a few millions to-day soon may cause a great deal of blood to flow, and money to be lost to France.

If it is replied that we cannot aid the Americans without drawing upon us a storm, I reply that this danger can be averted if the plan be adopted which I have so often proposed, to aid the Americans secretly.

The fact that Vergennes allowed this memoir to go up to the King is revealing of his new decision as to policy, as is the fact that on March 1 Vergennes sent a despatch to Grimaldi, the Spanish Foreign Minister, asking if Spain would be prepared to join France in rendering secret assistance to the Americans. Beaumarchais's arguments are generally credited with having overcome the scruples of Louis XVI. . . .

The King followed the advice of Vergennes and Beaumarchais, with results so fatal to that young monarch, so beneficial for America. He decided for secret assistance to the Colonists and directed, May 2, 1776, that one million *livres* be supplied to them, in the shape of munitions, through Beaumarchais, disguised as a private trader under the fictitious name of Roderigue Hortalez and Company. [Controller General of Finance Anne-Robert-Jacques] Turgot resigned May 12, leaving Vergennes as the dominating influence in the government. Thus, before an American agent had set foot on the soil of France, the French Ministry, actuated by coolly calculated motives of European international policy connected with the principle of the balance of power, had decided to offer secret assistance to the Colonies and was looking to a war with Great Britain as soon as the opportune moment should arrive. Informed by Louis XVI of his recent gift of a million, "under the title of a loan," Charles III of Spain matched it with another million, to be distributed to the Americans through the same source, according to an understanding already reached between the two courts. It was the first of a series of loans and subsidies from both powers which enabled the United States to go forward with the rebellion.

THE FALL OF SAVANNAH

ARCHIBALD CAMPBELL

George Washington's strategy of avoiding direct confrontations could not bring the Americans a decisive victory, but by 1778 he had achieved a stalemate in the northern colonies. At that point the action shifted to the southern colonies, where again the British won most of the battles.

Lieutenant Colonel Archibald Campbell was one of the few British officers whose reputation was actually enhanced by the American Revolution. After fighting in the Seven Years' War, where he was wounded at the Battle of Quebec, he served in India as a military engineer. He returned to America in 1776 in command of the British Seventy-first Highlanders but was promptly captured when General Richard Howe abandoned Boston without alerting other British ships of his retreat. Campbell's troops sailed into the city unaware that it was in enemy hands. Campbell spent the next two years as a prisoner of war. He was finally released during a prisoner exchange that involved the return of captured patriot leader Ethan Allen to the Americans. Campbell returned to his command and led numerous successful campaigns in Georgia, including the capture of Savannah in 1779. He gained a reputation as a humane soldier in a region where the war had taken on a particularly brutal character. This selection is a businesslike report on the capture of Savannah from Lieutenant Colonel Campbell to his superior, Lord George Germain.

Archibald Campbell, "Lieutenant Colonel Archibald Campbell to Lord George Germain," *The Spirit of 'Seventy-Six: The Story of the American Revolution as Told by Participants*, vol. II, edited by Henry Steele Commager and Richard B. Morris, Bobbs-Merrill, 1958.

I n consequence of Sir Henry Clinton's orders to proceed to Georgia with His Majesty's Seventy-first Regiment of Foot, two battalions of Hessians, four battalions of Provincials and a detachment of the Royal Artillery, I have the honor to acquaint your lordship of our having sailed from the Hook on the 27th of November, 1778, escorted by a squadron of His Majesty's ships of war under the command of Commodore [Peter] Parker; and of the arrival of the whole fleet off the island of Tybee on the 23rd of December thereafter, two horse-sloops excepted.

THE LANDING AT GERRIDOE'S PLANTATION

Having no intelligence that could be depended upon with respect to the military force of Georgia or the disposition formed for its defence, Sir James Baird's Highland company of light-infantry, in two flat-boats, with Lieutenant Clark of the Navy, was dispatched in the night of the 25th to seize any of the inhabitants they might find on the banks of Wilmington Creek. Two men were procured by this means, by whom we learned the most satisfactory intelligence concerning the state of matters at Savannah, and which settled the Commodore and I in the resolution of landing the troops the next evening at the plantation of one Gerridoe, an important post. This post was the first practicable landing-place on the Savannah River; the whole country between it and Tybee being a continued tract of deep marsh, intersected by the creeks of St. Augustine and Tybee, of considerable extent, and other cuts of water, impassable for troops at any time of the tide.

The *Vigilant*, man-of-war, with the *Comet*, galley, the *Keppel*, armed brig, and the *Greenwich*, armed sloop, followed by the transports in the divisions, in the order established for a descent, proceeded up the river with the tide at noon; about 4 o'clock in the evening the *Vigilant* opened the reach to Gerridoe's plantation and was cannonaded by two rebel galleys, who retired before any of their bullets had reached her: a single shot from the *Vigilant* quickened their retreat.

The tide and evening being too far spent, and many of the transports having grounded at the distance of five or six miles below Gerridoe's plantation, the descent was indispensably delayed till next morning. The first division of the troops, consisting of all the light-infantry of the army, the New York Volunteers and first battalion of the Seventy-first under the command of Lieutenant-colonel Maitland, were landed at break of day on the river-dam, in front of Gerridoe's plantation, from whence a narrow causeway of six hundred yards in length, with a ditch on each side, led through a rice-swamp directly to Gerridoe's house, which stood upon a bluff of thirty feet in height above the level of the rice-swamps.

The light-infantry, under Captain Cameron, having first reached the shore, were formed and led briskly forward to the bluff, where a body of fifty rebels were posted, and from whom they received a smart fire of musketry, but the Highlanders, rushing on with their usual impetuosity, gave them no time to repeat it: they drove them instantly to the woods and happily secured a landing for the rest of the army. Captain Cameron, a spirited and most valuable officer, with two Highlanders, were killed on this occasion, and five Highlanders wounded.

THE ASSAULT ON SAVANNAH

Upon the reconnoitering the environs of Gerridoe's plantation, I discovered the rebel army, under Major-general Robert Howe, drawn up about half a mile east of the town of Savannah, with several pieces of cannon in their front. The first division of troops, together with one company of the second battalion of the Seventy-first, the first battalion of Delancey's, the Wellworth, and part of the Weissenbach regiment of Hessians, being landed, I thought it expedient, having the day before me, to go in quest of the enemy rather than give them an opportunity of retiring unmolested.

A company of the second battalion of the Seventy-first, together with the first battalion of Delancey's, were accordingly left to cover the landing-place, and the troops marched for the town of Savannah.

The troops reached the open country near Tatnal's plantation before three o'clock in the evening and halted in the great road about two hundred paces short of the gate leading to Governor Wright's plantation, the light-infantry excepted, who were ordered to form immediately upon our right of the road, along the rails leading to Governor Wright's plantation.

The enemy were drawn up across the road at the distance of eight hundred yards from this gateway. One half, consisting of Thompson's and Eugee's [Huger's] regiments of Carolina troops, were formed under Colonel Eugee, with their left obliquely to the great road leading to Savannah, their right to a wooded swamp, covered by the houses of Tatnal's plantation, in which they had placed some riflemen. The other half of their regular troops, consisting of part of the first, second, third and fourth battalions of the Georgia brigade, was formed under Colonel Elbert, with their right to the road and their left to the rice-swamps of Governor Wright's plantation, with the fort of Savannah Bluff behind their left wing, in the style of second flank; the town of Savannah, round which they had the remains of an old line of intrenchment, covered their rear. One piece of cannon was planted on the right of their line, one upon the left, and two pieces occupied the traverse, across the great road, in the centre of their line. About one hundred paces in front of this traverse, at a critical spot between two swamps, a trench was cut across the road, and about one hundred yards in front of this trench, a marshy rivulet ran almost parallel the whole extent of their front, the bridge of which was burned down to interrupt the passage and retard our progress.

I could discover from the movements of the enemy that they wished and expected an attack upon their left, and I was desirous of cherishing that opinion.

Having accidentally fallen in with a Negro who knew a private path through the wooded swamp upon the enemy's right, I ordered the first battalion of the Seventy-first to form on our right of the road and move up to the rear of the light-infantry, whilst I drew off that corps to the right as if I meant to extend my front to that quarter, where a happy fall of ground favored the concealment of this manoeuvre, and increased the jealousy of the enemy with regard to their left. Sir James Baird had directions to convey the light-infantry in this hollow ground quite to the rear and penetrate the wooded swamp upon our left, with a view to get round by the new barracks into the rear of the enemy's right flank. The New York volunteers, under Colonel Trumbull, were ordered to support him.

During the course of this movement, our artillery were formed in a field on our left of the road, concealed from the enemy by a swell of ground in front, to which I meant to run them up for action when the signal was made to engage, and from whence I could either bear advantageously upon the right of the rebel line, as it was then formed, or cannonade any body of troops in flank which they might detach into the wood to retard the progress of the light-infantry.

The regiment of Wellworth was formed upon the left of the artillery, and the enemy continued to amuse themselves with their cannon without any return upon our part till it was visible that Sir James Baird and the light-infantry had fairly got round upon their rear. On this occasion I commanded the line to move briskly forward. The well-directed artillery of the line, the rapid advance of the Seventy-first Regiment and the forward countenance of the Hessian regiment of Wellworth instantly dispersed the enemy.

A body of the militia of Georgia, posted at the new barracks with some pieces of cannon to cover the road from Great Ogeeche, were at this juncture routed, with the loss of their artillery, by the light-infantry under Sir James Baird, when the scattered troops of the Carolina and Georgia brigades ran across the plain in his front. This officer with his usual gallantry dashed the light-infantry on their flank and terminated the fate of the day with brilliant success.

Thirty-eight officers of different distinctions, and four hundred and fifteen non-commissioned officers and privates, one stand of colors, forty-eight pieces of cannon, twenty-three mortars, ninety-four barrels of powder, the fort with all its stores, agreeable to the inclosed return, and, in short, the capital of Georgia, the shipping in the harbor, with a large quantity of provisions, fell into our possession before it was dark, without any other loss on our side than that of Captain Peter Campbell, a gallant officer of Skinner's light-infantry, and two privates killed, one sergeant and nine privates wounded. Eighty-three of the enemy were found dead on the Common, and eleven wounded. By the accounts received from their prisoners, thirty lost their lives in the swamp, endeavoring to make their escape.

Guerrilla Resistance in the Swamps of South Carolina

Paul A. Thomsen

The war in the South had a very different character from the war in the North. The war in the North was clearly a war between a European power and its breakaway colonies. Most of the soldiers in British uniform were actually from Britain and felt they were fighting on foreign soil. In the South the war seemed more like a civil war. Most of the soldiers in British uniform were American loyalists fighting against their own neighbors. As a result, the war in the South was particularly brutal, with atrocities committed on both sides. However, as in the North, the Revolution was won by avoiding direct confrontation, picking battles wisely, and eventually fighting the British to a draw. In this selection Paul A. Thomsen, who writes for *American History* magazine, describes how General Francis Marion employed this strategy to drive the British out of South Carolina and earn his nickname, "the Swamp Fox."

B y the fall of 1780, Charles Earl Cornwallis, the military governor in the rebellious colony of South Carolina, was feeling increasingly frustrated. Especially galling to the British general was a rag-tag band of guerrillas whose pinprick attacks had routed American Tories and even well-trained British

Paul A. Thomsen, "The Devil Himself Could Not Catch Him," *American History*, vol. 35, August 2000. Copyright © by *American History*. Reproduced by permission.

regulars. "The whole country between Pedee and Santee [rivers] has ever since been in an absolute state of rebellion, every friend of Government has been carried off, and his plantation destroyed," Cornwallis raged. "Some parties had even crossed the Santee and carried terror to the gates of Charlestown."

Yet only six months earlier Cornwallis had reported, with some satisfaction, that he had "put an end to all resistance in South Carolina." In truth, the American cause had looked bleak in the summer of 1780. Charleston had surrendered to the British in May, and on August 16 at the battle of Camden, Cornwallis's army had soundly beaten forces commanded by General Horatio Gates, the hero of Saratoga. In addition, British cavalry leader Banastre Tarleton had triumphed in a series of bold and lightning-fast attacks against Rebel forces. Just two days after Camden, Tarleton routed Patriots under Thomas "The Gamecock" Sumter at Fishing Creek. Sumter, who had literally been caught napping, was forced to flee coatless and on an unsaddled horse to avoid capture. "It was a perfect rout, and an indiscriminate slaughter," Tarleton said.

THE SWAMP FOX

Still, the Rebels continued to bedevil the British. One of the main sources of Cornwallis's frustration was a small band of men commanded by Francis Marion, a man who would become legendary for his skillful exploitation of the swamps and backwoods of South Carolina. Tarleton himself would give Marion the nickname by which he is still remembered: "The Swamp Fox."

The Revolutionary War battles in the northern colonies tend to receive the most attention in the history books, but the fighting in the south was even more bitter and divisive, in South Carolina, especially, the conflict had the character of a civil war, with American Tories loyal to King George III battling their neighbors. Personal animosity ran deep and led to savage reprisals by Rebels and Tories alike. It was, wrote one of Marion's men years later, "such a bloody warfare . . . as is seldom recorded in the annals of even civil commotion."

A number of American heroes emerged from the struggle, men like Sumter, cavalry leader "Light Horse Harry" Lee, Nathanael Greene, and Francis Marion. "While Sumter stands conspicuous for bold daring, fearless intrepidity and always resolute behavior; while Lee takes eminent rank as a gallant Captain of Cavalry, the eye and the wing of the southern liberating army under Greene," wrote William Gilmore Simms in 1844, "Marion is proverbially the great master of strategy—the wily fox of the swamps—never to be caught, never to be followed,— yet always at hand, with unconjectured promptness, at the moment when he is least feared and is least to be expected. His preeminence in this peculiar and most difficult of all kinds of warfare, is not to be disputed."

Born around 1732 in Berkeley County, South Carolina, Marion initially hoped for a career as a sailor but changed his mind after a shipwreck forced him and his crew members to survive for a week aboard a lifeboat, with only a ship's dog for nourishment. In 1759, when sporadic border disputes erupted into the Cherokee War, the short, scrawny, and swarthy young colonial volunteered his services as an Indian fighter. Marion, with other future revolutionaries like Sumter, William Moultrie, and Andrew Pickens, fought alongside British infantry against the Cherokees. "He was an active, brave and hardy soldier, and an excellent partisan officer," said Moultrie. On one occasion Marion and his men deliberately walked into a Cherokee ambush so they could buy time for the rest of the army to circle around and fall on the enemy from the rear. It was the kind of tactic Marion would later employ to great effect against the British.

Marion took up arms again for the American War of Independence. When the British tried to capture Charleston in June 1776, Major Marion was one of the Americans under Colonel Moultrie who thwarted them at the Battle of Sullivan's Island. Four years later the British returned and took Charleston, but an accident kept Marion from being captured when the city fell in May. In March he had been at a dinner party where the host had locked the doors so his guests would have to participate in some serious drinking. Marion, who drank little if at all, departed by jumping from a second-story window, but broke his ankle. Unable to fight, he returned to his home on the Santee River north of Charleston to recuperate and often had to hide from British troops searching for Rebels.

By August his ankle had mended, and he and a band of about 20 men joined up with [Horatio] Gates' army. The regulars of the Continental Army were unimpressed by Marion and his men. Wrote one officer, "[T]heir appearance was in fact so burlesque that it was with much difficulty the diversion of the regular soldiery was restrained by the officers; and the general himself was glad of an opportunity of detaching Colonel Marion, at his own insistence, towards the interior of South Carolina, with orders to watch the motions of the enemy and furnish intelligence."

Lieutenant Colonel (later Brigadier General) Marion left Gates to take command of militia in South Carolina's Williamsburg district. His initial band consisted of 60 ill-equipped fighters ranging from teenagers and Cherokee War veterans to the elder settlers of the territory who had been on the run since the British invasion the previous May. The demoralized band of Patriots had taken refuge in eastern South Carolina's swampy woodlands. When Marion arrived at the makeshift camp, he wore a crimson jacket and a leather cap with a silver crescent inscribed with the words "Liberty or Death." "He was a stranger to the officers and men, and they flocked about him to obtain a sight of their future commander," recalled William James, who joined Marion's men when he was only 15. "He was rather below the middle stature, lean and swarthy. His body was well set, but his knees and ankles were badly formed, and he still limped upon one leg. He had a countenance remarkably steady; his nose was aquiline, his chin projecting; his forehead large and high and his eyes black and piercing. He was then 48 years of age; with the frame capable of enduring fatigue and every privation necessary for a partisan."

Within days, Gates and the Continentals who had sneered at Marion and his men lost to Cornwallis at Camden. Upon receiving the news, Marion calculated his enemies' next likely course of action and immediately turned to intercept them. Near Nelson's Ferry, he made a surprise dawn attack on the 63rd Guard and Prince of Wales Regiment. Though the British infantry's ranks had been bolstered by Tory replacements, Marion's men killed 22 regulars, took two Tories as prisoners, and freed more than 150 Continentals taken prisoner at Camden. The Rebels suffered only one fatality.

Cornwallis responded by sending Major James Wemyss to take care of the nettlesome band. Outnumbered, Marion left the region. Wemyss responded with an orgy of burning, pillaging, and hanging that only served to drive more men to Marion's brigade. Even Cornwallis realized the futility of Wemyss's heavy-handed tactics when he received the major's report. "Your account is not so agreeable," he responded.

During the next few months Marion and his men conducted a series of pinprick attacks against the British and their Tory allies. At Britton's Neck they caught a Tory contingent unawares and managed to kill several of them, drive off their horses, and send the survivors fleeing into the wilderness, at the cost of only two wounded Patriots. At a swampy spot called Blue Savannah, Marion found a Tory force that outnumbered him almost four to one. Falling back on the tactics he had learned in the Cherokee War, Marion detached some of his men with orders to skirmish with the Loyalists, then feign a retreat to lure the enemy into an ambush.

Like all guerrilla leaders, Marion faced difficulties unknown to a regular army. Often miles away from a physician and dangerously low on munitions, he could afford few casualties. Many of Marion's men were farmers, and experience taught him to let them return to their homesteads for planting, harvesting, or other family necessities, asking only that they return as soon as possible. As a result, the number of men under his command varied widely, ranging from only a handful to around 500. At one point his numbers were so low that Marion threatened to resign his command and join the Rebel army in North Carolina. He regained his spirits only after more volunteers finally began to trickle into camp.

Marion's strength lay in his ability to move and strike quickly where he was least expected. "The general's favourite time for moving was at the sitting sun, and then it was expected the march would continue all night," wrote William James. "But the present time, and afterwards, before striking any sudden blow, he has been known to march sixty or seventy miles, without taking any other refreshment, than a meal of cold potatoes and a drink of cold water, in twenty-four hours. During this period men were but badly clothed in homespun, which afforded little warmth. They slept in the open air, according to their means, either with or without a blanket. They had nothing but water to drink. They fed chiefly upon sweet potatoes, either with or without fresh beef. And they submitted to this without a murmur; but all sighed for salt! for salt! that first article of necessity for the human race."

"BLOODY BAN" JOINS THE HUNT

During the following weeks Cornwallis threw every free regiment at Marion's forces, but none came close to capturing the wily and cautious partisan commander. Relentlessly striking Tory patrols, British convoys, and enemy encampments, Marion quickly grew from a minor embarrassment into a major threat to British supply lines. Cornwallis realized that he needed a skilled hunter with a reputation for ruthless pursuit. He found those qualities in 26-year-old Lieutenant Colonel Banastre Tarleton.

Although young, Tarleton was a cool and efficient soldier who excelled at tracking and neutralizing rebel factions. The Americans hated the man they called "Bloody Ban" after his troops bayoneted Rebels attempting to surrender at the Waxhaws (near Lancaster), South Carolina. Sometimes ruthless but always ready to strike when least expected, Tarleton had proven himself to be a worthy adversary.

In the summer of 1780 a case of yellow fever put Tarleton out of action, but he studied Marion's tactics while in his sickbed. "MR. Marion by his zeal and abilities showed himself capable of the trust committed to his charge," he wrote. "He collected his adherents at the shortest notice, and after making excursions into the friendly districts, or threatening the communications, to avoid pursuit he disbanded his followers. The alarms occasioned by these insurrections, frequently retarded supplies on their way to the army, and a late report of Marion's strength delayed the junction of the recruits who had arrived from New York for the corps in the country."

Tarleton finally rose from his sickbed after he received a letter he'd been anticipating. Cornwallis was finally sending him to "get at MR. Marion." Joining with the 64th British Infantry Regiment, "Bloody Ban" set out to follow his orders.

Tarleton had not been the only one studying his adversary. Marion's scouts had also been keeping watch on Tarleton. While ill he had been of little consequence, but in November the British colonel was spotted leaving Charleston with a large body of men. Marion quickly ordered 150 of his militia to gather at Nelson's Ferry, anticipating that Tarleton would pass there. After two days of futile waiting, Marion learned that Tarleton and his men had taken another route.

The scouts soon located their quarry. Marching the better part of the night, Marion's men reached a defensible position in the woods before setting up camp for the night. They hadn't settled in when Marion noticed the telltale flickering of campfires beyond the woods, evidence that Tarleton had arrived. But before Marion could order his men to their horses, a Colonel Richard Richardson dashed into the camp with news. Tarleton had arrived at the Richardson family plantation, but the British force was twice the size of Marion's and carried two field pieces. Worst of all, Tarleton was gaining information about the Americans' plans from a Tory prisoner who had escaped from their camp, and had prepared an ambush.

Fearing the prisoner would lead "Bloody Ban" to the brigade's campsite, Marion ordered an immediate retreat across a large swamp called the Wood-yards and through what one member later recalled as "the most profound darkness." After marching some six miles to a defendable pass, Marion called a halt.

"Now we are safe!" he declared.

He was right to be cautious, for Tarleton's guide did direct the British to Marion's first camp. Their commander easily deduced Marion's escape route and followed his prey, dividing his corps into several smaller, more rapidly advancing groups, spread out so that the Rebels could not double back.

In the past Tarleton had made his attacks quickly, routing his enemies before they were even aware of his approach. Facing Marion, he moved more deliberately. By the time the British officer finally resolved to move forward and attack, Marion and his men had once again faded into the swamps. This time he marched his men through woods, swamps, and bogs with neither roads nor paths. By dusk the Rebels had traveled 35 miles down the Black River to Benbow's Ferry (about 10 miles above Kingstree). There, Marion ordered trees felled across the area's only roadway and once more prepared his men to set an ambush for the British.

Tarleton had determined that Marion's route was impassable for his contingent and ordered a course parallel to the Rebels' probable line of retreat. Traveling about 25 miles through barely passable terrain, Tarleton finally halted at a wide and deep body of murky water called Ox Swamp. Here he decided to give up the chase. "Come my boys," he declared to his men. "Let us go back, and we will soon find 'The Gamecock,' but as for this damned old fox, the devil himself could not catch him." Tarleton spurred his horse away from the swamp, leaving behind the nickname by which Marion is still remembered.

"Had Tarleton proceeded with his jaded horses to Benbow's," William James later recalled, "he would have exposed his force to such sharp shooting as he had not yet experienced, and that in a place where he could not have acted either with his artillery or cavalry." Unable to capture the Swamp Fox, Tarleton took out his frustration on the local population by burning homes and de-

stroying livestock. He came down especially hard on the
Richardson plantation, burning all the livestock in the barn,
torching the house, and forcing the family to watch as his men
dug up the body of General Richard Richardson, Colonel
Richardson's father, who had died six weeks previously. Tarleton
said he wanted to teach the rebellious population the "'Error of
Insurrection,' as he put it, with the application of terror—the traditional and usually ineffective tactic of regulars trying to defeat
guerrillas," as John Buchanan wrote in *The Road to Guilford Courthouse*, his history of the Revolution in South Carolina.

THE BRITISH ABANDON SOUTH CAROLINA

Several weeks after the aborted pursuit, secure in his winter retreat on Snow's Island, Francis Marion received news about
Bloody Ban in a letter from General Nathanael Greene, who had
taken over for Gates. At the Battle of Cowpens, militia under
General Daniel Morgan had badly mauled Tarleton and his
British regulars. "The action lasted fifty minutes and was remarkably severe," Greene wrote. "Colonel Tarleton had his
horse killed and was wounded, but made his escape with 200
of his troops." From this point on until the war's end, Tarleton's
fortunes flagged.

Tarleton's decline merely reflected that of the British effort in
South Carolina. A few months later, Cornwallis abandoned the
colony. Unable to staunch the wounds Marion and other American leaders were opening across his occupied territory, and
with his army weary and bloodied in a long campaign that
ended with a narrow, costly victory over Greene at Guilford
Courthouse, the military governor declared he was "quite tired
of marching about the country in quest of adventures." Cornwallis decided to take his army north to Virginia—where he
found his final confrontation of the war at Yorktown.

Cornwallis's defeat sealed the fate of the Loyalist cause in the
colonies. Many of South Carolina's Tories fled for British-
controlled territory as the region's Patriot movement returned
to prominence. Marion remained in South Carolina and continued to make himself a nuisance to the remaining British
forces, so much so that one of his adversaries fumed that the
Rebel guerrilla leader "would not fight like a gentleman and a
Christian."

Marion suffered his greatest personal loss of the war when
his nephew, Gabriel, was captured and killed by Tories. "As the

general had no children, he mourned over this nephew, as would a father over an only son," William James wrote, "but he soon recollected that he had an example to set, and shortly after publicly expressed this consolation for himself—that his nephew was a virtuous young man—that he had fallen in the cause of his country, and he would mourn over him no more."

After the war, Marion continued his career of public service as a state senator, married a wealthy cousin, Mary Esther Videau, in 1786, and died on February 27, 1795, well on his way to becoming a legend. "History affords no instance wherein an officer has kept possession of the country under so many disadvantages as you have," General Greene once wrote him. "To fight the enemy bravely with the prospect of victory is nothing, but to fight with intrepidity under the constant impression of a defeat, and inspire irregular troops to do it, is a talent peculiar to yourself."

Founding a New Nation, 1781–1783

—— CHAPTER 6 ——

THE ARTICLES OF CONFEDERATION

One argument against independence was that the colonies needed a central authority to maintain peace and arbitrate disputes. Under Britain, the government in London supplied that central authority. On the same day that the Second Continental Congress began considering independence—June 7, 1776—it also established a committee charged with planning a permanent central government. That committee produced the Articles of Confederation.

The final version of the Articles of Confederation was agreed to by the Continental Congress on November 15, 1777, but it was not ratified by the states until March 1, 1781. The new central government created by the Articles of Confederation was named "The United States of America," and the governing body of that new nation was referred to as "the United States in Congress assembled." This governing body was closely patterned after the Continental Congress. Each state could send up to seven delegates to Congress, but each delegation could cast only a single vote. There was no provision for executive or judicial branches of government. Congress had the power to wage wars; conduct foreign affairs, including Indian affairs; issue money; and establish post offices. To resolve various land disputes among the states, Congress took possession of disputed western lands. However, Congress had no power to impose taxes and could not force states to comply with its laws. These limitations made the central government too weak to be effective, and in 1789 the Articles of Confederation were replaced by the Constitution of the United States.

"The Articles of Confederation," *The Annals of America, Volume 2: Resistance and Revolution, 1755–1783*, Chicago: Encyclopedia Britannica, 1976.

Article I. The style of this confederacy shall be "The United States of America."

Article II. Each state retains its sovereignty, freedom, and independence, and every power, jurisdiction, and right which is not by this confederation expressly delegated to the United States in Congress assembled.

Article III. The said states hereby severally enter into a firm league of friendship with each other, for their common defense, the security of their liberties, and their mutual and general welfare, binding themselves to assist each other against all force offered to, or attacks made upon them, or any of them, on account of religion, sovereignty, trade, or any other pretense whatever.

Article IV. The better to secure and perpetuate mutual friendship and intercourse among the people of the different states in this union, the free inhabitants of each of these states, paupers, vagabonds, and fugitives from justice excepted, shall be entitled to all privileges and immunities of free citizens in the several states; and the people of each state shall have free ingress and regress to and from any other state and shall enjoy therein all the privileges of trade and commerce, subject to the same duties, impositions, and restrictions as the inhabitants thereof respectively, provided that such restrictions shall not extend so far as to prevent the removal of property imported into any state, to any other state of which the owner is an inhabitant; provided also that no imposition, duties, or restriction shall be laid by any state on the property of the United States, or either of them.

If any person guilty of or charged with treason, felony, or other high misdemeanor in any state shall flee from justice, and be found in any of the United States, he shall, upon demand of the governor or executive power of the state from which he fled, be delivered up and removed to the state having jurisdiction of his offense.

Full faith and credit shall be given in each of these states to the records, acts, and judicial proceedings of the courts and magistrates of every other state.

Article V. For the more convenient management of the general interests of the United States, delegates shall be annually appointed in such manner as the legislature of each state shall direct, to meet in Congress on the first Monday in November, in every year, with a power reserved to each state to recall its delegates, or any of them, at any time within the year and to send others in their stead for the remainder of the year.

No state shall be represented in Congress by less than two nor by more than seven members; and no person shall be capable of being a delegate for more than three years in any term of six years; nor shall any person, being a delegate, be capable of holding any office under the United States for which he, or another for his benefit, receives any salary, fees, or emolument of any kind.

Each state shall maintain its own delegates in a meeting of the states and while they act as members of the Committee of the States.

In determining questions in the United States in Congress assembled, each state shall have one vote.

Freedom of speech and debate in Congress shall not be impeached or questioned in any court or place out of Congress, and the members of Congress shall be protected in their persons from arrests and imprisonments during the time of their going to and from, and attendance on, Congress, except for treason, felony, or breach of the peace.

CONGRESS IS RESPONSIBLE FOR FOREIGN POLICY

Article VI. No state, without the consent of the United States in Congress assembled, shall send any embassy to, or receive any embassy from, or enter into any conference, agreement, alliance, or treaty with any king, prince, or state; nor shall any person holding any office of profit or trust under the United States, or any of them, accept of any present, emolument, office, or title of any kind whatever from any king, prince, or foreign state; nor shall the United States in Congress assembled, or any of them, grant any title of nobility.

No two or more states shall enter into any treaty, confederation, or alliance whatever between them without the consent of the United States in Congress assembled, specifying accurately the purposes for which the same is to be entered into and how long it shall continue.

No state shall lay any imposts or duties which may interfere with any stipulations in treaties entered into by the United States in Congress assembled with any king, prince, or state, in pursuance of any treaties already proposed by Congress, to the courts of France and Spain.

No vessels of war shall be kept up in time of peace by any state except such number only as shall be deemed necessary by the United States in Congress assembled for the defense of such state or its trade; nor shall any body of forces be kept up by any state in time of peace except such number only as in the judgment of the United States in Congress assembled shall be deemed requisite to garrison the forts necessary for the defense of such state; but every state shall always keep up a well-regulated and disciplined militia, sufficiently armed and accoutered, and shall provide and constantly have ready for use, in public stores, a due number of field pieces and tents and a proper quantity of arms, ammunition, and camp equipage.

No state shall engage in any war without the consent of the United States in Congress assembled unless such state be actually invaded by enemies, or shall have received certain advice of a resolution being formed by some nation of Indians to invade such state, and the danger is so imminent as not to admit of a delay till the United States in Congress assembled can be consulted; nor shall any state grant commissions to any ships or vessels of war, nor letters of marque or reprisal, except it be after a declaration of war by the United States in Congress assembled, and then only against the kingdom or state and the subjects thereof against which war has been so declared and under such regulations as shall be established by the United States in Congress assembled, unless such state be infested by pirates, in which case vessels of war may be fitted out for that occasion and kept so long as the danger shall continue or until the United States in Congress assembled shall determine otherwise.

Article VII. When land forces are raised by any state for the common defense, all officers of or under the rank of colonel shall be appointed by the legislature of each state respectively, by whom such forces shall be raised, or in such manner as such state shall direct, and all vacancies shall be filled up by the state which first made the appointment.

Article VIII. All charges of war and all other expenses that shall be incurred for the common defense or general welfare, and allowed by the United States in Congress assembled, shall be defrayed out of a common treasury, which shall be supplied by the several states in proportion to the value of all land within each state, granted to or surveyed for any person, as such land the buildings and improvements thereon shall be estimated according to such mode as the United States in Congress assembled shall from time to time direct and appoint. The taxes for paying that proportion shall be laid and levied by the authority and direction of the legislatures of the several states within the time agreed upon by the United States in Congress assembled.

Article IX. The United States in Congress assembled shall have the sole and exclusive right and power of determining on peace and war, except in the cases mentioned in the sixth article—of sending and receiving ambassadors—entering into treaties and alliances, provided that no treaty of commerce shall be made whereby the legislative power of the respective states shall be restrained from imposing such imposts and duties on foreigners as their own people are subjected to or from prohibiting the exportation or importation of any species of goods or commodities whatsoever—of establishing rules for deciding in all cases what captures on land or water shall be legal, and in what manner prizes taken by land or naval forces in the service of the United States shall be divided or appropriated—of granting letters of marque and reprisal in times of peace—appointing courts for the trial of piracies and felonies committed on the high seas and establishing courts for receiving and determining final appeals in all cases of captures, provided that no member of Congress shall be appointed a judge of any of the said courts.

CONGRESS IS RESPONSIBLE FOR RESOLVING DISPUTES BETWEEN STATES

The United States in Congress assembled shall also be the last resort on appeal in all disputes and difference now subsisting or that hereafter may arise between two or more states concerning boundary, jurisdiction, or any other cause whatever, which authority shall always be exercised in the manner following: Whenever the legislative or executive authority or lawful agent of any state in controversy with another shall present a petition to Congress stating the matter in question and praying for a hearing, notice thereof shall be given by order of Congress to the legislative or executive authority of the other state in controversy, and a day assigned for the appearance of the parties by their lawful agents, who shall then be directed to appoint, by joint consent, commissioners or judges to constitute a court for hearing and determining the matter in question. But if they cannot agree, Congress shall name three persons out of each of the United States, and from the list of such persons each party shall alternately strike out one, the petitioners beginning, until the number shall be reduced to thirteen. And from that number not less than seven nor more than nine names, as Congress shall direct, shall in the presence of Congress be drawn out by lot, and the persons whose names shall be so drawn, or any five of them, shall be commissioners or judges to hear and finally determine the controversy, so always as a major part of the judges who shall hear the cause shall agree in the determination. . . .

If either party shall neglect to attend at the day appointed, without showing reasons, which Congress shall judge sufficient, or being present shall refuse to strike, the Congress shall proceed to nominate three persons out of each state, and the secretary of Congress shall strike in behalf of such party absent or refusing. . . . The judgment and sentence of the court to be appointed, in the manner before prescribed, shall be final and conclusive. . . . If any of the parties shall refuse to submit to the authority of such court, or to appear or defend their claim or cause, the court shall nevertheless proceed to pronounce sentence or judgment, which shall in like manner be final and decisive, the judgment or sentence and other proceedings being in either case transmitted to Congress and lodged among the acts of Congress for the security of the parties concerned. Provided that every commissioner, before he sits in judgment, shall take an oath to be administered by one of the judges of the supreme or superior court of the state where the cause shall be tried, "well and truly to hear and determine the matter in question, according to the best of his judgment, without favor, affection, or hope of reward": provided, also, that no state shall be deprived of territory for the benefit of the United States.

All controversies concerning the private right of soil claimed under different grants of two or more states, whose jurisdictions as they may respect such lands, and the states which passed such grants are adjusted, the said grants or either of them being at the same time claimed to have originated antecedent to such settlement of jurisdiction shall, on the petition of either party to the Congress of the United States, be finally determined as near as may be in the same manner as is before prescribed for deciding disputes respecting territorial jurisdiction between different states.

The United States in Congress assembled shall also have the sole and exclusive right and power of regulating the alloy and value of coin struck by their own authority or by that of the respective states—fixing the standard of weights and measures throughout the United States—regulating the trade and managing all affairs with the Indians not members of any of the states, provided that the legislative right of any state within its own limits be not infringed or violated—establishing or regulating post offices from one state to another, throughout all the United States, and exacting such postage on the papers passing through the same as may be requisite to defray the expenses of the said office—appointing all officers of the land forces in the service of the United States excepting regimental officers—appointing all the officers of the naval forces, and commissioning all officers whatever in the service of the United States—making rules for the government and regulation of the said land and naval forces, and directing their operations.

The United States in Congress assembled shall have authority to appoint a committee, to sit in the recess of Congress, to be denominated "A Committee of the States," and to consist of one delegate from each state; and to appoint such other committees and civil officers as may be necessary for managing the general affairs of the United States under their direction—to appoint one of their number to preside, provided that no person be allowed to serve in the office of President more than one year in any term of three years; to ascertain the necessary sums of money to be raised for the service of the United States, and to appropriate and apply the same for defraying the public expenses—to borrow money or emit bills on the credit of the United States, transmitting every half-year to the respective states an account of the sums of money so borrowed or emitted—to build and equip a navy—to agree upon the number of land forces, and to make requisitions from each state for its quota, in proportion to the number of white inhabitants in such state, which requisition shall be binding. . . .

Thereupon the legislature of each state shall appoint the regimental officers, raise the men and clothe, arm, and equip them in a soldier-like manner, at the expense of the United States; and the officers and men so clothed, armed, and equipped shall march to the place appointed and within the time agreed on by the United States in Congress assembled. But if the United States in Congress assembled shall, on consideration of circumstances, judge proper that any state should not raise men or should raise a smaller number than its quota and that any other state should raise a greater number of men than the quota thereof, such extra number shall be raised, officered, clothed, armed, and equipped in the same manner as the quota of such state, unless the legislature of such state shall judge that such extra number cannot be safely spared out of the same, in which case they shall raise, officer, clothe, arm, and equip as many of such extra number as they judge can be safely spared. And the officers and men so clothed, armed, and equipped shall march to the place appointed and within the time agreed on by the United States in Congress assembled.

THE APPROVAL OF NINE STATES IS REQUIRED

The United States in Congress assembled shall never engage in a war, nor grant letters of marque and reprisal in time of peace, nor enter into any treaties or alliances, nor coin money, nor regulate the value thereof, nor ascertain the sums and expenses necessary for the defense and welfare of the United States, or any of them, nor emit bills, nor borrow money on the credit of the United States, nor appropriate money, nor agree upon the number of vessels of war to be built or purchased or the number of land or sea forces to be raised, nor appoint a commander in chief of the Army or Navy, unless nine states assent to the same; nor shall a question on any other point, except for adjourning from day to day, be determined unless by the votes of a majority of the United States in Congress assembled.

The Congress of the United States shall have power to adjourn to any time within the year, and to any place within the United States, so that no period of adjournment be for a longer duration than the space of six months, and shall publish the journal of their proceedings monthly, except such parts thereof relating to treaties, alliances, or military operations as in their judgment require secrecy; and the yeas and nays of the delegates of each state on any question shall be entered on the journal when it is desired by any delegate; and the delegates of a state, or any of them, at his or their request, shall be furnished with a transcript of the said journal, except such parts as are above excepted, to lay before the legislatures of the several states.

Article X. The Committee of the States, or any nine of them, shall be authorized to execute, in the recess of Congress, such of the powers of Congress as the United States in Congress assembled, by the consent of nine states, shall from time to time think expedient to vest them with; provided that no power be delegated to the said committee, for the exercise of which, by the Articles of Confederation, the voice of nine states in the Congress of the United States assembled is requisite.

Article XI. Canada acceding to this Confederation, and joining in the measures of the United States, shall be admitted into and entitled to all the advantages of this union; but no other colony shall be admitted into the same unless such admission be agreed to by nine states.

Article XII. All bills of credit emitted, moneys borrowed, and debts contracted by or under the authority of Congress, before the assembling of the United States, in pursuance of the present Confederation, shall be deemed and considered as a charge against the United States, for payment and satisfaction whereof the said United States and the public faith are hereby solemnly pledged.

Article XIII. Every state shall abide by the determinations of the United States in Congress assembled on all questions which by this Confederation are submitted to them. And the Articles of this Confederation shall be inviolably observed by every state, and the union shall be perpetual; nor shall any alteration at any time hereafter be made in any of them; unless such alteration be agreed to in a Congress of the United States and be afterward confirmed by the legislatures of every state.

And whereas it has pleased the Great Governor of the world to incline the hearts of the legislatures we respectively represent in Congress to approve of, and to authorize us to ratify the said Articles of Confederation and Perpetual Union. Know ye that we the undersigned delegates, by virtue of the power and authority to us given for that purpose, do by these presents, in the name and in behalf of our respective constituents, fully and entirely ratify and confirm each and every of the said Articles of Confederation and Perpetual Union and all and singular the matters and things therein contained. And we do further solemnly plight and engage the faith of our respective constituents that they shall abide by the determinations of the United States in Congress assembled on all questions which by the said Confederation are submitted to them. And that the articles thereof shall be inviolably observed by the states we respectively represent and that the union shall be perpetual. In witness whereof we have hereunto set our hands in Congress.

THE ANTISLAVERY MOVEMENT DURING THE AMERICAN REVOLUTION

HERBERT APTHEKER

The grievances that sparked the American Revolution involved rather mundane fiscal matters: Taxes, tariffs, and trade restrictions. But the rhetoric used to express these grievances often dealt with high ideals: rights, equality, and freedom. Even William Pitt, speaking against the Stamp Act, had asked rhetorically, "When were they [the Americans] made slaves?" Of course the irony that this high rhetoric was being used on behalf of a people who themselves traded in, and owned, slaves was not lost on everyone. The rhetoric of the Revolution encouraged opponents of slavery to challenge the legality of slavery in courts and to agitate for the passage of laws prohibiting slavery. In the end, the results of these efforts were disappointing. At the end of the revolutionary period slavery was still legal in most states, and the issue was considered too divisive to be raised in a new nation.

Herbert Aptheker is a distinguished scholar of African American history and has written numerous books on the subject. Before his death, W.E.B. Du Bois selected Aptheker to edit his personal papers and correspondence, and to assist in the preparation of his autobiography. In this selection, Aptheker describes the rise in antislavery sentiment due to revolutionary rhetoric,

Herbert Aptheker, *Essays in the History of the American Negro*, New York: International Publishers, 1964. Copyright © 1964 by International Publishers Co., Inc. Reproduced by permission.

but gives a generally negative assessment of the practical results achieved during this period.

T he struggle of the American colonies for political and economic freedom from Great Britain gave a considerable impetus to the anti-slavery movement. This was anxiously watched and, where possible, aided by the Negro people themselves. In order fully to appreciate the role of the Negro in the American Revolution it is necessary to trace the story of this development and to observe that while some definite advancement was made yet no general clear-cut victory was achieved.

THE RHETORIC OF THE REVOLUTION

In the early literature, setting the stage for the revolutionary upsurge, notice is taken of the inconsistency in struggling for political and economic freedom while depriving hundreds of thousands of their personal freedom. This may, for example, be found in the writings of James Otis, the early leading theoretician of the Revolution, who, in his famous pamphlet called *Rights of the British Colonies* published in Boston in 1764, denounced slavery, affirmed the Negro's inalienable right to freedom and, at least by implication, upheld his right instantly to rebel against his enslavers.

Some of the later literature became even more bold, as when the Reverend Isaac Skillman in his *Oration upon the Beauties of Liberty* (published in Boston in 1772, and in its fourth printing by 1773) demanded the immediate abolition of slavery. In this work the reverend gentleman went as far as abolition literature was ever to go in asserting the slave's right to rebel, for, said he, this act would conform "to the laws of nature."

These same years witnessed the height of Anthony Benezet's anti-slavery work, as well as that of Benjamin Franklin and Benjamin Rush, each of whom widely spread his views. It is also an interesting sign of the spirit of the times to note that the addresses delivered at the commencement exercises of Harvard University at Cambridge, Massachusetts, in July, 1773, were concerned with "the legality of enslaving the Africans." Similar sentiments were expressed by Abigail Adams in telling her husband, John, in September, 1774, upon the discovery of a slave conspiracy in Boston, that "it always appeared a most iniquitous scheme to me to fight ourselves for what we are daily robbing and plundering from those who have as good a right to freedom as we have."

And it is to be remembered that the first article Thomas Paine, the international tribune of the people, ever wrote for publication was entitled "African Slavery in America" and appeared in a Pennsylvania paper of March 8, 1775. In this work Paine denounced slavery, demanded that it be abolished and that the Negroes be given land and the opportunity of earning a livelihood as well as personal liberty.

EFFORTS TO END SLAVERY

There are, too, besides these instances of individual protest (and the above is meant only as a sampling of that type of anti-slavery activity) many evidences of organized opposition to the institution of slavery during the Revolutionary period. Of very considerable importance in this activity, even during this early period, was the work of the Negro people themselves. We have, for example, evidence in John Adams' diary note of November 5, 1766, that Massachusetts slaves attempted, by bringing an action of trespass in the local courts against their masters, to challenge the entire legal concept of slavery. Adams, in reporting his own presence at one such unsuccessful effort, remarked that he had "heard there have been many." But this type of action proved futile.

The Negro people then turned to the application of mass pressure by the presentation of petitions to the legislatures appealing for liberation. There is record of at least eight such attempts, the first of which, appealing for the possibility of earning money with which to purchase freedom, was presented to the Massachusetts General Court in April, 1773. Two months later other slaves petitioned Governor [Thomas] Gage and the same General Court to grant them their freedom, together with land, for, said the Negroes, "they have in common with other men a natural right to be free." Still another "Petition of a Grate Number of Blackes" reached these same individuals in May, 1774, again asking for freedom as a natural right and denouncing slavery as sinful and evil. The next month, and the next year, still other petitions, of similar tenor, were presented.

In the spring of 1775 the Negroes of Bristol and Worcester in Massachusetts petitioned the Committee of Correspondence of the latter county to aid them in obtaining freedom. This resulted in a convention held in Worcester on June 14 at which it was re-

solved by the white inhabitants present "That we abhor the enslaving of any of the human race, and particularly of the Negroes in this country, and that whenever there shall be a door
opened, or opportunity present for anything to be done towards
the emancipation of the Negroes, we will use our influence and
endeavor that such a thing may be brought about." Again, in
January, 1777, many slaves of Massachusetts presented to the
Council and House of Representatives of that State a prayer for
freedom remarking that "they Cannot but express their Astonishment that It has Never Bin Considered that Every Principle
from which America has Acted in the Cours of their unhappy
Deficulties with Great Britain Pleads Stronger than A thousand
arguments in favours of your petitioners."

Slavery was a controversial issue during the American Revolution.

Finally, so far as the available records show, there was the interesting petition for liberty presented by twenty Negroes of
Portsmouth in November, 1779, to the New Hampshire legislature. This declared, in the precise reasoning of the Revolutionary movement itself, "That the God of Nature gave them life and
freedom, upon the terms of most perfect equality with other
men; That freedom is an inherent right of the human species, not
to be surrendered, but by consent, for the sake of social life."

Protests against slavery having an organized and mass origin also arose from the midst of the white people. Thus the religious Society of Friends, or Quakers, made considerable advances during the years of the Revolution towards wiping
slavetrading and slaveholding out of their group and by about
1785 this had generally been accomplished.

Governmental groups also took some steps in that direction.
In 1770 several petitions urging the end of slavery were received
by the Connecticut legislature, which the next year forbade the
slave trade. The New Jersey Assembly also received, in 1773,
anti-slavery petitions from groups of citizens in six counties.
Rhode Island declared, in 1774, that any Negro slave thereafter
brought into the region was to be free, and the preamble to this
law stated that this action was taken because "the inhabitants
of America are generally engaged in the preservation of their
own rights and liberties, among which that of personal freedom
must be considered as the greatest, and as those who are desirous of enjoying all the advantages of liberty themselves
should be willing to extend personal liberty to others." It is,
however, to be observed that the law did not free the slaves (of
which there were some 3,500) then in Rhode Island, though
later legislation permitting them to join the army did, as we
shall see later, have the effect of liberating several hundreds of
Negroes in that state.

Other legal acts or declarations of an anti-slavery outlook
were common. The Braintree, Massachusetts, town meeting, for
example, early in 1774 adopted a resolution promising to ab-
stain from the slave trade and to boycott all who engaged in
that business. Within a year of this action other localities, such
as Providence, Rhode Island; Chester County, Pennsylvania;
Delaware and Georgia, either considered or passed similar measures. The New York City delegation to the Provincial Congress
of the State, headed by John Jay, future first Chief Justice of the
United States Supreme Court, urged, in 1777, the adoption of a
gradual emancipation law. This came close to adoption and
might well have been passed had not John Jay been forced to
absent himself due to the death of his mother. Twenty-two years
were to pass before New York enacted such a law.

The constitution adopted in Vermont in July, 1777, contained
a specific clause appended to the Declaration of Rights directly
forbidding the enslavement of any individual, whether "born
in this country or brought from over sea." In 1780 an emanci-

pation bill was considered by the Connecticut legislature. A law gradually abolishing slavery, and written by Thomas Paine and George Bryan, was passed in Pennsylvania on March 1, 1780.

The liberty and equality clauses in the Massachusetts constitution of 1781 and in the New Hampshire constitution of 1784 were generally considered to have ended, for all practical purposes, the institution of slavery in those states, while in the latter year, 1784, Connecticut enacted a gradual emancipation law. It is also to be noted that Virginia in May, 1782, considerably eased the requirements for the manumission of slaves, but this liberal law, under which hundreds of Negroes were granted their freedom, was repealed within five years.

Similar tendencies came forward too, though rather weakly, on the national scene. Thus, part of the agreement reached in the Continental Association of 1774 called for an end to the foreign slave trade as an expression of both an anti-slavery and an anti-British feeling, the latter because the commerce in slaves was, to a considerable extent, carried on by English merchants. The Continental Congress repeated this action in April, 1776, by resolving that the importation of slaves should stop.

THE REVOLUTION DOES NOT END SLAVERY

There was, of course, latent anti-slavery sentiment in the final Declaration of Independence, particularly in its brave assertions "that all men are created equal, that they are endowed with certain unalienable Rights, that among these are Life, Liberty, and the pursuit of Happiness." It is, moreover, interesting to note that [Thomas] Jefferson's original draft of this immortal manifesto of revolution contained an overt and powerful anti-slavery declaration. In his list of grievances against the British monarch, Jefferson had originally included this statement:

> He has waged cruel war against human nature itself, violating its most sacred rights of life and liberty in the persons of a distant people who never offended him, captivating and carrying them into slavery in another hemisphere, or to incur miserable death in their transportation thither. This piratical warfare, the opprobrium of *infidel* powers, is the warfare of this *Christian* king of Great Britain determined to keep open a market where MEN should be bought and sold.

But this was, at the request of delegates from South Carolina and Georgia, and certain of the slave-trading New England states, deleted from the final copy. Other acts of an even more reprehensible character must be told if we are to understand the actions of a huge number of slaves in seeking freedom where they could—and particularly by flight to the armies of the British.

North Carolina, for example, passed a law in 1777 making the manumission of slaves difficult because "the evil and pernicious Practice of freeing Slaves in this State, ought at this alarming and critical Time to be guarded against by every friend and Well-wisher to his Country." South Carolina, in 1780, reached the depths of infamy, for it then passed a law granting a prime slave as part of the bounty to be given to soldiers volunteering for service in the Revolutionary army. As a matter of fact, this state, together with Georgia, made a practice of partly paying their officials' salaries by giving them slaves.

It may then be declared that the Negro people did receive some benefits from their own agitational efforts and from the increase in anti-slavery sentiment that accompanied the Revolutionary movement, but it is necessary to observe that these benefits generally came late in the period, were rarely far-reaching, and that the attitude of the Southern states, where, of course, the real evil of slavery was concentrated, was not one warranting hope or enthusiasm on the part of the Negro people. Where the Negro could serve his native land and obtain his freedom he gladly did so, but where he discovered that his native land denied him his craving for liberation he turned elsewhere—to arson, rebellion, flight—for it was liberty he wanted, not high-sounding speeches.

THE PROGRESS OF WOMEN DURING THE AMERICAN REVOLUTION

JOAN R. GUNDERSEN

The social changes of the eighteenth century were not necessarily beneficial for women. The increased wealth that came with the consumer revolution meant more leisure, at least for middle-class women, but men and women became increasingly segregated by separate social roles. Women managed the home and family; men took responsibility for public, legal, and business affairs outside the home. This meant that women lost much of the status and authority that they had enjoyed in earlier colonial America. The image of women changed as well. They were increasingly seen as too emotional to be trusted with important public matters, including governing the new country.

Joan R. Gundersen teaches history at Elon College. She specializes in history of law and women's studies, and she is the author of numerous articles on women's history. In this selection she describes the setbacks that women suffered during the revolutionary period.

D espite separate tasks in the household, men and women at the beginning of the eighteenth century lived in a gender-integrated world. Women were expected to fill in for their husbands on the farm or at the business, as a parent,

Joan R. Gundersen, *To Be Useful to the World: Women in Revolutionary America, 1740–1790*, New York: Twayne, 1996. Copyright © 1996 by Joan R. Gundersen. Reproduced by permission.

and sometimes even in court. The household was a place of business and community. Neighbors walked in unannounced; visitors shared family beds and meals. Rooms in a home were multipurpose. People slept, ate, and worked in the same spaces. There were public places in a community, such as the church, courthouse, tavern, market, or capitol, but women visited these as well as men. The home was not separate from public life. Men had some public positions that women could not hold, but women could participate by assuming certain roles.

By 1790 middle- and upper-class families made the home a place of retreat and nurture. They decided which visitors to receive, and had formal spaces set aside for visiting. Individuals linked work to public spaces in order to separate it from the domestic duties of women. Men developed a public life and world, while women cultivated a network of female friends in the private garden of the home. This separation had profound effects for all women and men, whether they lived their lives according to the new social rules or not. Fused with political rhetoric from the Revolution, the split between public and private provided a new role for women: the republican mother.

WOMEN WITHDRAW FROM LEGAL AFFAIRS

Many spaces—social, economic, emotional, and political—took on new shapes in the last half of the century. Women withdrew from the courthouse, for example. . . . Prosecution patterns changed so that proportionately fewer women were defendants in criminal cases, and their appearances for civil matters also diminished. Probate issues had brought many women to court at the beginning of the century. When there was no will, widows had first rights to administer their husbands' estates; in wills men often named their widows as sole administrators. Women also reported on management of the property given to underage children. Although some women went out of their way to settle out of court, most took care of their business. By the middle of the century, men used their wills to surround widows with other executors, or to exclude her. In Amelia County, Virginia, the percentage of widows named as executors dropped from 65 percent when the county was new to 43 percent in 1775. Additionally, men changed the kinds of bequests they left their wives to life interests or income and the right to use a portion of a house. Sons received direct control of the land. Not surprisingly, the share of wealth held by women dropped. In

Boston, women's share of taxes (a measure of personal property) went from 7.1 percent in 1687 to 5.3 percent in 1771, although the percentage of single women in the population was similar. Thus women managed less property and had less control over it (although life interests could be sold) than they had earlier, and had less reason to come to court.

By the middle of the century colonial debt included a number of interest-bearing and time-certain forms of borrowing. Courts moved to more formal and technical pleas, a process certainly helped by the development of a legal profession. Uncontested debt collection swelled court dockets. Women seldom appeared in these cases. Connecticut women appeared in about 19 percent of civil suits in the early decades of the century, about 10 percent at mid-century, and only 4 to 5 percent by 1775. Women's names appeared mainly with their husbands' and usually as collectors of debts, rather than as debtors. In other words, women made little use of new credit opportunities. Although women were involved in a higher number of civil suits, the percentage of suits involving women dropped. In the last half of the century almost all men in Connecticut appeared in court for some reason, but less than one in 10 women did.

Changing land-sale practices also affected women. Under English law, married women had an undivided third interest in all the couple's real property. A woman had to give up this dower interest for a land sale to be final. England used a complicated series of documents followed by a private interview of the wife by a judge to ensure she had not been coerced. Virginia and Maryland were the first colonies to develop a simpler procedure whereby both the husband and wife signed a joint deed. Because courts recognized that women might be coerced, many colonies eventually required wives to appear in court to confirm the deed. Colonial court decisions in the 1740s reinforced the interview requirement. New York and Pennsylvania added the interview requirement shortly before the War for Independence. These interviews brought many women to court. However, in 1748 Virginia passed a law allowing a justice to interview the woman at home, making her appearance in court unnecessary. . . .

WOMEN'S SOCIAL CONNECTIONS

Neighbors witnessed wills and deeds, appraised estates, testified in court, and stood bond for one another. They gossiped, shared tasks, and provided mutual aid. Neighbors also shared games and amusements, meeting at social occasions such as funerals and weddings. Although it might appear that women led more isolated lives than men since infant care and domestic duties limited travel and visiting, women visited in spite (or because) of these impediments. The lower density of population in rural areas increased the distances women traveled, but did not prevent visits. Childbearing caused women to travel. Women returned to their birth families to be at "home" for childbirth, or women in their families came to them. Nursing women did take "a sucking child" with them on social visits. They also used a trip to begin weaning. Illiteracy promoted local travel for women, since they needed to find someone who could write to compose a letter or draw up a deed. There is evidence to suggest that illiterate women attended court days specifically for this purpose.

For many eighteenth-century women, visiting was "the heardest work" they did. Part of visiting was "business" with her neighbors, buying and selling home and garden products. Such visits cut across class lines. Other visits maintained social status within the community, or extended kin and friendship ties outside the local neighborhood. Shifts in the relative importance of these three kinds of friendships mark the development of a separate women's sphere.

Both women's increased literacy and better systems of communication allowed women to build long-distance networks of friends. By 1750 enough middle- and upper-class women had achieved the practical literacy to sustain networks by correspondence. Women wrote letters to fill gaps between visits, and to extend neighborhood patterns of visiting. They requested small favors—the purchase of sewing supplies, the sending of preserved foods—and exchanged gossip. Letters sent advice and emotional support, and discussed religion. Such extended networks found a home for an orphan, and a publisher for works of poetry. Women began patterning their friendships on models they read, and let model form-books shape their written "conversation" with friends.

[Benjamin] Franklin's position as postmaster general for the colonies meant that he contributed directly to the development of communications. Consumers invested in horses and vehicles to travel the new post roads and other colonial roads. When it was necessary, women drove the wagons or chairs (a two-wheeled open carriage) themselves, and could fix a broken hitch with their ribbons and garters. Rural women visited less during weather extremes and harvests, and when sickness peaked. Where a town was nearby, women's travel was more evenly scattered throughout the year, but weather and sickness interfered at times. As one New York woman noted after delaying a sleigh trip in January 1747, "all convayances by Water are shut up & the weather has been so extreem hard that there was hardly any travelling any way for a week past. . . ."

Family ties reinforced women's friendships. Sisters and cousins called each other "Friend." Women also turned to their peers, whether related or not, to find a "Sister of my heart." Women brought together by religion, especially during revivals, called each other sister and shared deep emotion as they met in small groups or corresponded. Literature brought others together. Such bonds could "cement a union . . . which was interrupted only by the removal of parties to distant places, and disolved [sic] only by their death." As men created a competitive culture for themselves (separate from women) in politics, taverns, and clubs, women sought each other's support and comfort. They certainly began to rely on each other more as witnesses to legal documents, and they began showing a preference for other women in their wills. Thus collectively these factors helped create a climate that nurtured the growth of women's networks.

An elaborate set of social events provided the excuses for visiting and travel for middle- and upper-class women like [Benjamin Franklin's daughter] Sally Franklin. Young women went to housewarmings, christenings, boat races, horse races, and balls. They went on daily visits and took chariot rides, alone or with adults. Young girls got into scrapes together, such as smashing the new family carriage when a horse bolted. Dancing school, rowing on the river, walks, riding, or skating in the winter brought young people together. When in town they went to tea and to the theater. At night family and friends might sing or play music, sometimes sitting informally on the front steps.

Even women from modest middle-class farm families could expect constant comings and goings. Quiltings and sewing and spinning frolics happened several times a year. In 1769 one woman of a Long Island farm recorded 28 sets of women visitors, most of whom stayed at least one night. She went to town frequently for church and visiting, although not as often as her daughter, who caught smallpox with three young friends while on a visit. The diarist also sailed to New England for 11 days at the beginning of August, and packed in at least three tea visits among the family business that caused the trip.

Many of these social events also involved men. Without the records men kept we would know much less about women's visiting, but their records are partial, for men missed much of what women did together. The diaries also document the extent to which men had lives separate from women. One married man's diary from the 1740s, for example, mentions no women for the first month and a half of entries. Few entries include his wife, even when she was with him on visits. Since they sometimes met on the road and came home together, it is clear she had an independent round of visits. His diary thus documents both shared and separate social lives for them as a married couple.

These "Custamary invitations of the Season" provided occasions for women to meet but did not guarantee friendship. Women built upon these beginnings by writing letters or journals where they could have a "Free interchange of Sentiments." Women's letters and diaries are much more available from the second half of the eighteenth century. This reflects not only the higher level of literacy among women, but their deliberate use of writing to maintain ties with other women, "whose mind was tun'd in unison with my own." Women celebrated friendship with other women in their poems and letters. The earliest-known journal by an American woman is actually a series of long letters, mailed periodically by Esther Edwards Burr to her friend Sarah Prince in the 1750s. The two women discussed literature and ideas. When Burr died in 1758, Sarah recorded the loss of her "Beloved of my heart." Women understood that such writings occupied a semipublic space, for most were shared with others. Esther left her journal open for her husband to read. . . .

THE PERCEPTION OF WOMEN

The second and third quarters of the eighteenth century show many signs of shifting gender constructs. Newspapers and their readers treated women as private individuals defined by special gender roles and characteristics. Articles acknowledged women's bravery in defense of others and in endurance of troubles, but seldom praised their independence. Stories showed women as victims or as subject to irrationality and passion. Many women appeared as unnamed background figures, part of the social landscape. Negative notices were more common than positive ones. Most positive notices were of deceased women, praised for their private virtues, piety, and domesticity. The focus on deviancy helped define social boundaries in a period where women's behavior was changing. When the *New York Weekly Journal* in 1740 and 1741 carried a satire series suggesting women would readily accept guardianship in order to be thought eternally young, it played to its readers' discomfort with women's status.

The underlying text of these newspaper articles was that women were getting out of control, that they did have power, that passionate women might rule rational men. Editors warned about extravagant dress and published poems showing women's faults. British writers took up the same themes, and American printers reprinted their works. In an essay widely read in the colonies, Henry Home, Lord Kaimes characterized women as destined to be mates for men, more sedentary and disposed to obedience, gentler, and less patriotic because their only connection to the state was through men. If treated with humanity and introduced to morality gradually, women would become trustworthy, "delicious companions, and uncorruptible friends." He granted women intellectual powers, but argued that they should not be educated to rival men. The ambivalence here is striking. Home advocated a level of equality necessary between friends and companions, yet saw equality as a threat since women might challenge men.

Women were, of course, getting more education. These discussions about women's roles proliferated as literacy became widespread among women. Women were also asserting themselves in evangelical religion, exercising more choice in courtship, and investing their mothering with new meaning. The shifting roles shaped women's activism during the Revolution. Women heard the political rhetoric about liberty and bondage resonate with religious overtones. Liberty was as much spiritual as political. The "yoke of Bondage" meant both sin and unjust British policies, such as the Stamp Act. Women's spinning bees demonstrated women's benevolence and piety as well as their patriotism. Women made virtue and piety their version of civic support.

Another subtext appearing in women's conversations was a valuing of youth and its image of a compliant and innocent, yet sexual, woman. Youth as a virtue for women was emphasized in several ways by midcentury. After 1730 women's portraits portrayed them as younger versions of themselves with their hair down. In contrast, men were made to look older and shown with symbols of their work. In general, women's clothes in portraits tended to resemble those of children. Novels had young women heroines, while older women often appeared as contributing villains. Americans began expecting older women to withdraw from amusements like dancing, and to dress somberly and slightly out of fashion. . . .

WOMEN AS TRANSMITTERS OF VALUES

In the mid–eighteenth century the world had not yet divided sharply into either sacred and secular or into public and private spheres. By the end of the century, clear lines of demarcation had appeared for both. Shifting understandings of gender were both partial cause and partial effect of religious change. Religion uncomfortably straddled the fence, with piety and faith firmly tied to the private home, and the institutional church defined as public. Women's growing identification with the private and domestic cemented the connection between femininity and piety.

Conservatives, troubled by some of women's actions, found comfort in giving motherhood a religious purpose. It is hard to oppose the idea that mothers should have a positive influence on their children. It did not challenge men's authority or contact with children. Formulaic phrases appearing in wills after 1770, however, refer to fathers as "honored" and mothers as "beloved," "tender," and "affectionate." Eulogies emphasized motherhood more. Evangelical religion and sentimental novels insisted a mother's influence was special. By 1800 those writing memoirs of their childhoods considered it obligatory to include scenes describing their mother's role in their religious education. Women's letters and journals include concerns about child development and their delight in things their small children did. By the end of the century, the role of mother would subsume activities previously seen as economic. Eliza Lucas Pinckney, who had managed rice and indigo plantations, saw child-rearing as her "Business." The woman who once contributed to family income by sewing a child's shirt, now saw that same action as nurture.

Several threads of thought shaped a new image of women. The religious revivals validated emotion and emphasized women's piety and virtue. According to the Scots Common Sense philosophers then teaching and writing, women served as the transmitters of customs and morals upon which government depended; [economist and philosopher] Adam Smith even argued that family love was the model for government. Literary sentimentalism emphasized domestic personal happiness, and gave women the larger share of sensibility and chastity. Women's withdrawal from some public arenas, their increased household duties, and the emphasis on the emotional support provided in companionate marriage all helped identify women with virtue and economic and legal dependence, and define the public sphere as male. Political rhetoric gave independence and dependence gender overtones.

THE TREATY OF PARIS, SEPTEMBER 3, 1783

The last major battle of the Revolution took place in 1781. Although the Battle of Yorktown was a defeat for the British, it was by no means decisive. It merely proved that the British would not be able to win the war without a further investment of lives and resources. However, by this time the British had lost their appetite for war. In 1782 the British prime minister, Lord Frederick North, stepped down and was replaced by a new minister who was willing to negotiate peace. Benjamin Franklin negotiated a provisional treaty, which was signed in Paris on November 30, 1782. A final version of the treaty was signed in Paris on September 3, 1783. The treaty was ratified by Congress on January 14, 1784.

Like many other seminal documents in American history, the Treaty of Paris of 1783 is brief and to the point. The following selection reproduces the entire document except the names of the signatories.

ARTICLE I

His Britannic Majesty acknowledges the said United States, viz. New-Hampshire, Massachusetts-Bay, Rhode-Island and Providence Plantations, Connecticut, New-York, New-Jersey, Pennsylvania, Delaware, Maryland, Virginia, North-Carolina, South-Carolina, and Georgia, to be free, sovereign and independent States; that he treats with them as such; and for himself, his heirs and successors, relinquishes all claims to the government, propriety and territorial rights of the same, and every part thereof.

"Treaty of Paris, September 3, 1783," *Documentary Source Book of American History, 1606–1926*, edited by William MacDonald, New York: The Macmillan Company, 1926.

ARTICLE II

And that all disputes which might arise in future, on the subject of the boundaries of the said United States, may be prevented, it is hereby agreed and declared, that the following are, and shall be their boundaries, viz. From the north-west angle of Nova-Scotia, viz. that angle which is formed by a line, drawn due north from the source of St. Croix river to the Highlands; along the said Highlands which divide those rivers, that empty themselves into the river St. Lawrence, from those which fall into the Atlantic ocean, to the northwesternmost head of Connecticut river, thence down along the middle of that river, to the forty-fifth degree of north latitude; from thence, by a line due west on said latitude, until it strikes the river Iroquois or Cataraquy; thence along the middle of said river into lake Ontario, through the middle of said lake until it strikes the communication by water between that lake and lake Erie; thence along the middle of said communication into lake Erie, through the middle of said lake until it arrives at the water-communication between that lake and lake Huron; thence along the middle of said water-communication into the lake Huron; thence through the middle of said lake to the water-communication between that lake and lake Superior; thence through lake Superior northward of the isles Royal and Phelipeaux, to the Long Lake; thence through the middle of said Long Lake, and the water-communication between it and the Lake of the Woods, to the said Lake of the Woods; thence through the said lake to the most northwestern point thereof, and from thence on a due west course to the river Mississippi; thence by a line to be drawn along the middle of the said river Mississippi until it shall intersect the northernmost part of the thirty-first degree of north latitude. South by a line to be drawn due east from the determination of the line last mentioned, in the latitude of thirty-one degrees north of the Equator, to the middle of the river Apalachicola or Catahouche; thence along the middle thereof to its junction with the Flint river; thence strait to the head of St. Mary's river; and thence down along the middle of St. Mary's river to the Atlantic ocean. East by a line to be drawn along the middle of the river St. Croix, from its mouth in the Bay of Fundy to its source, and from its source directly north to the aforesaid Highlands which divide the rivers that fall into the Atlantic ocean from those which fall into the river St. Lawrence; comprehending all islands within twenty leagues of any part of the shores of the United States, and lying between lines to be drawn due east from the points where the aforesaid boundaries between Nova-Scotia on the one part, and East-Florida on the other, shall respectively touch the Bay of Fundy and the Atlantic ocean, excepting such islands as now are, or heretofore have been within the limits of the said province of Nova-Scotia.

ARTICLE III

It is agreed that the people of the United States shall continue to enjoy unmolested the right to take fish of every kind on the Grand Bank, and on all the other banks of Newfoundland; also in the gulph of St. Lawrence, and at all other places in the sea, where the inhabitants of both countries used at any time heretofore to fish; and also that the inhabitants of the United States shall have liberty to take fish of every kind on such part of the coast of Newfoundland as British fishermen shall use (but not to dry or cure the same on that island); and also on the coasts, bays and creeks of all other of his Britannic Majesty's dominions in America; and that the American fishermen shall have liberty to dry and cure fish in any of the unsettled bays, harbours and creeks of Nova-Scotia, Magdalen islands, and Labrador, so long as the same shall remain unsettled; but so soon as the same or either of them shall be settled, it shall not be lawful for the said fishermen to dry or cure fish at such settlement, without a previous agreement for that purpose with the inhabitants, proprietors or possessors of the ground.

ARTICLE IV

It is agreed that creditors on either side, shall meet with no lawful impediment to the recovery of the full value in sterling money, of all bona fide debts heretofore contracted.

ARTICLE V

It is agreed that the Congress shall earnestly recommend it to the legislatures of the respective states, to provide for the restitution of all estates, rights and properties, which have been confiscated, belonging to real British subjects, and also of the estates, rights and properties of persons resident in districts in the possession of his Majesty's arms, and who have not borne arms against the said United States. And that persons of any other description shall have free liberty to go to any part or parts of any of the thirteen United States, and therein to remain twelve months, unmolested in their endeavours to obtain the restitution of such of their estates, rights and properties, as may have been confiscated; and that Congress shall also earnestly recommend to the several states a reconsideration and revision of all acts or laws regarding the premises, so as to render the said laws or acts perfectly consistent, not only with justice and equity, but with that spirit of conciliation, which on the return of the blessings of peace should universally prevail. And that Congress shall also earnestly recommend to the several states, that the estates, rights and properties of such last mentioned persons, shall be restored to them, they refunding to any persons who may be now in possession, the bona fide price (where any has been given) which such persons may have paid on purchasing any of the said lands, rights or properties, since the confiscation. And it is agreed, that all persons who have any interest in confiscated lands, either by debts, marriage settlements, or otherwise, shall meet with no lawful impediment in the prosecution of their just rights.

ARTICLE VI

That there shall be no future confiscations made, nor any prosecutions commenced against any person or persons for, or by reason of the part which he or they may have taken in the present war; and that no person shall, on that account, suffer any future loss or damage, either in his person, liberty or property; and that those who may be in confinement on such charges, at the time of the ratification of the treaty in America, shall be immediately set at liberty, and the prosecutions so commenced be discontinued.

ARTICLE VII

There shall be a firm and perpetual peace between his Britannic Majesty and the said States, and between the subjects of the one and the citizens of the other, wherefore all hostilities, both by sea and land, shall from henceforth cease: all prisoners on both sides shall be set at liberty, and his Britannic Majesty shall, with all convenient speed, and without causing any destruction, or carrying away any negroes or other property of the American inhabitants, withdraw all his armies, garrisons and fleets from the said United States, and from every port, place and harbour within the same; leaving in all fortifications the American artillery that may be therein; and shall also order and cause all archives, records, deeds and papers, belonging to any of the said states, or their citizens, which in the course of the war may have fallen into the hands of his officers, to be forthwith restored and delivered to the proper states and persons to whom they belong.

ARTICLE VIII

The navigation of the river Mississippi, from its source to the ocean, shall forever remain free and open to the subjects of Great-Britain, and the citizens of the United States.

ARTICLE IX

In case it should so happen that any place or territory belonging to Great-Britain or to the United States, should have been conquered by the arms of either from the other, before the arrival of the said provisional articles in America, it is agreed, that the same shall be restored without difficulty, and without requiring any compensation.

CELEBRATIONS AT THE END OF THE AMERICAN REVOLUTION

KENNETH SILVERMAN

One aspect of civic culture that history tends to record is the manner in which great events are celebrated. Parades and pageantry have been part of American culture from the beginning, and we even consider a certain style of small-town parade, with its marching bands, floats, civic leaders in convertibles, and, of course, red, white, and blue on everything, to be characteristically American. Of course, the first such civic displays had not yet evolved this characteristic flavor. The first American parades borrowed symbols from Roman culture. Ancient Rome, like the new United States, was a republic, not a monarchy, and American patriots identified with the old Roman republic (not with the later Roman empire). Hence ancient Roman motifs, such as pillars and arches, expressed the spirit of American patriotism, much as red-white-and-blue floats do today.

In this selection Kenneth Silverman, an associate professor of English and a graduate adviser in American civilization at New York University, describes a parade held in Philadelphia to celebrate the end of the American Revolution. Even back then everyone loved fireworks, but in this case the combination of fireworks with Roman motifs was not entirely successful.

Kenneth Silverman, *A Cultural History of the American Revolution*, New York: Thomas Y. Crowell, 1976. Copyright © 1976 by Kenneth Silverman. Reproduced by permission.

On what day peace returned to America is not a matter of fact but of definition. The complex negotiations abroad moved forward in September 1782, when the English ministry authorized its representative to treat with the commissioners of the "13 United States." The phrase tacitly granted the point on which the American commissioners had insisted— a prior concession of independence. On November 30, 1782, a preliminary peace treaty was signed in Paris. Reports of the signing soon reached America, but the text did not arrive until March 1783. Even so, the preamble stated that the treaty would not become operative until Great Britain and France also agreed on peace terms. Many members of Congress suspected a ploy to create distrust among the allies and within America. [George] Washington more than anyone else remained cautious, intent on keeping the country "in a hostile position, prepared for either alternative, war or peace." On March 26, however, he received news of the conclusion of a treaty between France and Britain, activating the British-American treaty. At last he allowed himself to feel "inexpressible satisfaction."

This time it was Washington who spoke prematurely. The formalities lasted another full year. A definitive treaty had first to be signed in Paris, then ratified by Congress, then the ratified definitive treaties had to be exchanged, a process which ended in mid-1784. Overlapping with what must be called the postwar period, the war for independence did not so much end as fade.

Parades in Philadelphia

Uncertain about which one of the interminable formalities meant certain peace, Americans in one place or another celebrated them all. Philadelphians—who had been rejoicing since Yorktown— tried to raise a "Grand Exhibition" in May 1783, after Congress ratified the preliminary articles. Subscriptions were circulated to create a "Superb Sopha" mounted on a triumphal car drawn by six white horses, decorated with portraits of the "Principal Officers that have persevered in the present contest." The procession was to be accompanied by vocal and instrumental music, thirteen large torches, and "thirteen times thirteen boys drest in white." For some reason, Philadelphians failed to subscribe; a substitute plan was proposed for a combined peace and July 4 celebration. A broadside announcement called for a march from the State House to the house of the French minister in a spirit of decent gaiety instead of Roman grandeur:

With drums and trumpets sounding,
Liberty and joy abounding;
Musick, strike up;
Boys, look fierce;
And widows, be gay;
The road's made plain, march on, march on,
Huzza for peace and Washington.

In December, after the definitive treaty was signed in Paris, elaborate scenery and emblematical transparencies were set up at Quesnay's French Academy, where twenty-five students dressed as shepherds gave several performances of "a BALLET representing the Return of Peace, and the Coronation of the Success of America."

A more splendid celebration was planned for January, and held one week after the definitive treaty was ratified by Congress. The Philadelphia Executive Council provided a handsome outlay of £600 to Charles Willson Peale to build a Roman arch, perhaps having in mind the triumphal arches constructed for the *Mischianza*. The work was ideally suited to an artist-technologist-tinkerer, and Peale devised a clever painting-building-machine. The structure consisted of three hollow arches, the center one being thirty-five feet high, independent of the surmounting statuary. Bracketed by two lower arches, it made an edifice more than fifty feet wide, stretching nearly across Market Street. Outside, the arches were covered with transparent paper painted with revolutionary scenes and mottoes. Inside were 1,200 lamps to illuminate the transparencies, and a network of ladders and platforms from which various mechanical devices could be manipulated by technicians. The construction of the framework was assigned to a group of carpenters, while a room in the State House was turned over to Peale for a painting studio. To aid him he employed an apprentice, Billy Mercer—a young deaf mute whose father had been the much-eulogized General Hugh Mercer killed at the battle of Princeton. Peale taught Billy to paint miniatures and oils, and in return received his help in grinding paint, washing brushes, and preparing the transparencies. The arrangement did not work out well, since the boy seems to have considered his chores degrading, and the unheated room in the State House was so cold that his heel became frostbitten.

Descriptions of the completed arch appeared at great length in several newspapers. They stressed how Peale had reconstructed "a building as used by the Romans," authentic down to the balustrades, cenotaphs, and Ionic pillars. Among the many transparencies were representations of the French king, of various war heroes, of the various states, and of the arts and sciences, as well as a "Pyramidal Cenotaph" with the names of fallen soldiers, a tree with thirteen fruitful branches, and a picture of *"Indians* building Churches in the Wilderness." Peale rendered Washington as [Roman general] Cincinnatus returning to his plough, with the motto VICTRIX VIRTUS—"Victorious Virtue." The central arch was crowned with a "Temple of *Janus,"* shut to represent the close of the war, its motto echoing the new U.S. Seal: NUMINE FAVENTE MAGNUS AB INTE-GRO SAECULORUM NASSITUR ORDO—"By divine favor, a great and new order of the ages commences."

The celebration was scheduled to begin at twilight on January 22. According to a route published in Philadelphia newspapers, citizens would march down Market Street, carriages passing through the center arch, pedestrians through the side arches. Atop the house of the president of Pennsylvania, nearby, Peale placed a figure of Peace, rigged so as to suddenly appear and to descend along a rope to the top of the arch. Here the Peace figure would ignite a central fuse, touching off the thousand lamps within a minute. As the arch and its paintings of Washington and other heroes began to colorfully glow, there would be a huge burst of fireworks from the top of the arch, opening the celebration.

FIREWORKS

The actual event was a disaster. The paper covering the arch had been varnished and oiled all over to make the paintings transparent, and was highly combustible. The fireworks, when triggered, exploded, shooting 700 rockets at the crowds on Market Street, injuring several spectators and killing one man. Stranded atop the arch in the firestorm, Peale tried to climb down the back side of the frame, which had been covered with sails to protect the candles inside from wind. Rockets bursting below him as he descended ignited his clothes; one, he feared, zoomed under his coat. Dropping twenty feet to the ground he broke several ribs. He made it to a nearby house, where he managed to extinguish his clothing, but he was badly burned. Taken home on a sleigh and bled by a surgeon, he remained in bed for three weeks and suffered from his injuries through the summer.

Luckily his brother James and eldest son Raphaelle, assigned to mobilize the figure of Peace from the president's house, were unhurt. Billy Mercer also escaped, but not without having his watch and knee buckles stolen as he fled through the crowd.

Some sympathetic Philadelphians raised money to rebuild the arch, this time without fireworks. Without much enthusiasm, Peale repeated the event on Chestnut Street on May 10, 1784, two days before the exchange of the ratified definitive treaties of peace.

CHRONOLOGY

1752

Benjamin Franklin flies a kite during a thunderstorm, proving the "single fluid" theory of electricity.

1754

April: The French build Fort Duquesne (on the site of modern Pittsburgh).

May: George Washington, at age twenty-one, delivers a formal warning from Governor Dinwiddie of Virginia to the French commander at Fort Duquesne to withdraw from British territory.

1755

July: General Edward Braddock is defeated trying to take Fort Duquesne.

1756

May: Great Britain officially declares war on France, beginning the Seven Years' War.

1757

July: British take Louisbourg, Nova Scotia.

1758

August: French General Montcalm, outnumbered five to one, defeats James Abercrombie in the Battle of Ticonderoga.

1759

July: British capture Fort Niagara, Ticonderoga, and Crown Point.

September: General James Wolfe defeats Montcalm at Quebec. Both Wolfe and Montcalm are killed.

1760

September: British capture Montreal.

1763

February: Treaty of Paris of 1763 brings the Seven Years' War to an end.

May–June: Pontiac's War: Ottawas and allied tribes destroy most British forts west of Niagara.

October: King George III issues a proclamation forbidding settlement west of the Appalachian Mountains.

1764

April: Sugar Act places a three-penny tariff on molasses from the West Indies; Currency Act prohibits colonies from issuing paper money.

1765

March: Stamp Act places a tax on printed material, the first "internal" tax to be levied on colonists.

May: Quartering Act requires colonial governments to pay for lodging of British soldiers.

1766

March: Stamp Act is repealed since almost all tax agents responsible for enforcing the act have resigned.

1767

Townshend Revenue Act places tariffs on various imported goods.

January: *The Prince of Parthia*, by Thomas Godfrey, is performed in Philadelphia, the first American drama to be produced professionally.

1770

William Billings publishes *The New England Psalm Singer*.

Phillis Wheatley's elegy to George Whitefield brings her international acclaim at age seventeen.

March: The Boston Massacre. British soldiers fire at a mob in Boston, killing five people.

April: All Townshend duties are repealed, except the duty on tea.

1771

Benjamin West exhibits his painting *The Death of General Wolfe*.

1773

Phillis Wheatley's *Poems on Various Subjects, Religious and Moral* is published in London.

December: Boston citizens dressed as Indians board three ships and dump their cargo of tea into Boston Harbor.

1774

The "Intolerable" Acts close Boston Harbor, end election of members of the Massachusetts assembly, annex western lands to Canada, and renew and strengthen the Quartering Act.

September: First Continental Congress convened in Philadelphia. It adjourns after passing a resolution declaring thirteen acts by the British Parliament to be contrary to British law.

1775

February: British troops attempt to seize a stockpile of weapons at Salem, Massachusetts. They turn back when confronted by a patriot militia. No one is killed.

April: British troops attempt to seize a stockpile of weapons at Concord, Massachusetts. They are turned back at Lexington Bridge by patriot militias.

First abolitionist organization, the Society for the Relief of Free Negroes Unlawfully Held in Bondage, is established in Philadelphia.

Second Continental Congress convenes in Philadelphia.

June: British troops in Boston force patriot militias to withdraw from Breed's Hill and Bunker Hill overlooking Boston.

Second Continental Congress appoints George Washington commander in chief of patriot forces.

July: Second Continental Congress passes the "Declaration of the Causes and Necessity of Taking Up Arms," a declaration authorizing the use of force against Britain.

1776

January: Thomas Paine's pamphlet *Common Sense* is printed and released.

July: Second Continental Congress declares the independence of the thirteen colonies from Britain.

New Jersey adopts a state constitution under which women are not excluded from voting. (This constitution was amended in 1807 to again exclude women.)

September: A one-man submarine, the *Turtle*, attacks a British
warship off Staten Island, the first submarine attack in history.

September–December: Washington's army, forced out of New
York, is pursued through New Jersey and across the
Delaware River.

1777

July: Vermont adopts a state constitution prohibiting slavery,
the first state to prohibit slavery.

September: British seize Philadelphia.

November: Congress agrees to a final version of the Articles of
Confederation.

December: Washington's Continental Army settles into winter
quarters at Valley Forge, Pennsylvania, where the men endure harsh conditions but also receive military training from
German expert Friedrich von Steuben.

1778

February: France recognizes the independence of the United
States.

June: After British attacks on French ships, France declares war
on Britain.

December: British seize Savannah, Georgia.

1780

May: Loyalist Americans under Banistre Tarleton massacre one
hundred Virginia rebels as they attempt to surrender at
Waxhaw Creek, South Carolina.

October: The Battle of King's Mountain ends with a massacre
of Loyalist forces by Virginia and Tennessee militia.

1781

Francis Hopkinson's *The Temple of Minerva* is performed in
Philadelphia, the first American grand opera.

March: The Articles of Confederation take effect after they are
ratified by Maryland, the thirteenth state to ratify them.
Congress disbands and reconvenes under the new Articles.

October: Cornwallis surrenders more than eight thousand men
to Washington at Yorktown, Virginia.

1782

March: Prime Minister Lord North resigns. Parliament authorizes peace with the United States.

1783

January: Treaty of Paris of 1783 brings the Revolutionary War to an official end.

FOR FURTHER RESEARCH

John Richard Alden, *The American Revolution, 1775–1783*. New York: Harper Brothers, 1954.

Fred Anderson, *Crucible of War: The Seven Years' War and the Fate of Empire in British North America, 1754–1766*. New York: Alfred A. Knopf, 2000.

Herbert Aptheker, *Essays in the History of the American Negro*. New York: International Books, 1964.

Eric W. Barnes, "All the King's Horses . . . and All the King's Men," *American Heritage*, vol. 11, no. 6, 1960.

Samuel Flagg Bemis, *The Diplomacy of the American Revolution*. Bloomington: Indiana University Press, 1957.

David Bjelajac, *American Art: A Cultural History*. New York: Harry N. Abrams, 2001.

Daniel J. Boorstin, *The Americans: The Colonial Experience*. New York: Random House, 1958.

John Buchanan, *The Road to Guilford Courthouse: The American Revolution in the Carolinas*. New York: Wiley, 1997.

Colin G. Calloway, *The American Revolution in Indian Country*. Cambridge, UK: Cambridge University Press, 1995.

Cary Carson, Ronald Hoffman, and Peter J. Albert, eds., *Of Consuming Interest: The Style of Life in the Eighteenth Century*. Charlottesville, VA: University Press of Virginia, 1994.

T.R. Clayton, "The Duke of Newcastle, the Earl of Halifax, and the American Origins of the Seven Years' War," *The Historical Journal*, vol. 24, no. 3, 1981.

Henry Steele Commager, *The Empire of Reason: How Europe Imagined and America Realized the Enlightenment*. Garden City, NY: Anchor Press, 1977.

———, *Jefferson, Nationalism and the Enlightenment*. New York: G. Braziller, 1975.

Henry Steele Commager and Richard B. Morris, eds., *The Spirit of Seventy-Six*. New York: Bobbs-Merrill, 1958.

Henry Steele Commager and Allan Nevins, eds., *The Heritage of America*. Boston: Little, Brown, 1941.

Ronald L. Davis, *A History of Music in American Life, Volume I*. Malabar, FL: Robert Krieger, 1982.

Wilma Dykeman, *With Fire and Sword: The Battle of Kings Mountain, 1780*. Washington, DC: National Park Service, 1978.

David Hackett Fischer, *Albion's Seed: Four British Folkways in America*. New York: Oxford University Press, 1989.

Thomas Fleming, *The First Stroke: Lexington, Concord, and the Beginning of the American Revolution*. Washington, DC: National Park Service, 1978.

———, "George Washington, Spymaster," *American Heritage*, vol. 51, no. 1, March 2000.

———, *Liberty! The American Revolution*. New York: Viking, 1997.

———, *1776: Year of Illusions*. New York: W.W. Norton, 1975.

Lawrence Henry Gipson, *The British Empire Before the American Revolution, Vol. 1–15*. New York: Alfred A. Knopf, 1939–1970.

———, *The Coming of the Revolution, 1763– 1775*. New York: Harper Brothers, 1954.

Joan R. Gundersen, *To Be Useful to the World: Women in Revolutionary America, 1740–1790*. New York: Twayne, 1996.

Christopher Hibbert, *Redcoats and Rebels: The War for America, 1770–1781*. London: Grafton, 1990.

Richard Hofstadter, ed., *Great Issues in American History, From the Revolution to the Civil War, 1765–1865*. New York: Random House, 1958.

Donald H. Kent, *The French Invasion of Western Pennsylvania, 1753*. Harrisburg: Pennsylvania Historical and Museum Commission, 1991.

Richard M. Ketchum, *Decisive Day: The Battle for Bunker Hill*. New York: Anchor Books, 1974.

———, *Saratoga: Turning Point of America's Revolutionary War*. New York: Henry Holt, 1997.

———, *Winter Soldiers: The Battles for Trenton and Princeton*. Gordon City, NY: Doubleday, 1973.

———, *The World of George Washington*. New York: Harmony, 1984.

Henry F. May, *The Enlightenment in America*. New York: Oxford University Press, 1976.

William McDonald, ed., *Documentary Source Book of American History, 1606–1926*. New York: Macmillan, 1926.

Richard B. Morris, *The American Revolution: A Short History*. New York: Van Nostrand, 1955.

James P. Myers Jr., "General Forbes' Road to War," *Military History*, vol. 18, no. 5, December 2001.

Benjamin Quarles, *The Negro in the American Revolution*. New York: W.W. Norton, 1961.

Clinton Rossiter, *The Political Thought of the American Revolution*. New York: Harcourt, Brace and World, 1963.

David Lee Russell, *The American Revolution in the Southern Colonies*. Jefferson City, NC: McFarland, 2000.

Arthur M. Schlesinger, *The Birth of a Nation: A Portrait of the American People on the Eve of Independence*. New York: Alfred A. Knopf, 1968.

William Seymour, *The Price of Folly: British Blunders in the War of American Independence*. London: Brassey's, 1995.

Kenneth Silverman, *A Cultural History of the American Revolution*. New York: Thomas Y. Crowell, 1976.

Paul A. Thomsen, "'The Devil Himself Could Not Catch Him,'" *American History*, vol. 35, no. 3, August 2000.

Barbara Tuchman, *The First Salute*. New York: Alfred A. Knopf, 1988.

Dale Van Every, *Forth to the Wilderness: The First American Frontier, 1754–1774*. New York: William Morrow, 1961.

Paul A.W. Wallace, *Indians in Pennsylvania*. Harrisburg: Pennsylvania Historical and Museum Commission, 1993.

Stephanie Grauman Wolf, *As Various as Their Land: The Everyday Lives of Eighteenth-Century Americans*. New York: HarperCollins, 1993.

William J. Wood, *Battles of the Revolutionary War, 1775–1781*. Chapel Hill, NC: Algonquin Books of Chapel Hill, 1990.

INDEX

Adams, Abigail, 52, 253–54
Adams, John
  on Boston Massacre, 140
  Declaration of Independence
    and, 203
  on Franklin, 34
  on homes of poor, 49
Adams, Samuel, 25, 74
African Americans
  Boston Massacre and, 23, 140
  Copley and, 140–41, 142
  poetry and, 21–22, 150, 151–53
  population of, in 1763, 129
  position of, after Revolutionary
    War, 31
  see also slavery
"African Slavery in America"
  (Paine), 254
agriculture, 60, 134–35
American Magazine, 160
American Monthly Museum
  (magazine), 160
American Philosophical Society,
  37
Americans
  characteristics of, 15–16, 17, 40,
    62, 128, 161
  development of identity as,
    15–17
  music and
    Billings and, 166, 168–69
    Hopkinson and, 161, 162–63
  painting and
    Copley and, 140–44
    West and, 137–40
  poetry and, 153

  use of symbols and, 31, 273,
    275–76
  diversity of, 15, 129
  effect of Bunker Hill on, 188
  population of
    patterns, 128
    in 1763, 127–28
    during Seven Years' War, 20
American School, The (Pratt), 137
Anderson, Fred, 103
Andre, John, 215–16, 218
antislavery movement
  African Americans in, 254–55
  effects of, 256–57
  organized efforts of, 254–56
  rhetoric of Revolution and, 252,
    253–54, 257
  Wheatley and, 153
Appalachian Mountains, 119,
  122
Aptheker, Herbert, 252
Arnold, Benedict, 28, 218–19
Articles of Confederation,
  243–51
  government under, 29
astronomy, 17–18
Atotarho, 60
Attucks, Crispus, 23, 140
Autobiography (Franklin), 41

Banneker, Benjamin, 18
Barnard, Thomas, 179, 183
Barnes, Eric W., 175
Barr, Joseph, 180
Bates, Ann, 216
"Battle of the Kegs, The"

287